Performance Evaluation of
Data Base Systems

Computer Science: Distributed Database Systems, No. 3

Harold S. Stone, Series Editor

President, The Interfactor, Inc.

Other Titles in This Series

No. 1 *Medusa: A Distributed Operating System* John K. Ousterhout

No. 2 *Dynamic Resource Allocation in Distributed Computing Systems* Charles R. Vick

No. 4 *Design and Analysis of the Distributed Double-Loop Computer Network (DDLCN)* Jacob John Wolf, III

No. 5 *Performance of Update Algorithms for Replicated Data* Hector Garcia-Molina

No. 6 *Automatic Transaction Decomposition in a Distributed Codasyl Prototype System* Frank Germano, Jr.

No. 7 *A Systematic Approach to the Management of Data on Distributed Data Bases* Benjamin Wan-San Wah

No. 8 *Update Synchronization in Multiaccess Database Systems* Milan Milenkovic

Performance Evaluation of Data Base Systems

by
Patrick M. K. Wong

Copyright © 1981, 1979
Patrick M. K. Wong
All rights reserved

Produced and distributed by
UMI Research Press
an imprint of
University Microfilms International
Ann Arbor, Michigan 48106

Library of Congress Cataloging in Publication Data

Wong, Patrick M. K.
  Performance Evaluation of Data Base Systems.

  (Computer science. Distributed database systems ; no. 3)
  Revision of thesis (Ph.D.)–Ohio State University, 1979.
  Bibliography: p.
  Includes index.
  1. Data base management.   I. Title. II. Series.
QA76.9.D3W66 1981   001.64'2   81-7623
ISBN 0-8357-1211-7   AACR2

Contents

List of Figures   *vii*

List of Tables   *ix*

Key to Mathematical Symbols   *xi*

Preface   *xiii*

Acknowledgments   *xv*

1   Overview of the Research   *1*
    The Research Problem
    A Point of Perspective
    General View of an Information System
    Problems Affecting Information Systems Performance
    Methodology
    Results and Extensions

2   Information System Analysis   *19*
    Establishing System Objectives and Constraints
    Investigation and Analysis of Alternative Procedures
    Performance Evaluation

3   Underlying Methodologies   *29*
    Relational Data Model
    Renewal Processes
    IPSS

4   Methodology   *61*
    Methodological Components
    Transformations
    Data Base Workload Measures

5 Verification of the Methodology   79
    IPSS/REL Design
    Testing and Verification
    IPSS/REL Language Statements
    Transformations
    Statistics
    Summary

6 Conclusions and Recommendations   101
    Recommendations for Extension of the Methodology
    Summary

Appendix A   Syntax and Semantics of IPSS/REL   109

Appendix B   Sample Run of a IPSS/REL Model   175

References   231

Index   237

Figures

1. Transformation From Query to Performance Measure   *3*
2. General Model of an Information System   *7*
3. Query to Performance Transformation of IPSS   *13*
4. Attribute and Query Transformations   *15*
5. Phases of System Development   *21*
6. Relationship Between Research Methodology and Underlying Methodologies   *30*
7. Graphical Representation of Information in a Data Base   *32*
8. Logical to Physical Data Base Mapping   *34*
9. Example of Hierarchy of Relational Data Base Models   *35*
10. Example of a Hierarchical View of a Data Base   *41*
11. Data Model for University Data Base Example Represented as a Tree Structure   *42*
12. Sample Occurrences of the University Data Model Segments   *43*
13. Network Representation of a Typical Data Model   *44*
14. Network Representation of the Company Data Base Example   *46*
15. A Subschema for the Company Data Base Example   *47*

16. Relationship Between Different Approaches to Data Base Management   48

17. One-to-One Mappings Between Hierarchical, Network, and Relational Approaches   50

18. Occurrences of Keys Over the Accession Number Space   53

19. Query to Performance Transformation of IPSS   57

20. Attribute and Query Transformations   63

21. Structure of IPSS/REL Model   81

22. Example of PDF   85

23. Example of an Attribute Definition   87

24. Transformation of Query to Record Addresses   93

25. Active Query Statistics   96

26. Cumulative Query Statistics   98

27. Discrete PDF: $F_x(\cdot)$ 125

28. Continuous PDF: $F_x(\cdot)$ 126

Tables

1.	Relations for the Library Information System	*39*
2.	IPSS/REL Implementation of Methodological Model	*82*
3.	Definition of PDF	*84*
A–1.	IPSS Statements and Functions for Multi-Attribute Analysis	*113*
A–2.	$COMM Conventions for ATTRIBUTE Statement	*122*
A–3.	$COMM Conventions for PDF Statement	*127*
A–4.	#COMM Conventions for SEARCH KEY Statement	*130*
A–5.	$COMM Conventions for ATTRIBUTE Statement	*151*
A–6.	#COMM Conventions for DF Statement	*156*
A–7.	$COMM Conventions for SEARCH KEY Statement	*160*

Key to Mathematical Symbols

Symbol used in text	Mathematical Symbol	Meaning
F-ALL	$\forall$	for all
T-EXT	$\exists$	there exists
ELM-OF	$\in$	element of
SUM$_i$	$\sum_i$	summation over the index i
G i,j (x)	$G_{ij}(x)$	
N-ELM-OF	$\notin$	not an element of
GIVEN	$\mid$	
.LT.	$<$	less than
.GT.	$>$	greater than
.LE.	$\leq$	less than or equal
.GE.	$\geq$	greater than or equal
.NE.	$\neq$	not equal
.EQ.	$=$	equal

Preface

Data base workload is an important factor in the performance of an information system. All data base operations are in response to this workload. This study presents a methodology for characterizing the data base workload. The methodology is part of an upward extension of the Information Processing System Simulator (IPSS) methodology. IPSS is being developed by a research team at Ohio State University under the direction of Dr. Thomas G. DeLutis. It is a special purpose simulation language and provides a comprehensive set of facilities for modeling a wide range of information systems.

This work is divided into six chapters. Chapter 1 is an overview of the research problem and the methodology resulting from this research. It also gives a synopsis of the salient features of the methodology and conclusions drawn from the research. Chapter 2 discusses the system analysis problem and its dependence on workload definition in detail. System analysis tools and the lack of data base workload characterization methodologies that support these tools are described. Chapter 3 presents three underlying methodologies basic to this research: the Relational Data Model, Renewal Processes, and IPSS. The methodological view of a data base is based on the relational data model. Attribute analysis is used to characterize the distribution of data base attributes. IPSS is used to model the underlying information system transformations. Chapter 4 describes the methodology. Chapter 5 discusses the verification activities for this research. These centered on the development of simulation constructs (IPSS/REL) that model systems from the developed methodological view. Examples that illustrate the use of IPSS/REL are given. The implementation, testing and verification procedures of the language constructs are also described in this chapter. Chapter 6 summarizes the research problem. The results of the research are discussed and future extensions are proposed.

Acknowledgments

I wish to express my deep appreciation to Dr. Thomas DeLutis for his guidance, direction and assistance throughout this research. I would like to thank Dr. Lawrence Rose for his stimulating ideas and helpful suggestions in preparing this study. Special thanks go to Dr. James Rush for his advice and help in understanding the problems associated with the design and evaluation of commercial information systems. I would also like to acknowledge the help and advice extended by Dr. Howard H. W. Mei, and thank Miss Mary Styer and Miss April Ours for typing this study.

This research was supported in part by the Office of Science Information Services of the National Science Foundation.

1
Overview of the Research

The Research Problem

Timely information is an important resource for every modern organization. It is needed for operational control, tactical and strategic planning, and decision-making at virtually all levels of the organization. The purpose of an information system is to provide information – knowledge, news, facts, data, learning, and lore [WEBS62] needed by an organization to support its decision-making functions. Examples of information systems range from small private libraries to large corporate information processing systems. The input to an information system usually consists of undigested data such as daily operational statistics, sales slips, or invoices. One of the major tasks of an information system is to classify, analyze, and reformat this data into information that suits a user's needs. For the purposes of this research, an information system means a computer-based information processing system.

Modern-day government and industrial organizations usually have to handle large amounts of data; generally the most cost-effective method for handling this data is a computer-based information processing system. However, these systems can become extremely complex, and hence costly, in order to meet the needs of the user community. Contributors to complexity are numerous; some are well defined while others are nebulous. Two major contributors to a system's complexity are the structure of its stored information and the information services required by its users. For example, complexity is dependent on the variety of users, the kind of user decision functions to be supported, the quantity, quality, and degree of structure in the source data, the required infrastructure of the stored data, and the type of interaction between the users and the system.

The complexity of contemporary information systems also makes the system performance evaluation task very difficult. Many system designs and evaluation tools have been developed [MEAD67, TIMM73, CARD73, LEFK69, SENK71] to assist the designer of information systems to develop

2 Overview of the Research

system architectures which satisfy user requirements in a cost-effective and beneficial manner. Contemporary design aids generally have one of the following drawbacks: they are either restricted to the evaluation of only a particular aspect of an information system, or they do not characterize the system's input stream in sufficient detail to develop an accurate workload profile for the system's data base functions. The first problem is solved by the Information Processing System Simulator (IPSS) methodology [DELU76, 77a, 78]. This methodology allows the designer to characterize and evaluate a wide range of information systems. Solving the second problem is the goal of this research.

System input streams can be viewed as series of user-generated queries or requests for information services. These queries can be characterized using a high-level, multi-attributed meta-language such as Relational Calculus [DATE75]. These queries are transformed by system processing into demands for data base services. Figure 1 illustrates the transformation of user queries to data base workload and then to performance measures. In this research, the data base workload is characterized as the list of objects that are required to satisfy the user queries. Typical objects in the data base workload are logical data base records, documents, and aggregated data from the data base. In the past the data base workload has either been ignored or characterized as a series of random requests to the data base due to the lack of workload characterization tools. For example, the workload may be treated as a series of logical record addresses uniformly distributed throughout the data base's logical record address space. Since changes in the workload directly affect the utilization and demand of different resources [GHOS72, LOWE68], a methodology for characterizing the data base workload is needed to effectively analyze the performance of alternative system designs.

In this research, a methodology has been developed for predicting and measuring the workload placed on the system's data base. The workload is developed by analyzing the interaction between the user's query structures and the inherent characteristics of the data base. The objectives of this research are threefold:

1. To develop a general model for the characterization of the system's data base information structure;
2. To define a general framework for characterizing user query structures; and
3. To provide a methodology to ascertain the data base workload via the interactions of the characterizations for items one and two.

Figure 1. Transformations from Query to Performance Measure

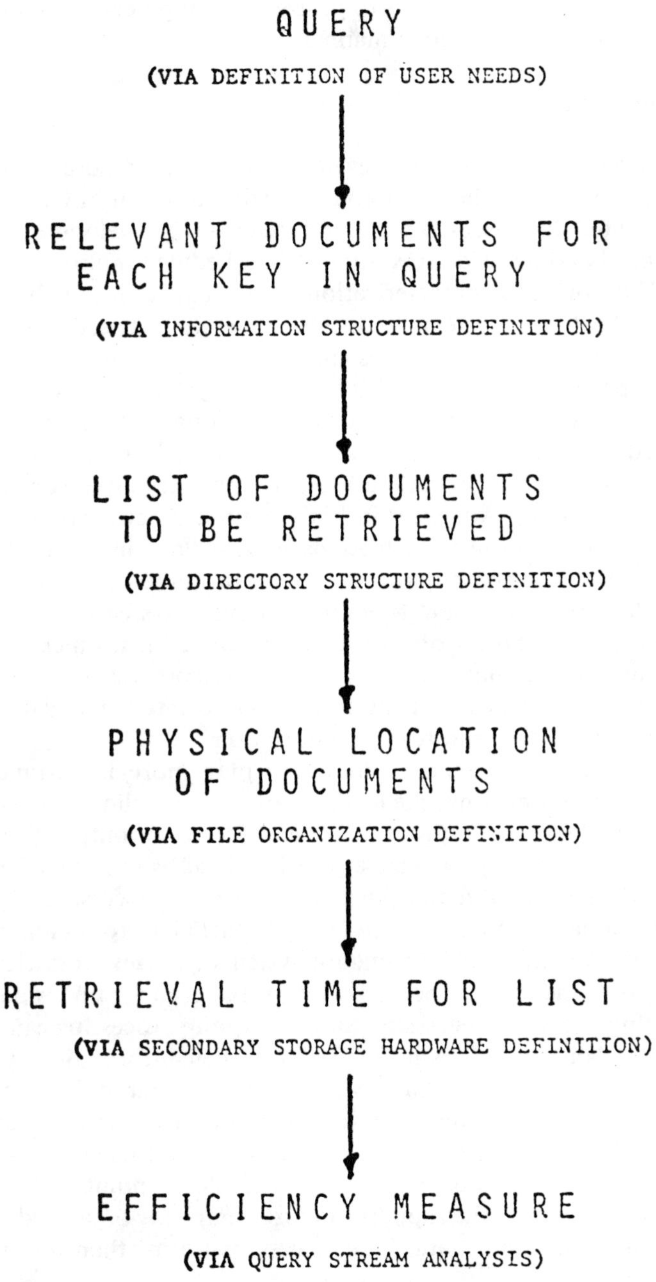

QUERY
(VIA DEFINITION OF USER NEEDS**)**

↓

RELEVANT DOCUMENTS FOR EACH KEY IN QUERY
(VIA INFORMATION STRUCTURE DEFINITION**)**

↓

LIST OF DOCUMENTS TO BE RETRIEVED
(VIA DIRECTORY STRUCTURE DEFINITION**)**

↓

PHYSICAL LOCATION OF DOCUMENTS
(VIA FILE ORGANIZATION DEFINITION**)**

↓

RETRIEVAL TIME FOR LIST
(VIA SECONDARY STORAGE HARDWARE DEFINITION**)**

↓

EFFICIENCY MEASURE
(VIA QUERY STREAM ANALYSIS**)**

Using this methodology, the designer will be able to develop a better estimate of system resource needs as a function of the data base workload. This in turn will enable organizations to utilize the computer-based information system in a more cost-effective manner.

A Point of Perspective

In this section, two trends in the development of contemporary information systems are discussed. The first trend is the development of large integrated multi-attributed data bases. The second trend is the development of on-line systems that handle a wide spectrum of unscheduled multi-attributed user queries. The workload characterizations developed in this methodology are directly applicable to systems with the above characteristics and are also applicable to less sophisticated systems.

In the past, the basic role of information systems has been to support clerical functions within organizations. Traditionally, these systems served the stewardship (accounting division) and in some instances provided first level data in support of operational control, but very little data for tactical or strategic planning. Advances in both computer hardware and software technologies and associated reductions in cost have increased the attractiveness of using the computer to provide information in support of more complex decision processes. Modern computer systems are capable of storing massive quantities of data and retrieving them quickly. Development of data base management systems and teleprocessing networks have further facilitated the implementation of large integrated data bases by reducing programming and telecommunication costs.

As information systems continue to play more important roles in support of decision making, the methods of data handling by these systems have changed. In the past, the schedule and format of output (e.g. reports) from an information system were a priori defined by the users. Traditional retrieving and storing of data using single attribute processing, e.g., organizing a personnel file by employee ID, was sufficient to handle the user's needs. As the function of information systems changes from clerical data processing to management decision support, the need for timely data and ad hoc reporting becomes a necessity. Single attribute processing can no longer meet the user's needs. Users no longer view their information system as a collection of single attribute files but as an integrated multi-attributed data base. The user's storage and retrieval operations are also multi-attributed, e.g., retrieving personnel records based on age, education, and salary instead of uni-attributed queries based on employee number. Multi-attributed operations require the support of more complexly organized data bases and generate different data base access patterns than do the more traditional systems.

For example, in traditional file organization the personnel data base is stored in employee number sequence and all queries would employ the same key to identify the records of interest. If the same data base is to support multi-attributed retrieval such as searching using education, age, department, and salary attributes, the file has to be sorted in different sequences, one for each use.

The development of multi-attributed data base structures (e.g., multi-list, inverted files, relational data base management systems, etc.) has improved a system's capability to support multi-attributed queries. These systems are much more difficult to design and evaluate. The information system designer can no longer evaluate the data base design based on single attribute queries, but has to evaluate the data base's performance against many different search patterns. A further complaint arises due to the fact that the way attributes are ordered and distributed within a data base significantly affects system performance.

The primary functions of an information system are storing information into and retrieving information from the system's data bases. Usually, the major processes are input/output (I/O) oriented as opposed to central processing unit (CPU) bounded. The users of an information system constitute the external environment of the system. The loading to the system is generated in response to this external environment. In the past, information systems operated in the batch processing mode. The loading on the system was in the form of a series of user requests, usually recorded on punch cards. These user requests are combined together, preprocessed (sorted) and stored in a temporary file called a transaction file. This transaction file is then processed sequentially against the data base or master file. The turn around time for a user request was usually long – several hours to several days. As information systems have become more management oriented, the long turn around time has become increasingly more undesirable. As a result, modern information systems are evolving away from batch to on-line and real-time processing environments.

Since in real-time systems many users communicate simultaneously with the system through computer terminals, system responsiveness is a critical performance criteria. Data base workload has been shown to be a major factor in achieving the desired response time. Real-time systems workload is the aggregate of many users working simultaneously on the system and the outputs required to satisfy their queries. Usually, the fast response time required of on-line systems precludes the possibility of improving system performance by combining or resequencing the user requests into batches. Since there is little resequencing of user requests, improvement in system performance must come from data base organization and management. This requires the analysis of data base accessing patterns. The multi-attributed nature of the integrated data base complicates the characterization and measurement of the loading of on-line systems. The unpredictability of user information requests is especially true in modern decision support systems and management information systems because these systems are designed to help many users solve complex and unstructured data referencing problems.

To satisfy the unpredictable needs of the users, high-level query languages have been developed to allow the user maximum flexibility in formulating the input query. These languages enable users to formulate queries in either English-like natural language or in more restricted programming language-like statements. User queries are characterized by Boolean expression.

General View of an Information System

In this section, a general model of an information system (figure 2) is defined. This model is used as an example of systems for which this research is applicable.

There are four basic components in this model:

1. Acquisition and characterization of documents,
2. Data storage,
3. Query analysis and processing, and
4. Data base retrieval and dissemination of results.

Each component is discussed in the following subsections.

Acquisition and Characterization of Documents

The basic information unit of storage and retrieval unit is called an 'object'. An object represents information about some logical entity. Objects that are used in an information system are records, reports, and documents. These objects arrive at the information system from external sources. Before these objects are stored in the system, they are classified. A consistent normalized organization of the object data is required so that it can be retrieved in a cost-efficient and consistent manner. An example of this process is found in the content analysis function used to classify and analyze documents to produce the normalized descriptors in libraries. In general, these normalized descriptors can be regarded as sets of attribute-value pairs that characterize the inputted documents. For example, the following attributes can be used to describe a collection of books: author, title, subject, publisher, and other attributes which characterize the contents of the books. For each document, values are asigned to these attributes. Examples

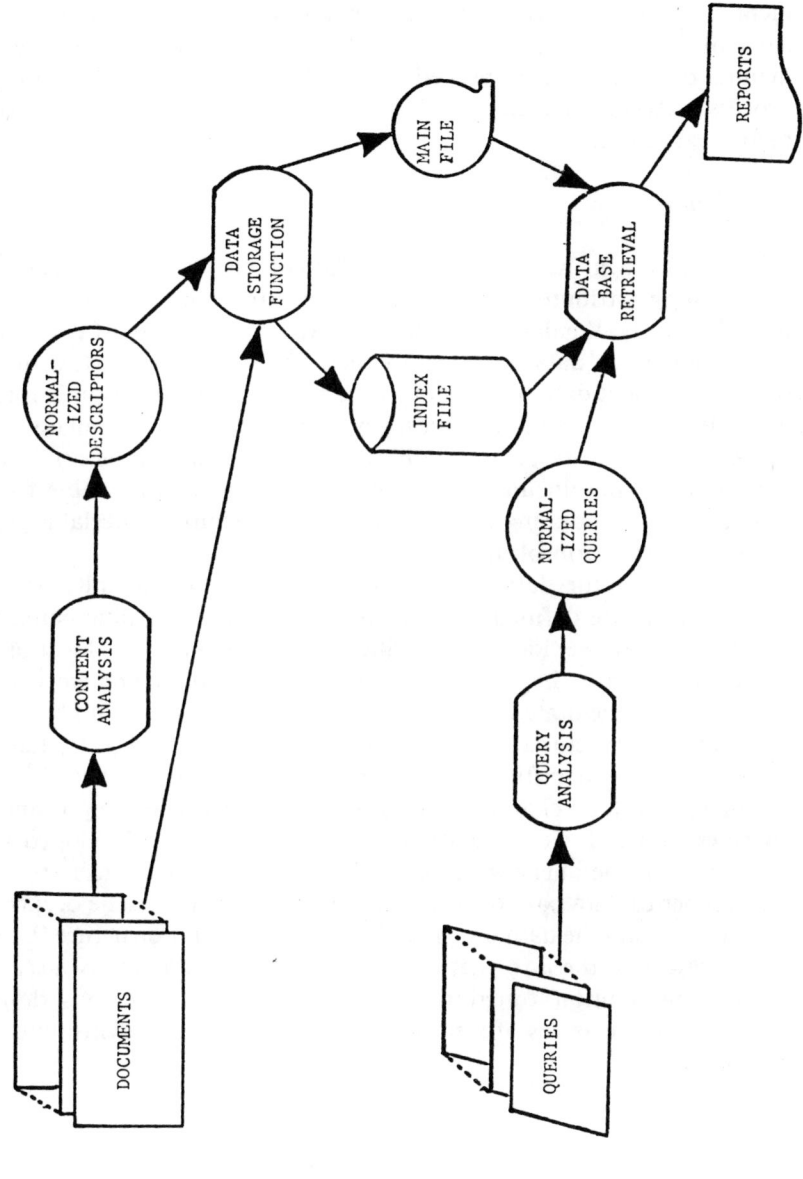

Figure 2. General Model of an Information System

8 Overview of the Research

of values for the subject attribute are: Engineering, Mathematics, or Physics. The basic requirement is that the content analysis is consistent, i.e., that it will produce the same set of attribute-value pairs for the same document and that the attribute-value pairs are reflective of the body of knowledge of the document being stored. Content analysis can be done either by manual or computerized procedures [MEAD67, LEFK69, SALT71]. This process creates the entities which constitute a system's data base and information structure.

Data Storage

After a document has been analyzed for content, both the document and the resulting attribute-value descriptors are stored in the appropriate data base. Logically, the data base can be viewed as consisting of two parts: the source document data base and the descriptor data base. Most often, the source document data base is not stored in computer-processable form. For example, in most automated library systems, the actual documents — books, journals, etc., are stored in the library stacks while bibliographical information about the documents is stored in computer-processable forms. In standard data processing facilities, the original source material is generally placed in some form of archival storage.

The descriptor data base is organized into logical units or objects. These objects are defined by their associated attribute-value pairs, two of which are the object identifier attribute (and value) and the location of the source document. The data base is assumed to have one or more attribute indexes which facilitate data base traversal. These logical data base indexes are generally structured so that all data base entities (objects) having the attribute can be identified. Since in most systems, on-line data is a shared resource, workload characteristics for on-line storage are important design considerations. However, workload profiles cannot be developed without knowledge of the query workload and the data base response profile (i.e., the number of data base records relevant to the queries). The occurrence of attributes within the data base is called the information structure [LEFK69]. In this research, the information structure is characterized by a set of probability distribution functions. These distribution functions define the number of occurrences of attribute value pairs and their distribution in the data base.

Query Analysis

The query will be assumed to be a user's statement of his information needs. The needs are expressed in a query language that is recognizable by the information system's query processor. All such language will be assumed to be comprised of three basic elements: a vocabulary, a set of operations on the vocabulary, and a set of syntax rules. The vocabulary defines what symbols or words are valid in the language. The syntactic rules tell how to combine the vocabulary via the operators into higher-level language elements, the highest level being the query itself. The function of the query analysis is to decode the syntactic unit into lower-level syntactic units and operations with the lowest level being the vocabulary. This query translation step is similar to the document content analysis step. In the document content analysis step the inputs are documents and the outputs are document descriptor records, while in the query translation step the inputs are queries expressed in a user language (which could be a natural language) and the outputs are a normalized format of descriptors and operators that identify content characteristics of candidate documents.

In this research, the output of the query translation is assumed to be a list of Boolean expressions in disjunctive normal form. That is, each query is translated to an expression of the form:

$$C_{11} \wedge C_{12} \wedge \ldots C_{1m_1}) \vee \ldots \vee (C_{nl} \wedge \ldots \wedge C_{nm_n}).$$

C_{ij} represents an attribute value relation (A_{ij} R V_{ij}) preceded optionally by a $\neg$ (NOT) operator. In the above expression, A_{ij} stands for an attribute, V_{ij} stands for a value, and R is one of the following relation operators: $<$ (less than), $\leq$ (less than or equal), $=$ (equals), $>$ (greater than), $\geq$ (greater than or equal), $\neq$ (not equal). The attribute value relations are connected by the logical operators: $\wedge$ (AND), $\vee$ (OR) and $\neg$ (NOT). The format of the above normalized query is similar to expressions in Propositional Calculus. These expressions are very general and are capable of characterizing the search requirements of most multi-attributed query languages [KORF66].

Data Base Retrieval

Data base retrieval is the process by which candidate documents are identified based on matching the attributes in the query with those in the descriptor record. Functionally, data base retrieval can be viewed as consisting of two phases. Phase 1 identified candidate records, i.e., the list of document ID. This may be the result of complex search processes, where the complexity of the searches is a function of the query structure and the data base attribute indexes. The resultant list of document ID's is used to retrieve the actual documents or the data base entities constituting the query response set. Often only a small portion of the document is in computer-processable form and additional mechanical or manual activities may have to be performed to obtain the complete documents. For computer-processable documents, a third phase may be entered: the extraction of the desired information and its assembly or summarization into an appropriate format for dissemination to the users.

The data base retrieval process usually places a large demand on a system's I/O resources and thus is a significant factor in the system's performance. Since the data base retrieval process is governed by the user workload, it is necessary to characterize the workload in order to ascertain its effect on system performance. In this research, the data base workload corresponds to the data base responses needed to satisfy the Boolean expressions.

Problems Affecting Information System Performance

This section discusses some system performance problems that can be addressed via the workload characterization developed in this research. Based on the general view of information systems given in figure 2, the following is a list of design and analysis problems addressed by the research.

Complexity of the Query Language

The performance of a system is dependent on the structure and content of the user queries. The system designer must decide whether to allow the users to express their queries in a high-level English-like query language or in a more restrictive query language with fixed vocabulary and simple syntax. In either case, the structure of the normalized query is the same. This normalized form can be stated in terms of Boolean expressions which are generally the outputs of computer based pseudo-natural language query parsers. The types of Boolean expressions generated by the parsers is one basis for evaluating the desirability of query languages.

Changes in User Query Stream Characteristics

The user query stream characteristics may change due to different groups of users utilizing the system at different points of time. The workload on the data base, however, is also affected by the query language because of the inherent complexity of the resultant Boolean expressions. The data base workload is also affected by the scheduling of queries based on query structure. The designer must determine how query stream characteristics affect the system performance. One of the goals of their research query was to permit stream characteristics to be easily modeled, permitting the designer to analyze the impact on the system input stream due to different query language features.

Generation of Document Attributes and Values

The system designer must describe the data base. A second goal of this research is to permit data base characterization based solely on the inherent attributes of the data to be stored in the data base. These characterizations can be developed from statistical analyses of attribute frequency or any other analysis procedure of the contents of the documents. If statistical analysis is used, the results from the analysis can be used to generate the data base distribution functions needed by the methodology developed in this research.

Indexing Breadth and Depth

The system designer must determine how many topics or attributes can be used to index the documents and how much information or how many possible values are assigned to each topic or attribute. In particular, the designer must decide how many attribute-value pairs should be used to index an average document. The above problems can be solved by varying the indexing breadth and depth and comparing the resulting workloads that are generated by the methodology.

Selection of Physical and Logical Data Base Organizations

The performance of an information system's data base is dependent on the storage organizations used for its data. There are many file organization methods (e.g., sequential, index sequential, random) and data base index strategies (e.g., multi-list, cellular multi-list, tree, inverted) that the system designer can use to organize the information system data base. Each has its own performance characteristics and the designer must determine the most appropriate data base schema based on the system's design objectives. One of the difficulties in comparing the different data base schemata is the derivation of a representative workload to test each organization. This research provides a methodology for developing data base workload profiles as a function of the user input stream and the system's information structure.

Selection of a Strategy for Managing a Data Base

The performance of an information system is dependent on the content of its data base. The content of the data base may change over time. The performance of a system may deteriorate due to the addition and deletion of information. The designer must develop criteria for determining when a data base should be reloaded so as to maintain performance profiles. Thus, an additional goal of the research was to provide a mechanism capable of assessing data base deterioration. This was accomplished by changing the distribution characteristics of attributes within the data base as a function of time since reorganization. By examining the changes in user workload resulting from the changes in the information structure, the designer can develop the required criteria for data base reorganization.

Methodology

Information system performance depends in large part on the data base workload. Two salient factors determine the user workload generation. They are the distribution of the data base attributes and the characteristics of the system loading generated by the user query stream. The above factors are not generally examined in detail in the design and evaluation process due to lack of systematic characterization and analysis procedures. Therefore, the goals of this research are:

1. To develop procedures for characterizing the distribution of data base attributes,
2. To develop procedures for characterizing the user queries and system loading generated by the user request stream,
3. To develop procedures for developing data base workload profiles as a function of the characterization developed in goals one and two.

A methodology that accomplishes the above goals has been developed. This methodology was based on three underlying methodologies: the relational data model [DATE75], stochastic renewal processes, and IPSS [DELU77a].

The relational data model provides a general logical view of an information system's data base. This model is capable of modeling a wide range of data base systems including hierarchical and network data bases [CODD70, TSIC73]. The information structure or data base content is characterized by attribute analysis employing stochastic renewal processes. In attribute analysis, the occurrences of data base attributes are characterized by probability distribution functions. The IPSS methodology views the information system as the series of transformations shown in figure 3. These are information system level transformations, application level transformations, DBMS level transformations, file management level transformations, and secondary storage level transformations. Except for the system level transformation, these conceptual transformations have been realized in the IPSS simulation language facilities in previous work. This research concentrates on the system level transformation, i.e., the transformation of the user input stream into the data base workload.

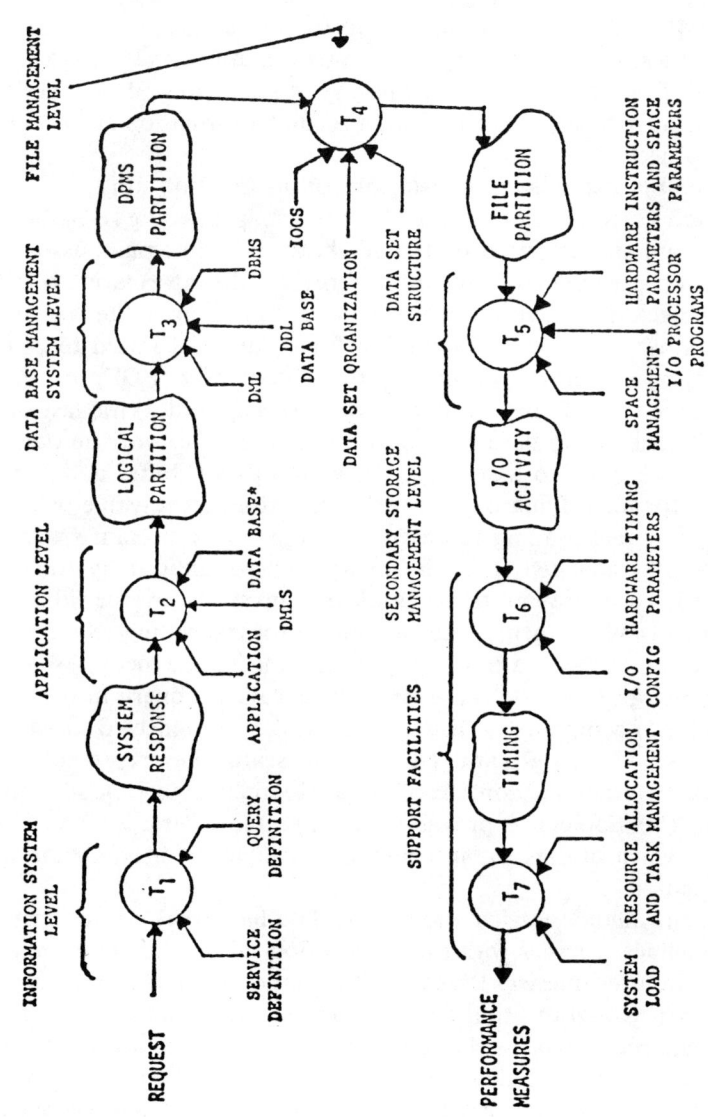

Figure 3. Query to Performance Measure Transformations of IPSS (DELU77a)

A methodological model for the system level transformation has been developed. This model represents the conceptual view of an information system. The methodological model characterizes the user workload as a function of the following methodological components and algorithms: (figure 4) data base, files, objects, attributes, values, distributions, search key, queries, system loading, query transformation, and workload transformation. The information system's data base is viewed as a collection of files. A file represents a collection of related information and is defined as a list of objects.

An object stands for a basic unit for information storage and retrieval. An object corresponds to a record in the data processing (DP) terminology. Objects are characterized by the attribute and value pairs associated with them. The attribute and value pairs represent the information that is stored in an object. The identity of objects with a given attribute is characterized by the four probability distribution functions (PDF) used to characterize the attribute. They are: a) the first occurrence PDF, b) the NEXT occurrence PDF, c) the number of occurrences, and d) the last occurrence PDF. These PDF's define the information structure of the data base. A fifth PDF is used to assign specific values to attributes and provides the method for identifying objects with selected attribute-value pairs.

The system loading represents the user input stream. Queries in this stream are translated (i.e., the query transformation) by some designer specified procedure into target Boolean expressions. As an aid to designing such a procedure, a generalized algorithm for translating relational calculus queries [DATE75] to a Boolean expression using the methodology has also been developed. A Boolean expression is called a query in the conceptual model and comprises a list of search keys connected by the logical operators: AND, OR, and NOT. Each search key represents an object retrieval criterion and consists of an (attribute, comparison operator, value) triplet. The Boolean expressions are inputted to the workload transformation which utilizes the information structure to produce the data base workload.

In the methodological model, the data base workload consists of a list of file names together with the objects (logical records) that are needed to satisfy the user queries. Based on the methodological model, a procedure for deriving equations that describe the user workload has been developed. These equations express the user workload as a function of the data base information structure and user input stream characteristics. Based on the methodological model, a set of language constructs and syntax has been developed. These constructs are implemented as extensions to the IPSS modeling and executional facilities.

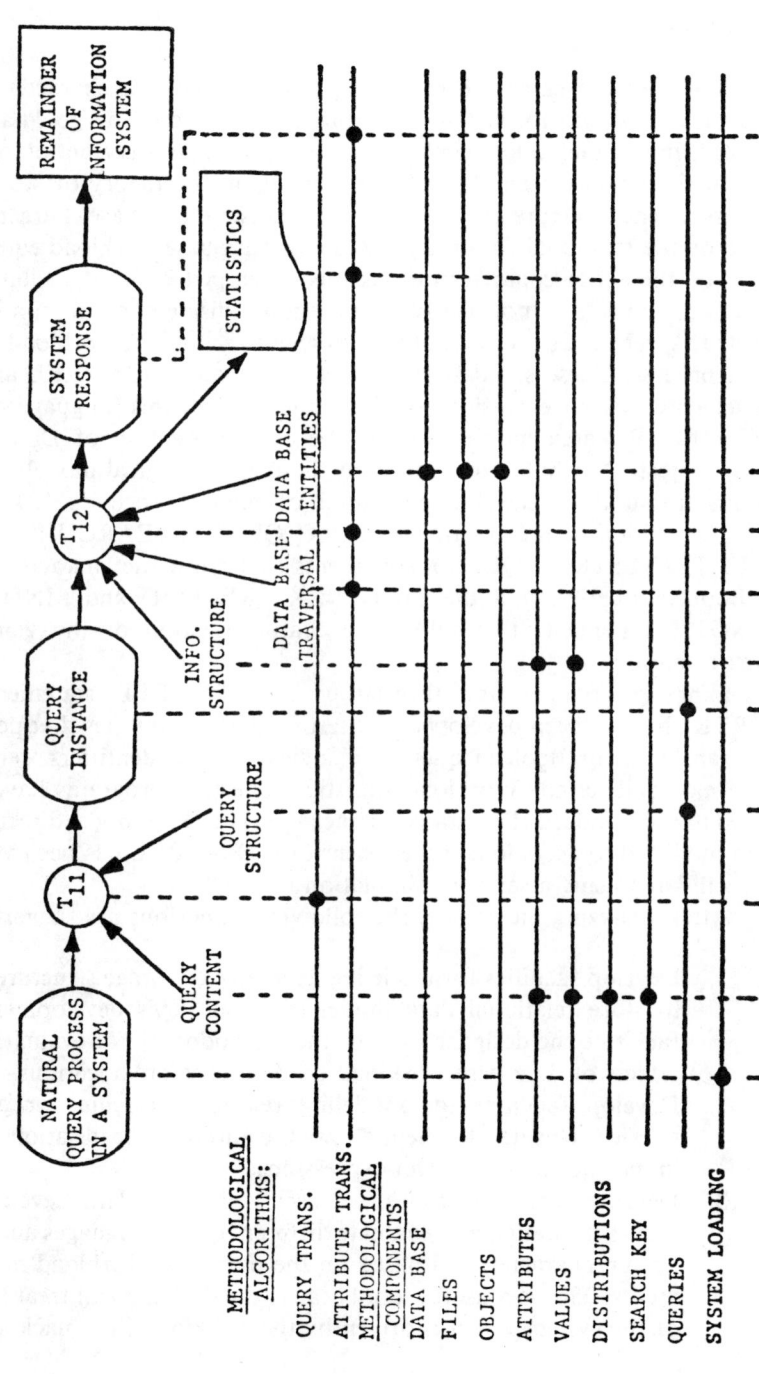

Figure 4. Attribute and Query Transformations

Results and Extensions

The goal of this research was to develop a methodology to characterize the data base workloads for system performance evaluation. This goal has been realized. In this methodological model, the ordering or distribution of data base attributes has been characterized based on the theory of stochastic processes. The structure of the data base and user queries are characterized based on the relational data model. A set of data base workload equations based on the above characterizations was developed. Since the solution to these equations are not easily computable, discrete event simulation constructs were created to permit the designer to model the workload generation process. These simulation constructs are called IPSS/REL and are implemented as an extension to IPSS. Included in this language are an ATTRIBUTE statement that allows the characterization of Data Base, Files, Object, Attribute, and values in the methodological model, a PDF statement that allows the characterization of renewal processes PDF's used in the definition of information structure, QUERY, SEARCH KEY, and CREATE/DESTROY QUERY statements that allow the characterization of Boolean queries, and the FIND NEXT RECORD and FIND LIST LENGTH statements that allow the characterization of the workload transformation.

Language parsers for translating the IPSS/REL statements to FORTRAN have been developed and tested. System routines that perform the translation of Boolean queries to logical record identifiers were also developed and tested. Workload statistics collection programs have been added to the standard IPSS statistics package. The IPSS model director has been modified to accomodate the extensions. IPSS/REL has been verified and validated using a series of simulation models.

After analyzing the results, the following extensions are suggested:

1. Develop facilities for modeling generalized storage structures used to store relational data model relations. This development will facilitate the designer's use of the methodology for evaluating the effects of data base workload on data base organizations,
2. Develop facilities for modeling relational calculus or algebra queries. This development allows the automatic translation of user input queries to Boolean expressions,
3. Develop further measures on user workload. This development allows the designer to evaluate different query languages and query stream characteristics based on the data base workload measurements. This is a useful tool because the designer can treat the rest of the system which is driven by the workload as a blackbox.

To summarize, a methodology for defining the data base workload for performance evaluation has been developed. The methodology expresses the workload as a function of the data base information structure and user input stream. The methodology is general and can be applied to a wide range of information systems.

2

Information System Analysis

This chapter discusses the problem associated with the analysis and evaluation of computerized information systems. The analysis and evaluation problems are examined from the point of view of the need to accurately define the system's workload in order to support configuration evaluations and performance analysis, especially as related to an information system's data base. The term 'system analyst' will be used in its generic sense, that is, a person or a group of persons in an organization that is in charge of one or more of the above duties. This chapter examines work done previously in this area and discusses the strengths and weaknesses of various tools which characterize and evaluate the workload of an information system. It will be shown that system analysis tools in the past have concentrated on the analysis of the internals of an information system such as memory management, task scheduling, and file management. Tools for analysis of the system workload such as the distribution of user requests, structure of the user queries, and the clustering of the user requested data are available. However, none of these are specific to the problems associated with on-line, real-time data base systems with heavy ad hoc, multi-attribute queries. It is because of the lack of data base workload analysis tools that this research began.

Aron [ARON69] discusses the evolution of information processing systems from their early data processing orientation to contemporary decision-support systems. Typically, early systems were record oriented and were used for clerical operations such as payrolls and invoicing. The analysis of these systems was relatively simple since the choice of hardware, software, and data base designs was limited and the workload of these systems followed a fixed pattern. As computers became faster and had better capability for storing and handling large volumes of both numeric and non-numeric data; more sophisticated, file-oriented information systems were developed. Typical systems were: the inventory system and the personnel records system. In an inventory system, data such as part number, part description, quantity, and cost could be stored in an inventory file and processed against daily sales and purchases file. The system analysis problem became more complex because there was a large number of combinations of software and hardware components. The query characteristics for these systems still followed a relatively fixed pattern since the types of information requested were relatively standard in terms of user population and query structure. With advances in hardware components, specifically, in large scale main memory and on-line rotating mass storage, have come advances in executive and data base management software. Together these advances have made on-line, real-time computer utilities practical and cost effective. Examples of such systems are: library information systems and passenger airline reservation systems. Information systems are evolving towards even more complex systems that utilize semantic as well as syntactic information to describe the system's data base. Characteristic of this evolution is the wide diversity of users and uses. The design problem is further complicated by the multiplicity of software and hardware components that can be used to build contemporary information systems. Both of these phenomenon have greatly increased the complexity of the analysis and design tasks. Parallel to the above evolution is the evolution of the data bases which these systems manage. Since data base design is critical to the overall performance of these systems, workload estimates are an essential ingredient to good data base performance assessment and configuration analysis. However, workload definition of these systems has become very complex due to the changing nature of the user population. Better and more sophisticated evaluative techniques are required to better support the system analysis function.

    System analysis is the application of systematic methodologies to large, complex, unstructured and future-oriented problems. System analysis when applied to information systems has a more restricted meaning: it consists of organizing, synthesizing and evaluating some aspects of an information system—hardware, software, data base, and users to develop a basis for designing and implementing a better system [COUG73]. In contrast to the more general definition of system analysis where the analysts evaluate and compare alternative ways of achieving objectives and make recommendations to a decision maker who ultimately selects one of the alternatives, an information system analyst often participates in all phases in system development—establishing system objectives and constraints, investigation and analysis of alternative procedures, selection of an alternative, detail design, and implementation (figure 5). In this research, emphasis is on data base workload definition so that the analysis and selection of alternatives can be performed in a more systematic and meaningful manner.

Figure 5. Phases of System Development

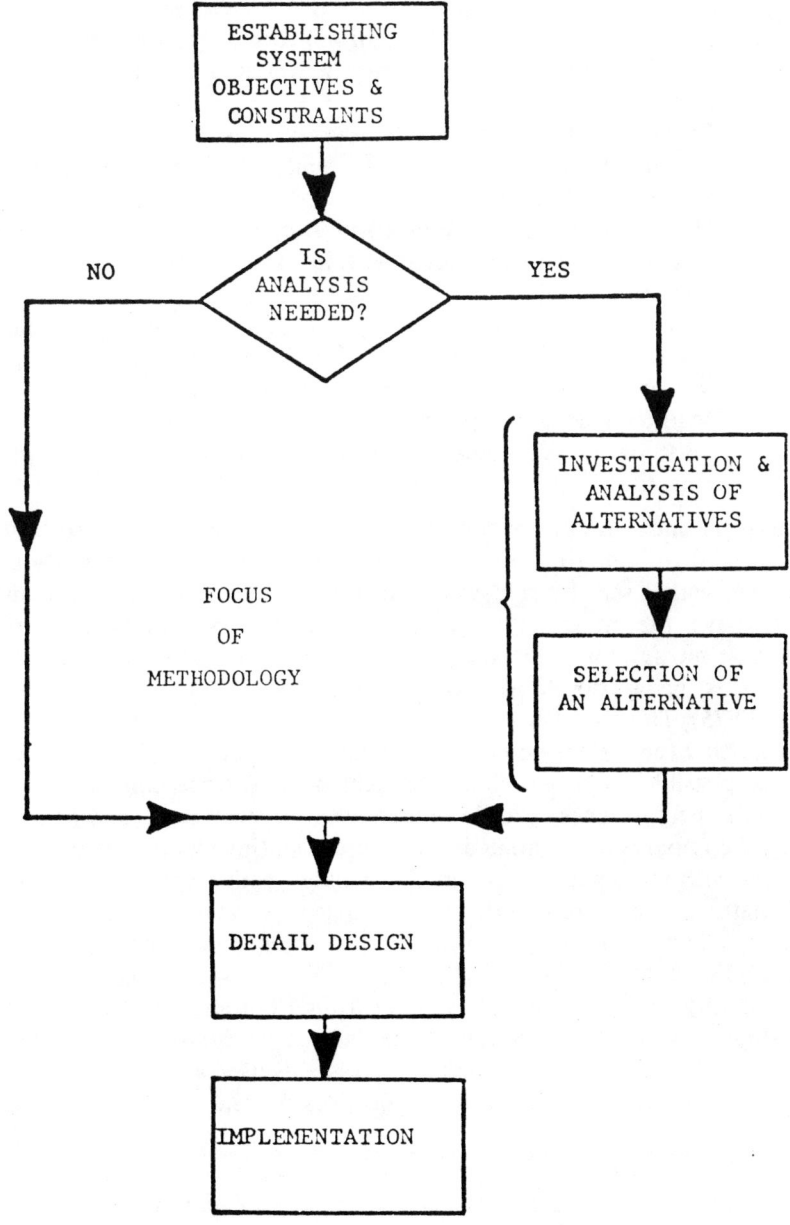

Establishing Systems Objectives and Constraints

Some of the reasons for starting an information system project are:

1. Establishment of new information processing requirements, e.g., a bank wanting to provide a new automated banking service to its customers.
2. Existence of problems in a current system, e.g., the average response time of an on-line information system has deteriorated to an intolerable extent.
3. Need to improve system performance, e.g., reducing the operating system overhead associated with information storage and retrieval operations.
4. Availability of new technology, e.g., the invention of inexpensive and large volume storage devices making possible the development of a large data base management system.
5. Maintenance of competitive edge, e.g., a company realizing that it must have a computerized information system for competitive reasons.

One of the most important but difficult tasks for an analyst is to translate the general reasons for an information system project into a well-defined problem with a set of exact systems objectives and constraints, the analyst must have the means to characterize all the potential users of the information system. The analyst must remember that the information system is being developed for the users and not for the computer [MART75]. This translates into a statement of the system's workload. After establishing the system objectives and constraints, the analyst formulates a list of possible solutions. The technical basis for the comparison is the system's performance profile under various workload scenarios. The analyst compares the estimated cost of investigating all or some of the alternatives with the potential savings that would result from choosing the best alternative. The formulation of information system objectives and constraints has been the subject of a number of papers and books [CHAN69, COUG73, KIMB72, MEAD67, WHIT69]. These references discussed general objectives in terms of system through-put and constraints in terms of response time. The function of the data base workload was not emphasized. In this research, a mathematical model is used as a systematic way of representing the system workload objectives for the data base subsystem.

Investigation and Analysis of Alternative Procedures

In general, there are extremely large numbers of alternative architectures available for a system's data base. The first goal for the analyst is to reduce the number of alternatives to a manageable size. Unfortunately, he can no longer rely solely on his past experience to make this judgment. Below we discuss the alternatives an analyst may have to consider, separating them into hardware and software aspects.

Hardware Selection

In many cases the analyst has to investigate different types of information processing equipment that can be used to support the workload requirements of the system. In terms of hardware, the analyst may have to consider different types of central processing units and memory. There are a large number of computer companies that manufacture CPU's and memory. The CPU's and memory configurations have a wide range of performance characteristics. In fact, selection of computers is such a complicated process that some large government and industrial organizations like the Air Force, the Navy, and Westinghouse have permanent computer evaluation and analysis teams [TIMM73].

Timmreck [TIMM73] indicated that the user workload can be modeled by the use of 'benchmarks'. This approach requires the maintenance of current system loading data and testing this against the alternative computer configurations. The drawback of this approach is that for a new system, the system loading data may not be available.

Another important set of hardware alternatives is the selection of on-line input-output and secondary storage devices. Information can be inputted or outputted from an information system in many different ways. Some of the common types of equipment used are: card reader, card punch, paper tape punch, printer, teletypewriter, graph plotter, cathode ray tubes, magnetic ink character reader, and optical character reader. Input-output devices are usually the direct interface between the users and the information system and strongly affect the opinions of users about the system.

Secondary storage units are also input-output units but they are usually used to store large amounts of data, i.e., the system's data base. Some of the common types of secondary storage units are: magnetic tape, magnetic drums, magnetic disks, data cells (magnetic strips storage). The number of input-output and secondary units alternatives are also very large because in addition to computer companies that manufacture these units there are a large number of peripheral equipment companies that manufacture only input-output or secondary storage units. Secondary storage units play an important role in the performance of an information system. Very often, the percentage of utilization of these devices determines the system's efficiency.

The user workload drives both the input-output and secondary storage devices. There are a number of studies on the strategies of allocating and storing data using these devices. Morgan [MORG74] gave a heuristic method for assigning files to either resident or non-resident disk devices. Through the use of queueing theory, Piepmeier [PIEP75] formulated equations for efficient distribution of I/O requests to a set of disks with differing operational characteristics. Lum [LUM75] gave an algorithm for allocating files in a hierarchical or multi-level storage organization. Salasin [SALA73] developed equations to predict data access time using different file structures in a hierarchy of storage devices. The problem with these studies is that the effect of the user workload is not considered due to the lack of tools for characterizing the user requests.

In order to process the large volume of user requests, some contemporary systems utilize concurrent and distributed processing. Chandy [CHAN76] described a method for allocating files in a distributed network through the use of integer programming techniques. [KUMA78] illustrated the use of simulation for evaluation of alternative configurations of highly concurrent computers. In these approaches, the user workload is viewed as a stream of random input-output requests to the system. Since the actual user requests to an information system are usually written in a high-level query language and are not completely random, a better workload characterization is needed. This is especially important in a distributed computer network environment because the user queries can be distributed based on the user workload, so as to optimize the usage of system resources.

Software Alternatives

The software alternatives are even more important than the hardware alternatives because during the lifetime of a system, software usually cost several times more than the hardware.

One of the important functions of the system's software is to provide a means of communication between the users and the information system. A language in which a user communicates his requests to the information system is called a Data Manipulation Language (DML). A system's workload is represented by a series of Data Manipulation Language commands. These commands may be embedded as part of user's programs written in a programming language such as Assembly, Cobol, Fortran, or PL/1. The kind of programming language(s) used determines the ease with which new software applications can be added and maintained.

When DML commands are embedded in user programs the workload is usually a series of simple attributed requests. That is, requests for records that contain a given attribute. Instead of having DML as part of a programming language, the system analyst may allow the user to communicate with the system through the 'query language'. These query languages allow the users to perform data manipulation functions such as retrieval, storage, modification, or deletion. The analyst should bear in mind that the user may not be a computer programmer and may not like to use complicated programming languages to retrieve information. On the other hand, the language should be flexible and powerful enough to allow the user to get all the information he needs [MEAD67]. In the case that a query language is used, the user workload is usually in the form of a series of multi-attributed queries. The complexity and frequency of the queries directly affect the system performance. Ghosh [GHOS75] discussed the advantages of clustering records that satisfied the same query and investigated the properties of files that have this type of organization. Cardenas [CARD73], in his performance evaluation methodology, characterized the user queries using a simple query complexity measure. This measure is based on the number of AND's and OR's in a Boolean expression. Both of these approaches are the first steps in the direction of characterizing the important effect of the user workload on system performance.

One important piece of software that supports the processing of the user workload is the operating system. An information system can usually be supported by one of several operating systems. Each operating system can have many alternative levels of implementation depending on what type of operating system facilities (e.g., job scheduling, memory management) are being provided. The design and implementation of operating systems are described in detail in [DONO72] and [SHAW74]. Saltzer [SALT74] gave equations for selecting optimal memory page size. Rosel [ROSE73] proposed a methodology to evaluate operating system dispatching schemes. Madnick [MADN74] discussed the performance of memory management, processor management, and device management schemes. The problem with these studies is that the analysis is based on random user inputs. A better characterization of the system usage pattern would allow these methodologies to evaluate different operating system resource allocation schemes more accurately.

The function of the user queries is to retrieve the relevant information from the system's data base. It is important that the data base be organized in such a manner that the requested data can be retrieved efficiently. There are many logical file organizations (e.g., inverted, multi-list, tree structured) and each of these organizations can be implemented using different physical storage organizations (e.g., sequential, indexed sequential, random) [KNUT73, BERZ71]. Each of these alternative logical or physical organizations has different performance characteristics such as memory utilization, access speed, and ease of update. The information analyst compares the alternatives and selects the appropriate logical and physical organizations for information systems.

In addition to designing logical and physical file organizations, the analyst may select a Data Base Management System (DBMS) to provide a high degree of independence between user application program and data and to improve programming productivity. A DBMS also facilitates systematic control of data and improves data base reliability and integrity. Currently, three data models are being used to implement DBMS's: (a) hierarchical, (b) network, and (c) relational. Date [DATE75], Martin [MART77], and Tsichritzis [TSIC77] provide excellent tutorials in these approaches. A system analyst may employ a DBMS for his information system using one of these models or he can use one of the commercially available DBMS such as: IMS by IBM (hierarchical), IDMS by Cullinare Corporation (network), or QBE by IBM (relational).

There are a large number of studies on the selection of data base organizations. Severence [SEVE74] and Lefkovitz [LEFK69] discussed the use of different storage structures. Cardenas [CARD75] has formulated equations for evaluating the access time and storage requirement of inverted file organizations as a function of data base content, query complexity, machine timing and blocking factor. Rothnie [ROTH74] developed a heuristic program for evaluating different combinations of inverted structures and multi-key hashing structures as a function of data and traffic characteristics. Siler [SILE76] described a stochastic model for evaluating alternative data retrieval systems organized under a combination of inverted lists, threaded list, and cellular list structures. Schneiderman [SCHN73] examined strategies for selecting the optimal data base reorganization points based on certain information structure and user activity characteristics. Maruyama [MARU76] gave a cost function that measures the system's overhead due to data base updates. This function computes the optimal data base reorganization point. Although all of these methodologies have indicated that the user workload is an important factor in selecting data base organizations, none of them have given adequate characterization of the user workload.

Performance Evaluation

The user workload is generated as a result of the interaction between the user requests (queries) and the data base's information structure. The characteristics of this workload are an important factor in system performance. Senko [SENK71] has illustrated that in several cases, the performance of a system using direct access devices is affected by the information organization structure and user search request characteristics. Boyse [BOYS75] described some simple analytical models for computer performance evaluation. Borovits [BORO77] gave a measure of system performance imbalance as a function of cost and utilization of system resources. Bucci [BUCC79] developed an analytical model of a distributed information system. This model related cost as a function of user's time, system rental, and system operations. Nunamaker [NUNA76] described a set of computer program procedures that can be used to facilitate the automation of analysis and design of information systems. Brownsmith [BROW79] described a performance evaluation methodology on the network DBMS approach. The effectiveness of these performance evaluation tools is dependent on how accurately the user workload can be characterized.

Although the workload characterization developed in this research can be applied to all the system analysis tools described earlier in this chapter, those tools restricted the analysis to specific components of the information system: file organization, task scheduling, and secondary storage utilization. Many of these tools can only be applied to systems that satisfied some specific set of conditions. A methodology that can be used to analyze a wide range of information systems is needed. The information system model developed here can be used to examine the interaction between the user workload and various system components. Through the use of this model, a wide range of information systems, from traditional information storage and retrieval systems [MEAD67] to modern day, relational types of systems [ZLOO77] can be studied. This general model is based on three underlying methodologies: the relational data model, the theory of stochastic processes, and the Information Processing System Simulator (IPSS) [DELU78]. These methodologies are discussed in the next chapter.

3

Underlying Methodologies

The purpose of this chapter is to provide a foundation for the research. The three underlying methodologies used in this research are discussed. These are:

1. *Relational Data Model:* To characterize the logical structure of an information system's data base from the user's perspective and to provide the basic structure for using attribute analysis to characterize an information system's information structure.
2. *Renewal Theory:* To characterize the distribution of attributes within an information system's logical data base and the basis for the attribute analysis characterization of data value dispersion.
3. *The Information Processing System Simulator (IPSS):* The IPSS methodology provides the basic framework for transforming user queries into data base workload definition.

Figure 6 illustrates the relationship between the methodology developed in this research and the underlying methodologies.

Relational Data Model

The relational data model is one of two widely used data models for characterizing the information system data bases. The other is the network (or CODASYL) data model. The advantage of the relational data model for this research is that the data bases it characterizes have no explicit or implicit implementation dependencies. Therefore, it takes a more user oriented perspective. It will be used to form the basis for characterizing the logical structure of the data stored in an information system in this research [CODD70] (E. F. Codd was the first author to propose the relational data model. Since then, a large number of studies on the relational data model have been conducted [DATE75, MART77, TSIC77]. Furthermore, the relational data model allows the information analyst to model the logical

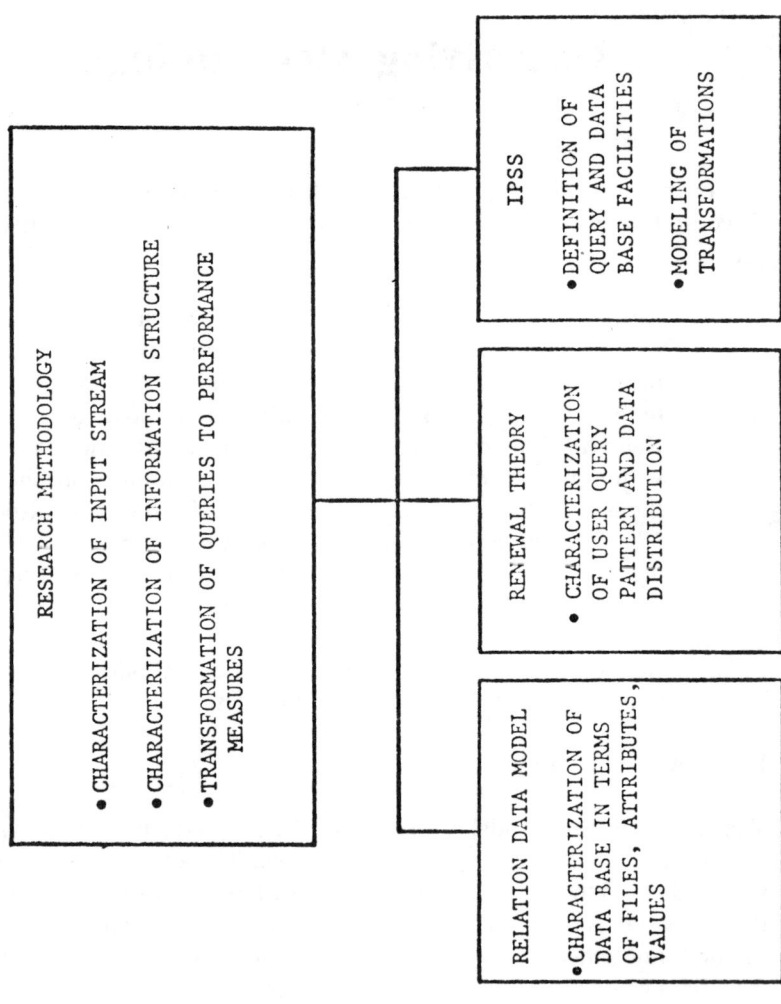

Figure 6. Relationship Between Research Methodology and Underlying Methodologies

relationship between various entities of the information system independent of how these entities are physically stored on hardware media. Using the relational model, the analyst can examine data base functions such as data integrity, redundancy control, data sharing, and data security from a logical point of view without worrying about the implementation details. In this research, the relational data model is used to characterize the logical structure of an information system's data base in term of files (relations) which are comprised of objects, attributes and values.

Conceptual Model of an Information System Data Base

Logically, an information system's data base can be characterized by a systematic ordering of information units. Each information unit is a triplet [LYON71] which consists of entity, attribute, and value. For example, consider a personnel data base which contains information about the following employees: Employee 1, last name is DOE and lives in Columbus; Employee 2, last name is SMITH and lives in Boston. The above information can be represented by the following triplets:

Entity	Attribute	Value	
(Person 1,	Last Name,	Doe	)
(Person 1,	City,	Columbus	)
(Person 2,	Last Name,	Smith	)
(Person 2,	City,	Boston	)

This information system data base can also be represented by clusters of points in a three dimensional space as shown in figure 7.

The function of a data base model is to provide a set of guidelines for clustering data points and manipulating the clusters. A DBMS is a specific language and syntax that performs these operations within an actual computer system. Additionally, the DBMS may have a high level language—a query language—that resembles a natural language such as English, for use by the information system user community. These clusters correspond to files in traditional information storage and retrieval systems and to relations in a relational data model. Entities within a relation correspond to traditional logical records, and data fields to attribute-value pair occurrences. For example, using the data base in the above example, a user can define a logical subset which consists of all the information about Person 1. This would be the set [(Person 1, Last Name = Doe), (Person 1, City = Columbus)]. The user can define another logical subset which consists of all the last names in the data base. This would be the set [(Person 1, Last Name = Doe), (Person 2, Last Name = Smith)]. Ideally, a data model should allow a user to group any possible combinations of a data base's

Figure 7. Graphical Representation of Information in a Data Base

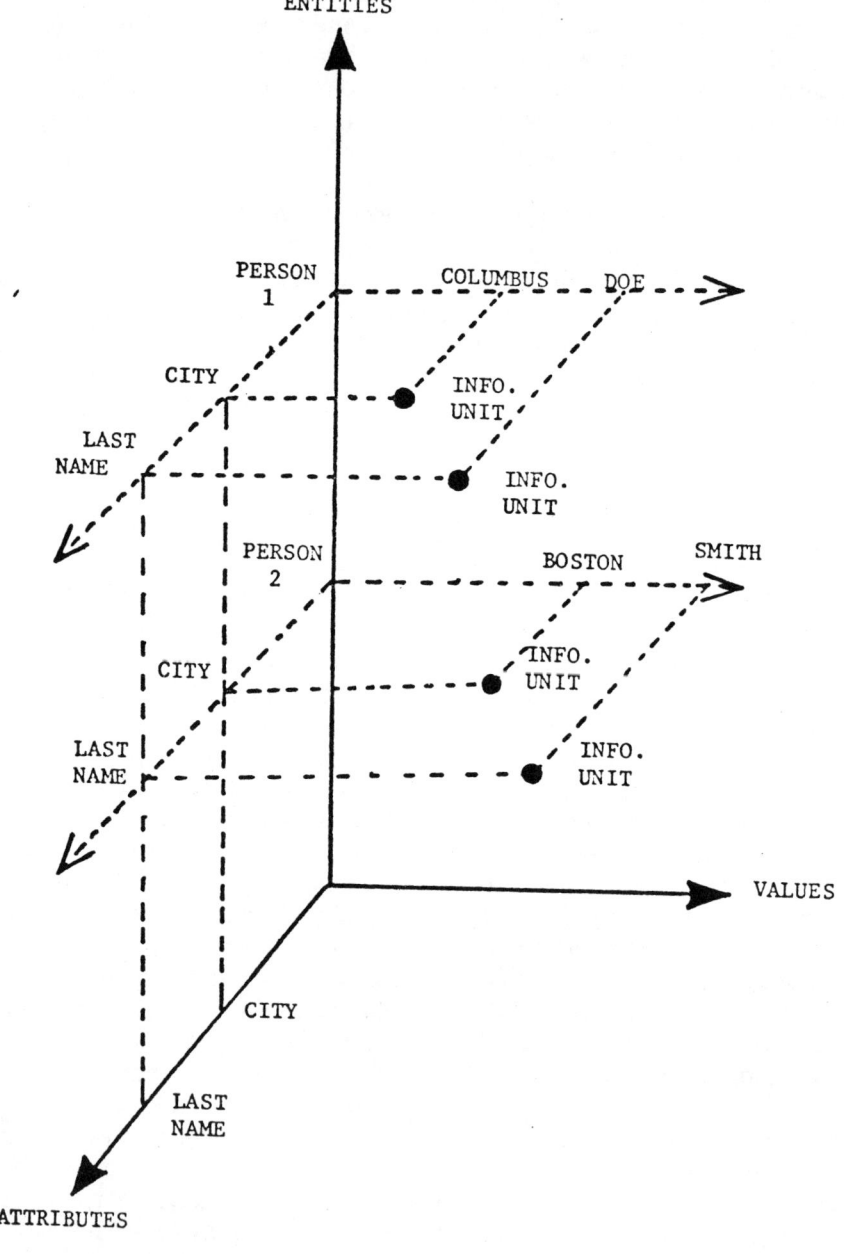

information units into logical subsets and to manipulate these objects. In actual implementation this is usually not possible because of efficiency considerations.

The above data base model described the data base from a users point of view. The data base model can also be described from a computer system point of view, that is, in terms of the software and hardware that are needed to support the data base model. In this use, the information units that comprise a data base are called the logical data base. These information units are stored on some physical storage media (e.g., drum, disk, or tape). It is the responsibility of the DBMS software to map a user's logical subsets of information units into physical storage addresses and to translate the user's logical subset manipulation instructions into physical storage access instructions. This characterization of DBMS is given in figure 8. The data base model developed in this research (described in chapter 4) is general enough to accomodate both the users and computer systems views of the data base.

Using the data base model, a user sees his data in a form provided by a higher level, non-programming logical data base and does not know its actual software system representation. Any changes in DBMS maintained schema formats such as changes from fixed length to variable length or from sequential to direct access would only affect the DBMS mapping function. Since the user views his data as logical objects in the logical data base, his programs (using these logical objects) will not be affected by these changes. Note that a relational data model is a meta-DBMS which is used to describe the salient features and capabilities of a class of DBMS's. Two important aspects of the relational data model is its DDL for defining data base schemata and its DML for traversing the data base in response to user queries. One important advantage of the relational data model is that it lends itself directly to Boolean operators in the user queries. Figure 9 shows a structural model of a relational data model based DBMS. Level 0 corresponds to the physical data base in the conceptual model. Levels 1 through 3 are parts of a more refined view of the logical data base.

Level 3 represents the user processes. For each user process there is a buffer through which the data submodel records are inputted or outputted. A DBMS would provide users with a special language called a Data Manipulation Language (DML) to input, output and manipulate data submodel records in the buffer area.

Since most users would be interested in only a small part of the data base as represented by the data model, Level 2 is introduced. Level 2 consists of a collection of data submodels. Each data submodel represents the part of the data model which a user's program may use. Beside partitioning the data model for the users (the partitions may overlap), Level 2 of

Figure 8. Logical to Physical Data Base Mapping

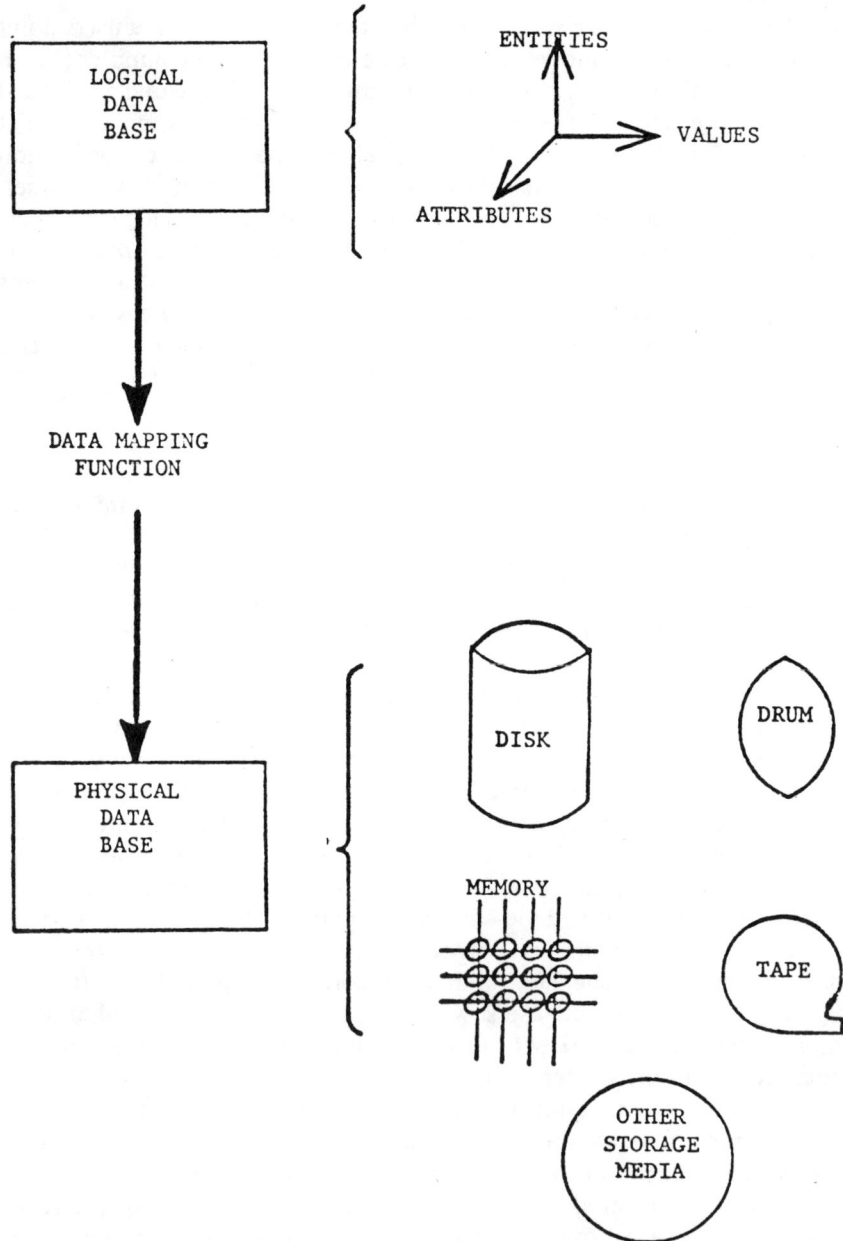

Figure 9. Example of Hierarchy of Relational Data Base Models

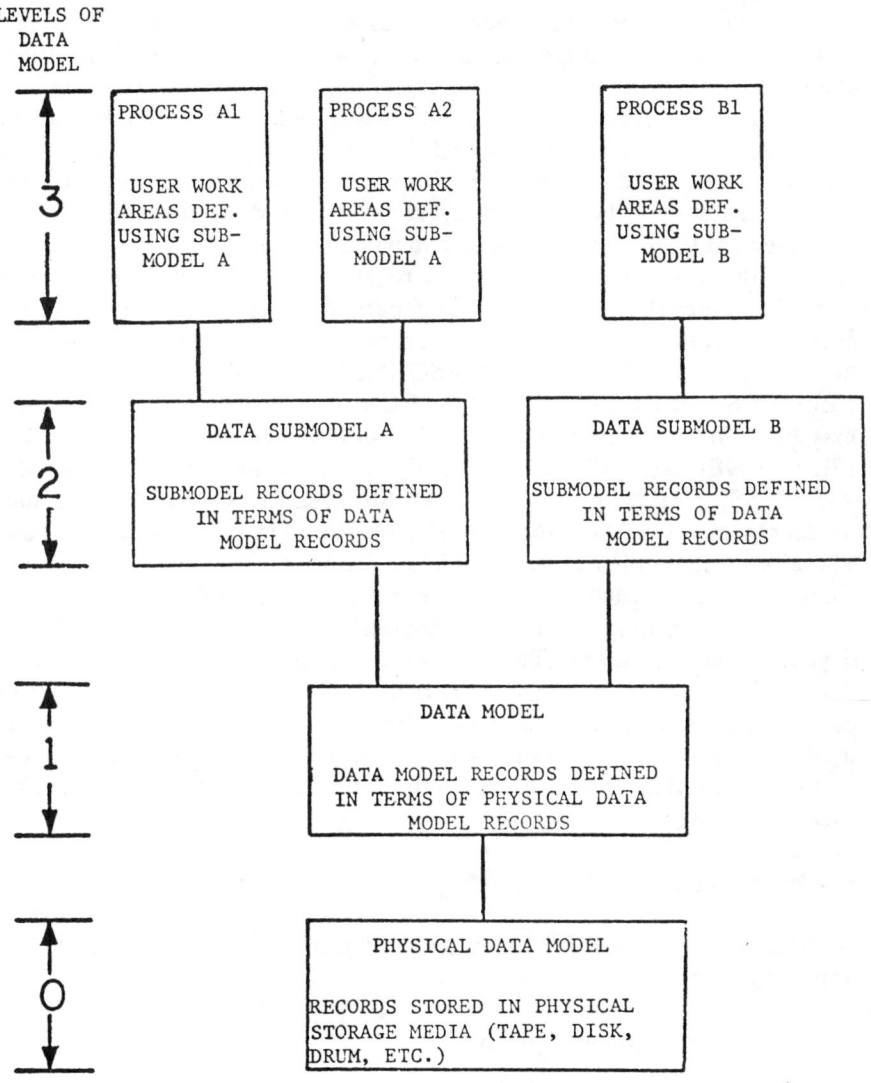

the logical data base also lets users view the structure of the data model records in a modified form. For example, the fields in a data submodel may be a subset of the fields in the corresponding data model record, and the field by which the data submodel records are sequenced may be different from the field by which the data model records are sequenced. The DBMS can use Level 2 to increase the security of the data base by restricting each user to the use of only those data submodels for which he has authorization.

Level 1 is called the data model. The data model allows users to view the whole physical data base as various types of data model records. The specific structure of these data model records depends on the approach used to implement the structural model, and will be discussed in the next section. Usually the structure of data model records is defined by using various symbolic names that represent various parts of the physical data base. For example, through the data model, users may see a data base as three types of data base records called PERSONNEL-RECORDS, INVENTORY-RECORDS and CUSTOMER-RECORDS. The structure of these records may be defined by specifying the fields within each record. For example, PERSONNEL-RECORDS may consist of four logical fields: NAME, ADDRESS, SALARY, and SOCIAL-SECURITY-NUMBER. The data model represents all the information that is stored in the physical data base. Therefore, the number of data model record types together with the corresponding record structures may be very large and complex.

At Level 0, data is stored as physical records on secondary storage devices. There are many file organizations (hashing, sorted, binary tree) that can be used to store the physical records. Also, there is a wide spectrum of secondary storage devices (disks, drums, bubble memory) that can be used to support the file organizations. The selection of file organizations and storage devices should be based on the processing requirements of the user workload.

Implementation Model of DBMS

At present there are three approaches of implementing a DBMS. These approaches are:

 1. The Hierarchical approach
 2. The Network approach
 3. The Relational approach

The major difference between these approaches lies in the way they implement the logical data base (i.e., level 1 to 3 of the conceptual model). In a DBMS, users do not see the physical data base. Very often they do not even see the data model because queries are prewritten as in a scheduled report. Each user only sees the data submodel for which he is authorized. Coordination between data bases is the responsibility of the system's data base administrator. His responsibilities include maintaining the mapping between the data model and the physical data base, maintaining the mapping between each data submodel and the data model, and specifying the set of instructions that each user is allowed to use to manipulate the data submodel records. For the users, the DBMS provides a data manipulation language to access the data model records. The DBMS also provides the following languages to the data base administrators:

1. A language to specify the mapping between the data model and the physical data base,
2. A language to define the data model,
3. A language to specify the mapping between the data submodels and the data model, and
4. A language to specify the data submodels.

The Relational Approach

In this section, the relational approach to data base management is described. The description of the relational data model follows the multi-level view of DBMS given in figure 7. Currently, several relational DBMS's have been developed. For example, the data base management systems QBE [ZLOO77] and System R [SYSR79] are relational systems.

The relational approach is based on the mathematical theory of relations. In the data model, all record types and links between these record types are represented by relations. Formally, given sets $D(1), D(2), \ldots, D(n)$, R is a relation on these sets if R is a set of n-tuples $(d(1), d(2), \ldots, d(n))$ where $d(i)$ belongs to $D(i)$ for $i = 1$ to n. That is,

R is a relation on $<D(1), \ldots, D(n)>$
    if and only if
R = $<(d(1), \ldots, D(n)) | d(i)$ belongs to $D(i), i = 1$ to $n>$

These ideas can best be illustrated by an example. Consider a data base for a library information system. Suppose the data base contains information about a group of libraries and a collection of periodicals. Each library may subscribe to one or more periodicals and each periodical may be subscribed to by one or more libraries. Using the relational approach, the data model is represented by three relations: a PERIODICALS relation which contains information about periodical publications, a LIBRARY relation which contains information about each library, and a SUBSCRIPTION relation which contains information about periodicals subscribed to by each library and libraries that subscribe to each periodical. An example of relations in table form is shown in Table 1.

The data submodels consists of a subset of the set of relations defined in the data model. For example, in the library information system data model, a submodel can be defined as consisting of only the PERIODICALS relation in Table 1. In this research, queries that are inputted to the data submodel level is considered to be in the form of Boolean expressions (Propositional Calculus expressions). These are expressions of domain and value conditions connected by the logical operators AND, OR, and NOT. For example, to retrieve all tuples in the PERIODICAL relation that described journals that are published monthly or bimonthly, the following Boolean expression can be used: TYPE = MONTHLY OR TYPE = BIMONTHLY. It is assumed that at the submodel level queries only work on individual relations.

At the user application level, a data manipulation language or data sublanguage can be used to access relations. The data sublanguage can be implemented as extensions to current high level languages or as subroutine calls. The relational approach can support two possible types of data sublanguages: the relational calculus language and the relational algebra language. Both of these languages are equally powerful and any user query which can be expressed in the form of First Order Predicate Calculus [KOR66] can be handled. An example of a first order predicate calculus expression is given below.

$$\forall \text{ PERIODICALS } \exists \text{ SUBSCRIPTION}$$
$$[\text{LIBRARY.LNO} = \text{SUBSCRIPTION.LNO} \wedge \text{PERIODICAL.PID} = \text{SUBSCRIPTION.PID}]$$

This expression represents the set of libraries that subscribe to all periodicals given in the PERIODICAL relation. The relational calculus language is a non-procedural language, i.e., a language in which a user specifies his request to the DBMS by defining the property of the information he wants instead of specifying the instructions (procedure) to obtain the information. Expressions in this language are extensions of first order predicate calculus expressions. The relational algebra language is a procedural language and instructions in this language consist of simple instructions that are similar to the union and intersection operations of mathematical set theory. For example, the command JOIN PERIODICAL.PID WITH SUBSCRIPTION.PID represents the combining of the PERIODICAL and SUBSCRIPTION relations to form a new relation

Table 1. Relations for the Library Information System Example

P.ID	PERIODICAL NAME	TYPE
1	COMPUTING SURVEYS	QUARTERLY
2	COMMUNI-CATIONS	MONTHLY
3	COMPUTER WORLD	WEEKLY
4	SOFTWARE ENGINEERING	BIMONTHLY
5	COMPUTERS	MONTHLY

LIBRARY NUMBER	PERIOD-ICAL ID	NO. OF SUBSCRIPTION
1	1	2
1	2	4
1	4	1
1	5	1
2	2	1
2	3	1
3	3	2
4	4	2
4	2	3
4	1	1

L.NO	LIBRARY NAME	STATE
1	A	OHIO
2	B	NEW YORK
3	C	MICHIGAN
4	D	CALIFORNIA

using the PID (periodical ID) as the link for combining the relations. Note that at this level, queries access multiple relations and these queries have to be translated to single relation queries at the submodel level.

Similarity of Relational Data Model to Other Data Models

Besides the relational approach, there are two other approaches to the modeling of logical data bases. These approaches are the hierarchical approach and the network approach. This section will give a brief description of each approach. It will be shown that the relational data model can characterize both the hierarchical and network data structures. The generality of the relational model in representing both the hierarchical and network models has been described by Date [DATE75]. Since the research methodology is based on the relational data model, data bases with either hierarchical or network structures can use the research methodology.

In the hierarchical approach, the entities in logical data bases are connected by tree-like structures. A typical hierarchical system is the Information Management System (IMS) developed by IBM [IBM75].

In IMS the data model is called the data base descriptor. The data model lets the users view the data base as a collection of ordered tree structures (forest). The roots of the tree structures are called the physical data base records (PDBR) and the nodes of the trees (including the roots) are called segments. The data model can be represented by a tree diagram as shown in figure 10.

There can be any number of each type of segment in the data model. For example, figure 11 shows a tree diagram representation of a data model which consists of information about department, courses and students in a university. A sample occurrence of these segments is shown in figure 12.

In the network approach the entities in the logical data base are connected by network-like structures. The basic typical network approach is given in the reports of the CODASYL Programming Language Committee [DBTG71, CODA73]. CODASYL is a language and programming package standardization committee composed of representatives from government and major industries. In the network data model the user views the data base schema as a network (or directed graph). The nodes of the network represent record types. The links between record types are a priori named associations and are called sets. (Note that a network set is different from the usual way a set is defined in mathematics.) Sets are used to permit data base traversal in response to a user query. A typical data base represented as a network diagram is shown in figure 13.

The data model is defined by specifying the different record types, and the sets that link these record types together. Since tree structures are

Figure 10. Example of a Hierarchical View of a Data Base

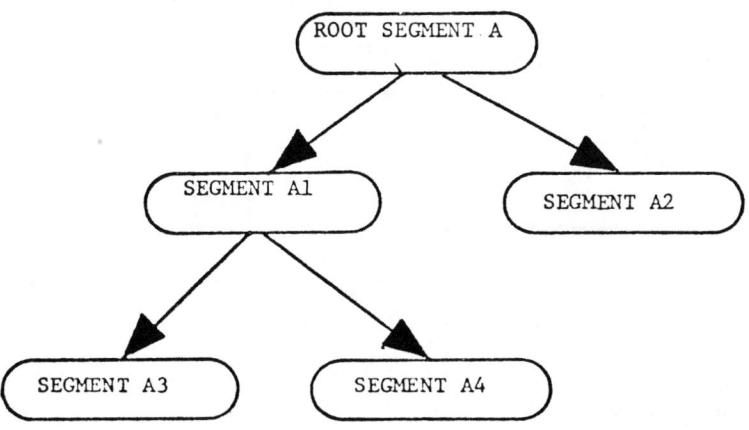

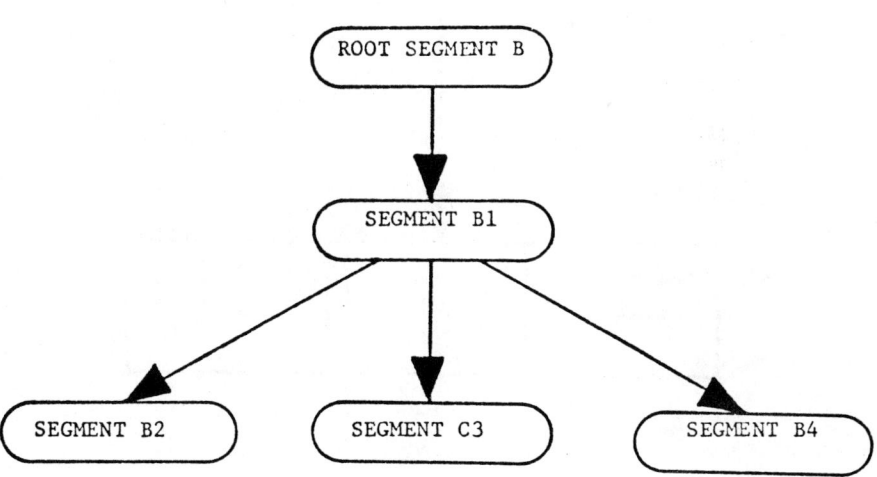

Figure 11. Data Model for University Data Base Example Represented as a Tree Structure

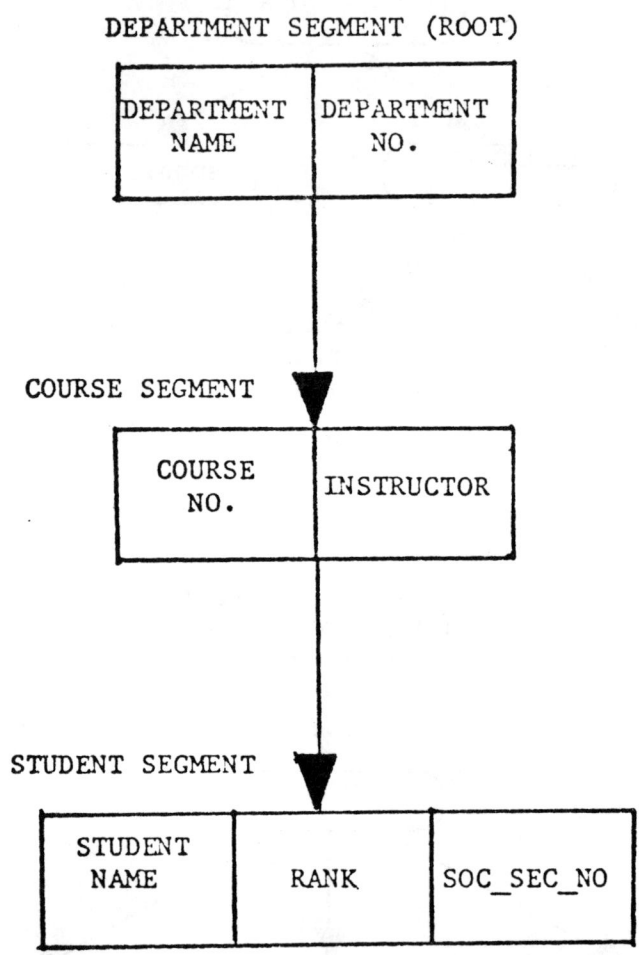

Figure 12. Sample Occurences of the University Data Model Segments

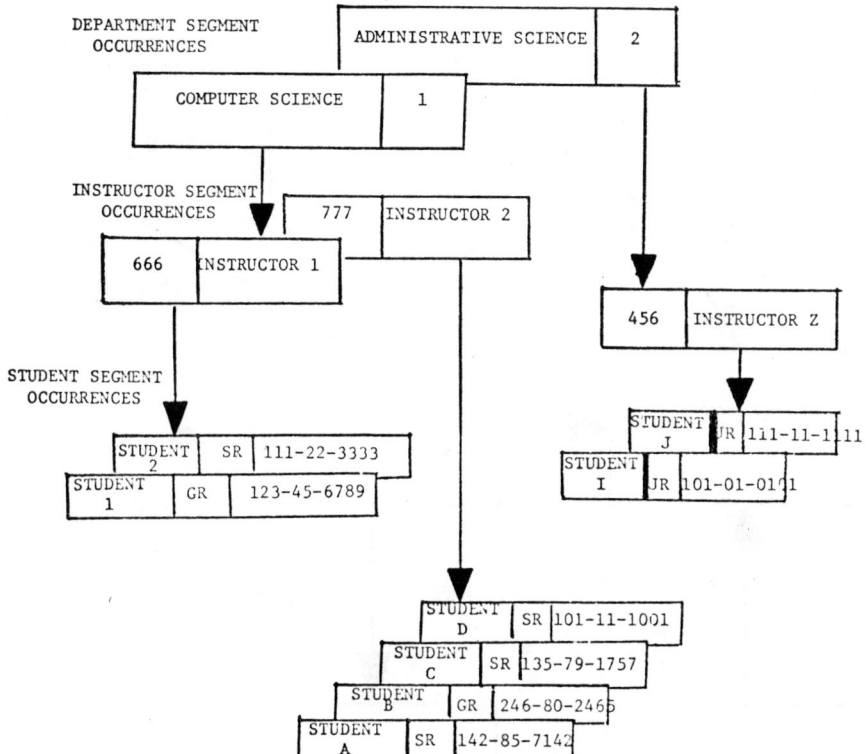

Figure 13. Network Representation of a Typical Data Model

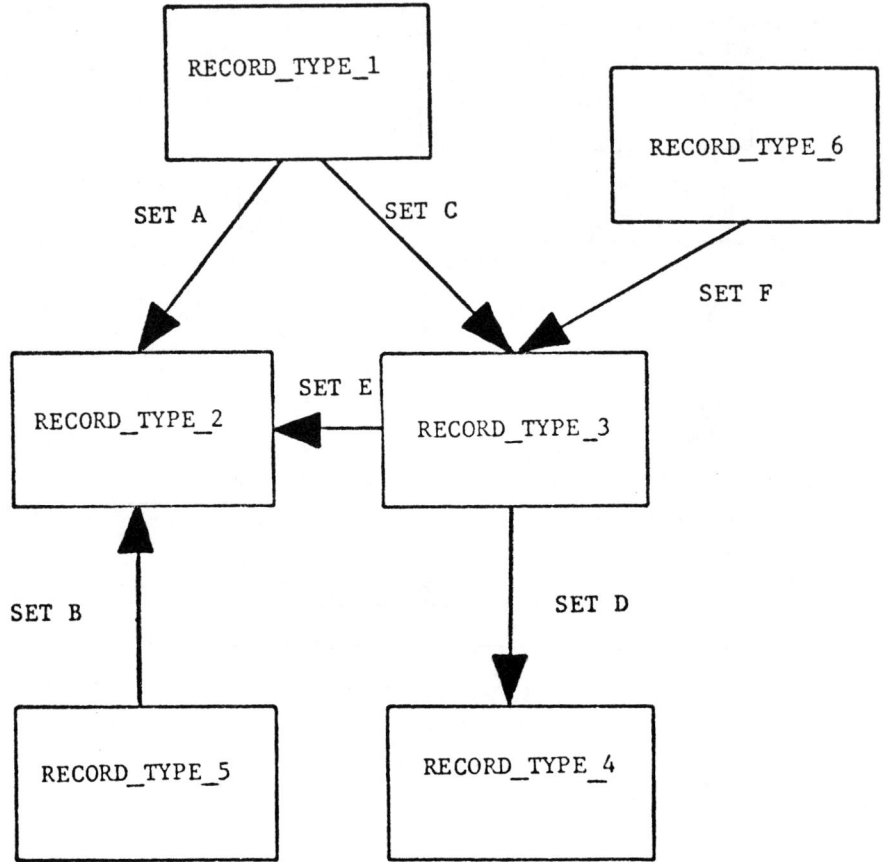

actually specialized network structures, all possible logical relations representable in the hierarchical approach can be represented in the network approach. The network approach is more general than the hierarchical approach. An example of the network representation of a data base is given in the following example. Suppose a company's data base consists of three types of records: DEPARTMENT-RECORDS, PROJECT-RECORDS, and EMPLOYEE-RECORDS. If the system designer wants to handle user requests of the forms: (1) find all employees of a given department and (2) find all employees of a given project, he can define the data model in the form of a network as shown in figure 14. In this figure, two DBTG sets are defined: the PROJECT-EMPLOYEE set that represents the link between PROJECT-RECORDS and EMPLOYEE-RECORDS, and the DEPARTMENT-EMPLOYEE set that represents the link between DEPARTMENT-RECORDS and EMPLOYEE-RECORDS.

Commonly, application level views (Level 2 in figure 15) are referred to as subschema. Each subschema consists of a network of records which is a subnetwork of the schema (a restriction for DBTG only). For example, in the company data base example, a subschema can be defined so that users of this subschema can see the department and employee records but not the project records or the relationship between the project records and the employee records. A graphical representation of this subschema is shown in figure 15.

Figure 16 illustrates the similarity between the three data models. As was mentioned earlier, hierarchical data models are tree structures and network data models are graph structures. Since tree structures are also graph structures, hierarchical data models can be represented by network data models. That is, there exists a one-to-one map from the hierarchical data models into the network data models.

In a network data model, the logical structure is completely described by a graph consisting of a collection of record types and a collection of arcs called 'sets'. Each record type corresponds to a relation in a relational data model. An arc that joins two records types (e.g., record type A to record type B) can be represented by a relation consisting of two domains. The first domain consists of record ID's of record type A and the second domain consists of the corresponding ID's of record type B. That is, if there is an arc joining record n of record type A to record m of record type B, then this arc is represented by the tuple (n,m) in the relational data model. The building of a relation to represent arcs also takes care of the case where 'sets' in network model have conditions for set membership because all membership conditions can be represented by arcs from the owner record instance to the member record instance. All of these arcs can be represented by the above relation. Since both the record types and arcs (sets) in the net-

Figure 14. Network Representation of the Company Data Base Example

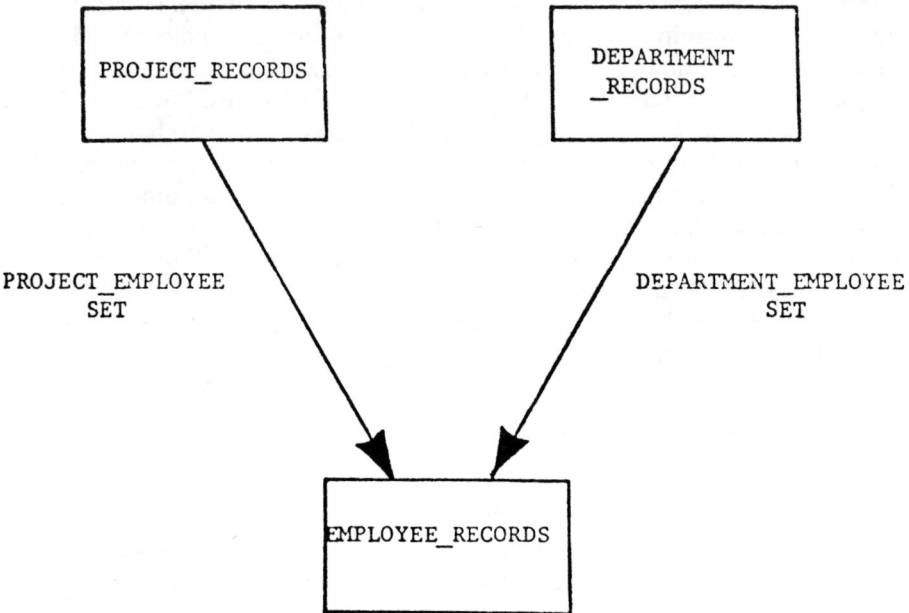

Figure 15. A Subschema for the Company Data Base Example

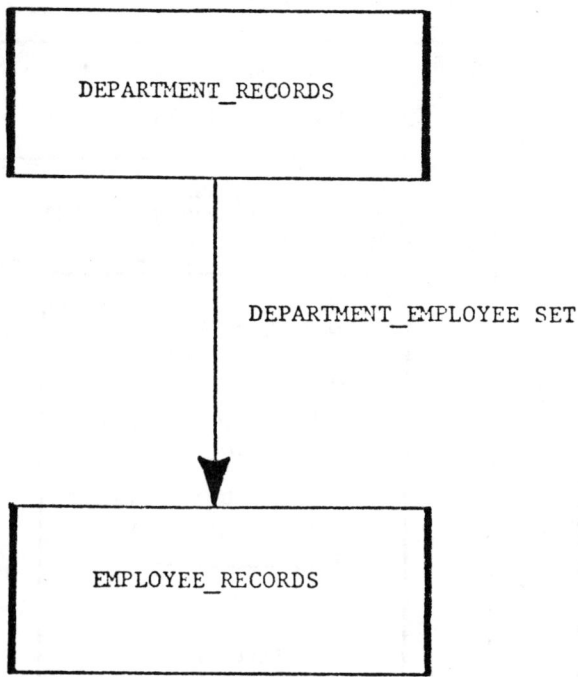

Figure 16. Relationship Between Different Approaches to Data Base Management

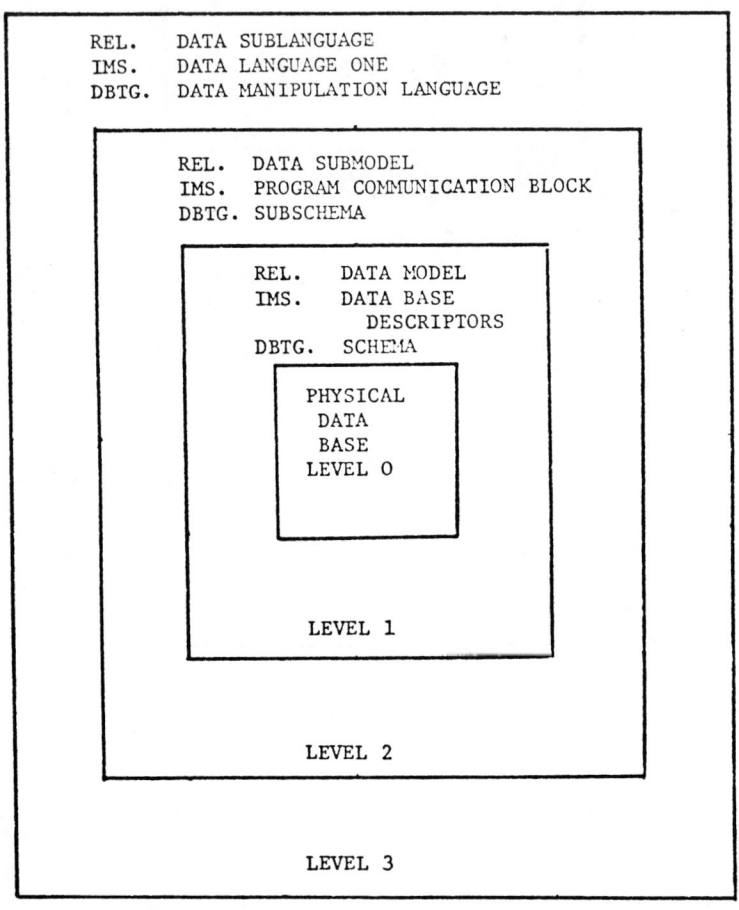

LEGEND: REL. RELATIONAL APPROACH
        IMS. INFORMATION MANAGEMENT SYSTEM (HIERARCHICAL APPROACH)
        DBTG. NETWORK APPROACH

work model can be represented as relations, any network model can be represented by a corresponding relational model. That is, there exists a one-to-one map from the network data models to the relational data models.

As was shown above, the hierarchical data models can be represented by network data models and network data models can be represented by relational data models (figure 17). Therefore, the relational data model is capable of representing the logical data structure of both the hierarchical and network approaches. Taking advantage of the generality of the relational approach, this research uses the relational data model as a basis for characterization of the logical data structure of information systems. Descriptions about this characterization are given in the methodological model in the next chapter.

Renewal Processes

In this research the distribution of data values (i.e., attribute-value pairs) in a data base is characterized by the renewal processes. The definitions of these renewal processes are based on the theory of stochastic processes. The following is a brief description of stochastic processes. A more detailed description of stochastic processes can be found in books by Karlin and Parzen [PARZ62 and KARL61]. Attribute Analysis, the use of renewal processes to characterize data collections, is also described below.

Probability theory is the study of random phenomena. All of the possible outcomes of a random phenomenon constitute a sample space. For example, consider a student records file in a university. Each record has a field called the rank field which has one of the following values: FR (freshman), SO (sophomore), JR (junior), SR (senior), or GR (graduate). If a record is selected at random from the student records file, the rank field will have one of the five possible values. The set of ranks, RANK = (FR, SO, JR, SR, GR), is a sample space. Since mathematically it is more convenient to manipulate numbers instead of sample space of objects, random variables are used to map objects of sample space to numbers. A random variable is defined as a function which assigns numeric values to the different outcomes defined by the sample space. A random variable is called a discrete random variable if the range of numeric values are integers. A random variable is called a continuous random variable if the range of numeric values are real numbers. Using the previous example, a random variable called R can be defined as a function that maps the sample space values FR, SO, JR, SR and GR to 1, 2, 3, 4 and 5 respectively. That is, $R(FR)=1$, $R(SO)=2$, $R(JR)=3$, $R(SR)=4$ and $R(GR)=5$.

A sample space together with the associated random variable defines the possible outcomes of a random phenomenon. The probability asso-

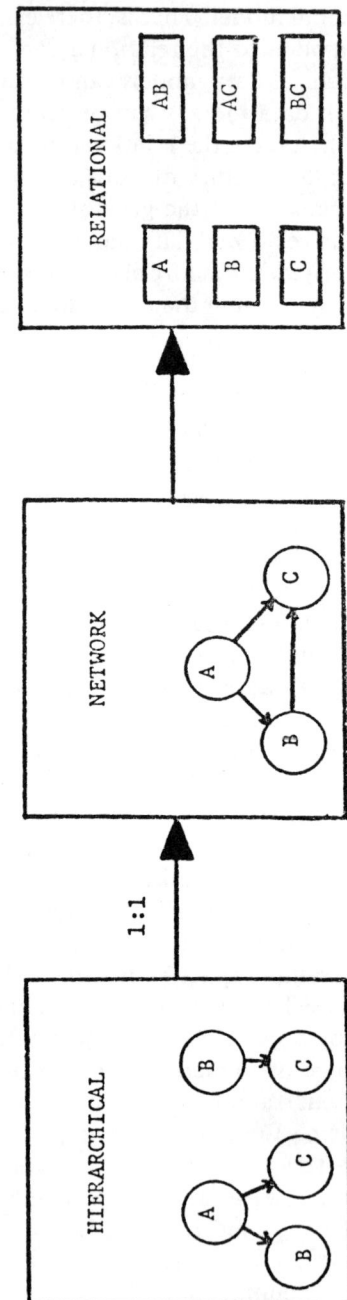

Figure 17. One-to-One Mappings Between Hierarchical, Network and Relational Approaches

Underlying Methodologies 51

ciated with each of these outcomes is defined by the probability function. For a discrete random variable, a probability function f is defined as a function which assigns probabilities to each number within the range of the random variable. The probability of a random variable X having the value t is denoted by $f(X=t)$. Using the previous example, let the probability of a randomly selected record having a rank of FR be 0.4, SO be 0.2, JR be 0.15, SR be 0.15, and GR be 0.1. The probability function g for the rank random variable R is defined as follows: $g(R=1)=0.4$, $g(R=2)=0.2$, $g(R=3)=0.15$, $g(R=4)=0.15$ and $g(R=5)=0.1$.

For both discrete and continuous random variables, the distribution of values is often expressed as the probability that the random variables are less than or equal to some value. The probability distribution function (pdf), or cumulative distribution function for a random variable X, is denoted by $F(x)$ and represents the probability that the random variable X is less than or equal to x. Using the student records file example, the probability distribution function G for the rank random variable R is defined as follows: $G(1) = g(R.LE.1) = 0.4$, $G(2) = g(R.LE.2) = 0.6$, $G(3) = g(R.LE.3) = 0.75$, $G(4) = g(R.LE.4) = 0.9$ and $G(5) = g(R.LE.5) = 1.0$.

Probability distribution functions are used to describe individual random variables. Stochastic processes are used to study a collection of random variables. A stochastic process is a family of random variables ($X(t)$, where $t \in T$). That is, the parameter t varies in an index set T and each $X(t)$ is a random variable. Many events that occur in an information system are governed by stochastic processes. For example, the total number of queries that arrive at an information system can be represented by the stochastic process ($N(t)$, where t .ELM-OF. T). Here, T represents the set of times between system start-up and system shut-down. $N(t)$ is a random variable that gives the total number of queries at a time, t. This type of stochastic process is also called a counting process. The occurrences of events correspond to a series of points, $t(0), t(1), t(2),...$, between 0 and infinity. The intervals between consecutive occurrences are called inter-arrival times and are denoted by $T(1), T(2),...$, where $T(i)=t(i)-t(i-1)$. Each inter-arrival time is a random variable. If the inter-arrival times, $T(1), T(2),...$, are independent and identically distributed positive random variables, the associated stochastic process is called a renewal process. For example, if the inter-arrival times between queries have independent and identical probability distribution functions, then the input stream of the information system can be described by a renewal process.

In DeLutis's "The Information Processing System Simulator" [DELU 68], renewal processes are used to characterize the occurrence of attributes in documents of an information system. This method was called attribute analysis. In this research, the characterization of information structure is developed based on ideas suggested by this approach.

52 Underlying Methodologies

Attribute analysis is a method of characterizing the occurrences of secondary keys in data base records. A data base is a collection of records containing one or more secondary keys, the collection of which constitutes the contents of the record. Records are assumed to arrive at the information system in an order which is not under the control of the system. Each of these records is assigned a consecutive number called an accession number. For each key, the occurrences of the key in the accession number space (data base) is represented by a stochastic process. Figure 18 shows the occurrences of the keys A, B, and C.

The occurrences of keys over the access number space of a data collection is characterized by three probability distributions (1) the renewal process PDF F(x) which describes how records with the same key are distributed over the accession number space, (2) for each key, the first occurrence PDF G(x) describes the arrival pattern of the first record that contains the key, and (3) for each key, the number of occurrences PDF N(x) gives the total number of records that contain the key. For example, if the occurrences of a key follow the Poisson process, then the renewal process PDF, the first occurrence PDF, and the number of occurrences PDF are given by the following equations: $G(x) = 1 - \exp(-ax)$, $F(y) = 1 - \exp(-ay)$ and $N(z) = \exp(-b))(b^{**}z)/(z!)$. In these equations, a and b are constants, exp is the exponential function, ** means 'raised to the power of', and ! indicates factorial. The above equations show that both the first occurrence and renewal PDF's follow the exponential distribution. The number of occurrence PDF is represented by the counting function for the Poisson process.

In this research, renewal processes are used to describe the occurrences of attributes in a data base. In DeLutis's work [DELU68] attribute analysis was performed on actual data collections and the equations obtained followed the form given by Zipf's Law [MEAD67]. That is, the inter-record distances are indirectly proportional to the frequency of occurrences. In another study [OCLC79] in which a library system data base was examined, the occurrences of subject headings (attributes) in the data base can be characterized by renewal processes. Also, if a data base is sorted using multiple attributes, the clustering of records with the same attribute can be described by renewal processes with equations in the form of Zipf's Law.

This concludes the discussion of renewal processes. The use of renewal processes to characterize information systems is described in the methodological model of chapter 4.

IPSS

The Information Processing System Simulator (IPSS) is a special purpose methodology and simulation language for the performance evaluation of

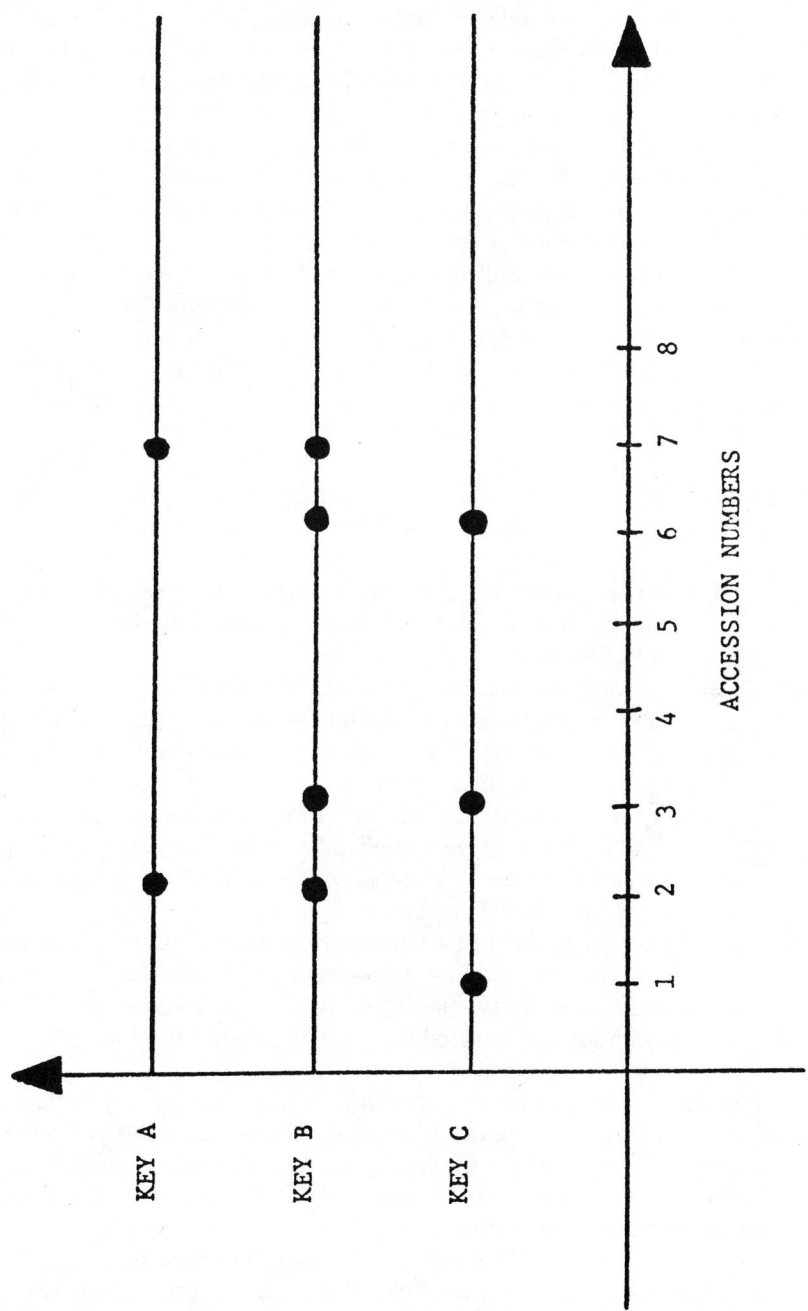

Figure 18. Occurrences of Keys Over the Accession Number Space

information processing systems. The IPSS simulation language was designed, developed and implemented by a research team headed by Dr. Thomas DeLutis at Ohio State University. IPSS has been discussed in detail by DeLutis [DELU76, DELU77a, and DELU78]. The following is a summary of the IPSS methodology.

IPSS has been designed to serve three distinct groups of users: the researcher, the information system analyst/designer, and the student. The most important departure from current simulation packages which IPSS embodies is its emphasis on the interrelationship between the application, the system software, and the I/O process. The language constructs permit the modeler to describe easily complex I/O activity for a wide variety of computer systems and applications. One important research area for which IPSS will be especially useful is the investigation of data structures/data manipulation operations for large on-line, real-time, integrated data base systems.

IPSS is a large research project; the total IPSS simulation package contains more than 50,000 PL/1 and FORTRAN statements. Included in this total is the software for the following IPSS subsystems:

1. Source statement processors—these are a set of IPSS language parsers written in PL/1 that translate the IPSS commands to FORTRAN.
2. Library management and listing facilities—these facilities allow the modeler to save, load, and list various IPSS model components stored in an IPSS library. The library management and listing routines are written in PL/1.
3. IPSS supplied simulation time facilities—these are special FORTRAN routines supplied by IPSS. These routines support the execution of an IPSS model. The calls to these routines are generated by the IPSS parsers.
4. Run time control software—these are special PL/1 programs that support the interface between the IBM S/370 Operating System and IPSS. These programs direct the loading and execution of compilers, linkage editors and IPSS load modules.

IPSS has been designed in a modular fashion to assist the continued development of both language and run control facilities. IPSS has been designed to facilitate the transfer of developed models to computer systems other than the IBM System/370. In this research facilities for modeling the user workload have been added to IPSS.

The underlying methodology is straightforward. Basically, it defines a sequence of processing transformations which successively alter the user query into performance measures. The transformations are not directly defined by the modeler but are produced indirectly via definitions of the appropriate information system components. It is the interaction of these components over simulated time that causes the desired transformations to occur. Currently, IPSS language constructs concentrate on a computer system's jobs, tasks, and resources. They provide the modeler with recognizable analogs to common operating system software, hardware devices, and input/output control system level files and operations. This level of detail is the nucleus for the continued upward expansion of IPSS descriptive and evaluative facilities and is the necessary first step in the realization of the methodology. Definitional statements for the telecommunication subsystems, i.e., lines, terminals, etc., are omitted. This omission is based on the complexity of this subsystem and on the ability to describe with IPSS its aggregate behavior at the central site.

The Information Processing System Simulator can also be viewed as a laboratory in which the researcher can investigate information system behavior under controlled and repeatable conditions. Model systhesis is conceptual and definitionally modular, allowing the researcher to modify complex designs with minimum effort. The modeler has the ability to define data base activity procedurally, and therefore can ascertain secondary storage behavior dynamically, a distinct advantage over the assigning of a priori values to secondary storage operations. This facility is one of the important benefits of IPSS. The ability to define system hardware and software in a modular manner also permits the designer to develop a model to the depth of functional detail desired. He has the capability of substituting system components between successive model evaluations without redefining the model. Furthermore, IPSS has extensive library facilities which enable hardware and software definitions to be stored for later inclusion into more extensive component definitions. The analyst, therefore, can concentrate his energies on the specific aspects of a particular problem instead of having to develop a complete model.

The ability to isolate functional components and to allow for their communication only through specific interfaces enhances a model's utility to the researcher, the analyst/designer, and to the student.

The definition of a model is the definition of a set of system resources and their interactions with each other. Resources are the hardware and software comprising the system.

Information Systems Resources are characterized by the attributes assigned to them. The IPSS methodology assumes that attributes can be either static or dynamic or a combination of both. Attribute values may be a priori assigned to resources, in which case they are parameters within the resource definition, or they can be dynamically calculated each time the attribute is referenced. IPSS allows the modeler to combine FORTRAN code and special IPSS statements and functions to define dynamic resource attributes. Static procedures are generally associated with hardware definitions. Each allocatable hardware resource is defined by a static type definition. These definitions, however, can reference other attributes of either static or procedural type.

The top-down modular design of IPSS eases many of the problems associated with the synthesis of a simulation model. Model analysis and sensitivity testing can be performed easily.

Figure 19 illustrates the design and simulation facilities of IPSS from the modeler's point of view. The modeler can view his system from three different perspectives: the IPSS Methodological View, the IPSS Modeling Facilities, and the IPSS Execution Facilities.

The IPSS Methodological View allows the modeler to transform general system knowledge about his information system into component knowledge of the system. The system knowledge represents all the information that the modeler has about his system. The component knowledge of the system allows the modeler to build a conceptual model of the information system. This conceptual model consists of four components. The service and interservice procedures component allows the definition of all system software. This component allows the modeler to describe the salient features of the application program, operating system, and data management system that he is interested in. The hardware resources and configuration component is a description of the hardware configuration of the system. This component allows the definition of hardware such as CPU, disk, drum, tape, channels, controllers, and unit record equipment at the level of detail required by the modeler. The data base resources and configuration component describes the file organizations and physical storage layout of the system. In addition, this component is capable of modeling the network view of DBMS. The user workload component represents the external events that stimulate the system. Since this component is the driving force of the information system, it is important that it be characterized accurately. In this research the user workload component has been expanded to allow the modeling of relational DBMS and high-level user requests in the form of Boolean expressions.

The IPSS Modeling Facility allows the modeler to translate the conceptual components given by the IPSS methodological view into a set of IPSS model components. As a result of this translation process, an IPSS simulation model is produced. There are six basic components in an IPSS model. The System Resources component defines the hardware and software resources of the system. This component allows the modeling of the hardware configuration including: CPU, I/O devices, and memory; the

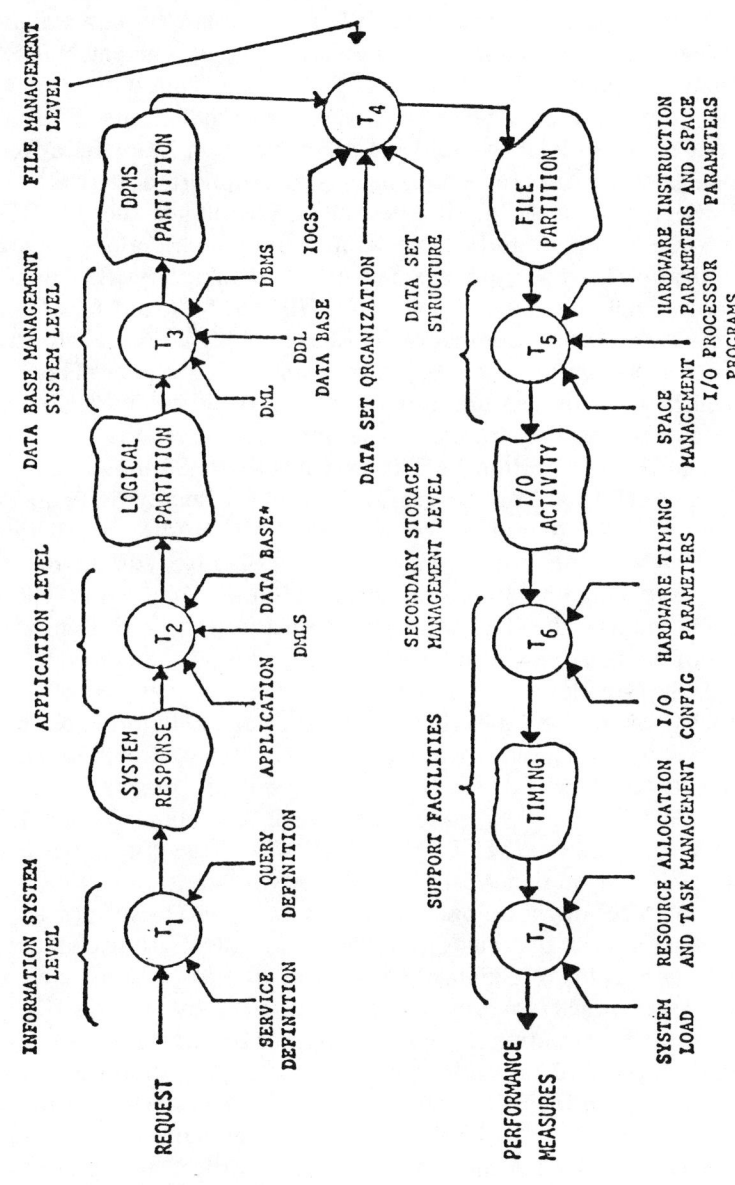

Figure 19. Query to Performance Measure Transformations of IPSS (DELU77a)

58 Underlying Methodologies

application software: query translation and processing programs; and executive software: task management and memory management routines. The Storage Structure component defines the storage structure of the information system's data base. This component uses 'data sets' and 'files' to model the logical data base structure. The mapping of data sets and files to physical storage is modeled using 'areas' and 'segments'. The Request Stream component defines the system service request stream. This component models user requests as a series of external events. These events are generated by an inter-arrival time procedure. The Data Base Access component defines the resources needed to support a network structured DBMS. This component supports DML commands such as GET, FIND and STORE. The Data Base Structure Component defines the logical data organization used to support a network structured DBMS. This component supports DDL statements such as: SCHEMA, SET and RECORD TYPE. The Model Director Component defines how facilities are selected from all the other five components to build a simulation model. This component established the interconnections between facilities from different components and specifies the simulation termination criteria.

The IPSS Execution Facility executes the IPSS model components to produce performance statistics. The execution facility performs the translation of IPSS source programs into FORTRAN, compilation of the FORTRAN modules to object modules, linkage editing of the object modules to a load module, and execution of the load module. The execution facility also uses the IPSS library to store and retrieve IPSS modules in the form of either IPSS source, FORTRAN, or object code.

IPSS provides a comprehensive set of statistics as part of the standard output from an IPSS model. Statistics such as operational, request stream, I/O activity, utilization, waiting, service, task, and activity statistics are automatically provided by IPSS. Queueing statistics on any System Resources facility can be collected using special IPSS commands. In addition, since IPSS allows the mixing of FORTRAN with IPSS code, the modeler can collect his own statistics using FORTRAN routines.

The IPSS methodology viewed the information storage and retrieval process as a series of transformations (figure 18). Each transformation represents a mapping of a higher level view of an information system to a lower level view. These transformations are discussed by DeLutis [DELU77a].

At the Information System level, inputs to this transformation are user requests expressed in a user query language. As a result of this transformation, a list of logical objects required to satisfy the user requests is built.

At the Application level, information that is necessary to support user applications is transformed into requests to the Data Base Management

System. As a result of this transformation, Data Manipulation Language commands are produced.

At the Data Base Management level, DML commands are processed. Using the data definitions given in the data model, a list of data base files and records that have to be accessed is generated.

At the File Management level, the data set, file and record requests are transformed into actual physical storage locations. File organizations such as sequential, hashed, and sorted organizations are represented at this level.

At the Secondary Storage Management level, I/O operations to the hardware system are generated. Typical of such I/O operations are seek, search, and data transfer operations. I/O scheduling is done at this level in order to optimize the physical access path. As a result of this transformation, performance measures are generated.

Transformations T_2 through T_7 have been realized by the IPSS methodology [BROW79, DELU78]. This research focuses on the investigation of the highest level of transformation, T_1: the transformation of a user query into data base workload. Workload is expressed as the system's response to a complex, multi-attributed stream of queries and is measured by the number of data base records needed to satisfy each input query.

4

Methodology

The purpose of this chapter is to present the methodology for the definition of data base workload. In this chapter, the methodology is described as a conceptual model. This model characterizes the salient features of an information system's workload in terms of the requirements on the data base subsystem. The baseline IPSS methodology shows that the information system performance is dependent on the following parameters:

1. system loading and distribution of different types of queries.
2. system hardware and physical storage methods.
3. information structure and logical storage organizations.

Figure 19 shows a more detailed analysis and transformation, T_1, that was described in chapter 3. This transformation is decomposed into two sub-transformations: the query transformation, T_{11}, and the attribute transformation, T_{12}.

The query transformation accepts user queries in a high-level query language such as relational calculus or relational algebra commands. The queries may reference several files simultaneously. At this level of transformation, a multi-file request is broken down into single file requests.

The attribute transformation accepts single file requests in the form of Boolean expressions (Propositional Calculus) and transforms these into a set of system response requirements. These system response requirements represent the workload to the remainder of the information system. Boolean expressions are used because these expressions are one of the most general mathematical abstractions of query languages [CODD70, DATE75]. Many query languages can be modeled by these expressions.

Basically, the methodology views the information system level transformation T_1 (figure 19) as a workload generator. A stream of user queries is transformed to a set of record identifiers which name the data base records (information objects) that satisfied the attribute-value conditions posed in the query. The workload is represented by a data base response pattern, i.e., those records which must be assessed for the system to generate a response to the user queries. This logical data base response pattern can be used to judge the efficiency of the logical data base organization. In addition, this logical data base response pattern can be used to drive the lower level transformations T_2 through T_7 (figure 19) to produce system performance statistics.

There are five information system attributes that support the system level transformation. These system attributes are: Query Content, Query Structure, Information Structure, Data Base Traversal, and Data Base Entities. The Query Content attribute describes what information is needed to satisfy user queries. The Query Structure attribute describes the structure of the query language and how the language can be translated to Boolean expressions. The Information Structure attribute describes how information is distributed throughout the data base. The Data Base Traversal Attribute describes the logical access mechanisms for traversing the data base. The Data Base Entities attribute describes the basic logical units in the data base.

The transformations T_{11} and T_{12}, together with the information system attributes represent the system knowledge level of the workload generation process. In this methodology, the system knowledge level is transformed into a set of conceptual methodological components and algorithms. These methodological components and algorithms represent the methodological view of the workload generation process. Figure 20 illustrates the relationship between the system attributes/transformations and the methodological components/algorithms. The following sections describe the methodological components and methodological algorithms used to characterize the user workload. A step-by-step approach is used to build up a set of equations that express the user workload as a function of the methodological components and algorithms.

Methodological Components

As shown in figure 20, the methodology includes the following methodological components: data base, files, objects, attributes and values, data distribution functions, search keys, queries, and system loading. Each of these components will be defined and discussed in the following sections.

Data Base

The data base is assumed to represent all the data that is stored in the information system. For the purposes of the methodology, it will be viewed as being one or more sets of related data called files. For example, in a library

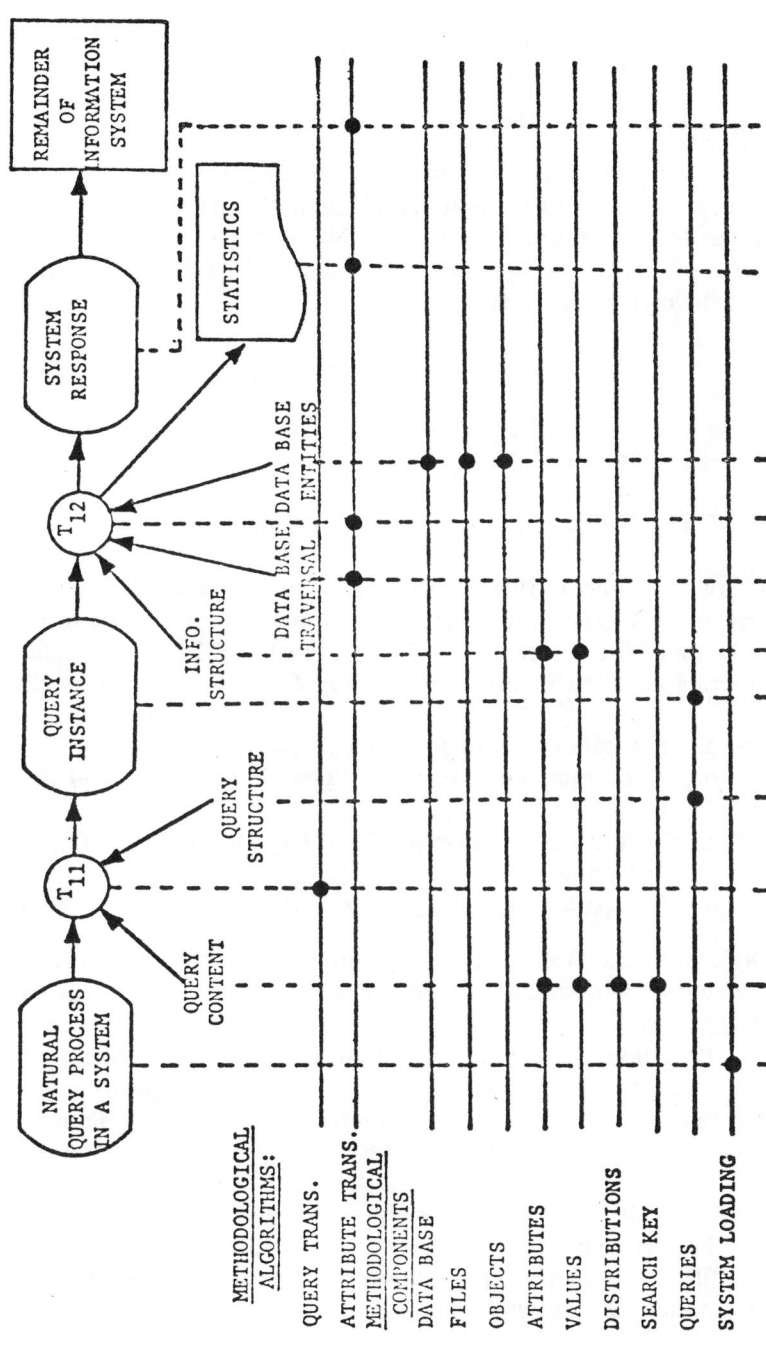

Figure 20. Attribute and Query Transformations

information system, the data base may consist of an author file, a subject file, and a bibliographical file. Mathematically, a data base (DB) is defined as a set of files (F):

$$DB = UNION\ (F(i), \text{ for } i = 1 \text{ to } n(DB))$$

where DB = Information System's Data Base, F(i) = i^{th} file within the data base, and n(DB) = total number of files in the data base. Note that UNION stands for the set union, i.e., UNION(S(i), for i = 1 to m), stands for the union of all the sets: S(1), S(2), ..., S(m). The data base defines the files that the user input stream can access.

File

A file will be defined as a collection of related data. Mathematically, a file, F, is a totally ordered set of objects:

$$F = UNION\ (O(j), \text{ for } j = 1 \text{ to } n\ (F))$$

where F = a file, O(j) = an object j which is the logical address in the file's logical record space, and n(F) = total number of objects in F. The total ordering of the objects in file, F, is defined as follows. R is called the total ordering associated with file F if R satisfies the following conditions:

a. the Reflexive property: O(x) R O(x),
b. Antisymmetric Property: if O(x) R O(y) and O(y) R O(x), then x = y,
c. Transitive Property: if O(x) R O(y) and O(y) R O(z), then O(x) R O(z),
d. Comparable Property: either O(x) R O(y) or O(y) R O(x).

O(x), O(y), and O(z) are arbitrary objects in F. The ordering R can be interpreted as follows: O(x) R O(y) means "Object, O(x), precedes Object, O(y)".

The above definition shows that a file has two mathematical characteristics: (a) a file is a set of objects, and (b) these objects are sorted or ordered. In order to simplify the mathematical notation, let O(x) R O(y) if and only if x.LE.y. The notation O(x).LE.O(y) will be used to substitute for the notation O(x) R O(y). O(x).LE.O(y) can be read as "the logical address of object, O(x), is less than or equal to the object O(y)."

The ordering of objects in a file is determined by one or more attributes in a file. For example, in a relational DBMS, the primary key of a relation determines the ordering.

Objects

An object is a description of some entity. For example, it can be used as a mathematical abstraction of a logical record in a traditional file system, or a tuple in a relational data base system. An object is the smallest information unit which a user can retrieve or store. Since an object describes some entity, it is made up of a set of descriptors called attribute-value pairs.

$$O = \begin{pmatrix} (t,v) \text{ such that:} \\ t \text{ ELM-OF } A(F) \text{ and } v \text{ ELM-OF } V(t) \end{pmatrix}$$

where O = an object in file F, t = an attribute, v = a value, $A(F)$ = a set of possible attributes associated with file F, and $V(t)$ = a set of possible values for attributes t (this may be an empty set). The objects represent the basic units requested users. The user workload is represented by the objects that are needed to satisfy the user queries.

Attributes and Values

Attribute and values are the basic terms in the methodology and therefore are not defined in terms of other methodological components. Attributes are common properties associated with the objects in a file. The distinctive features of an object are indicated by the attribute-value pairs that it contains. For example, in a bibliographical records file, each record is an object and the possible attributes may be: AUTHOR, TITLE, YEAR, and PUBLISHER. A specific object may contain the following attribute-value pairs: AUTHOR—'J. Doe', TITLE—'Introduction to Data Base Organizations', YEAR—'1978', and PUBLISHER—'XYZ Co.'. Note that the above example is one of many possible ways of selecting attribute-value pairs to describe the bibliographical record. For instance, instead of AUTHOR as an attribute, each AUTHOR NAME can be viewed as an attribute. That is, 'J. Doe' can be an attribute. There is exactly one value associated with this attribute (in other words, the set of values associated with the attribute is the same as the attribute itself). The above two ways of viewing the author information shows that the methodology is flexible and can be used to model only those areas that are of interest to the information system designer or analyst. The distribution of attribute-value pairs determines the information structure of the data base. In the attribute transformation process, the attribute-value distributions are used to locate the objects that constitute the data base workload.

Methodology

Probability Distribution Functions

Since the way information is distributed in a data base largely determines the performance of an information system, in the mathematical model this distribution of information is characterized by a set of probability distribution functions. These include a: (a) first occurrence PDF, (b) next occurrence PDF, (c) number of occurrences PDF, (d) last occurrence PDF, and (e) value PDF.

First Occurrence PDF

In order to locate objects that contain the attribute t the first object that contains this attribute determines the starting point of the search process. This first occurrence of attribute t is characterized by the first occurrence PDF. Let fr/t/(m) be the probability that attribute t first occurs in object O(m).

$$fr/t/(m) = Pr(\text{ t N-ELM-OF } O(1), O(2), \ldots O(m-1)$$

$$\text{and t ELM-OF } O(m))$$

Then the first occurrence PDF, FR/t/(m) is given by:

$$FR/t/(m) = fr/t/(1) + fr/t/(2) + \ldots fr/t/(m)$$

In the above definition, the notation Pr(e) stands for 'the probability of event e'. Also, "t ELM-OF O" is the shorthand notation for "(t,v) ELM-OF O, T-EX v". Similarly, "t N=ELM=OF O" is the shorthand notation for "(t,v) N=ELM=OF O, F=ALL v". The first occurrence pdf, FR/t/(m), is the probability that attribute t occurs in one of the first m objects. The reason that the first occurrence of an attribute in a file is treated as a probability is because objects in a file may be in a dynamic state, i.e., they are constantly being added, deleted, or modified. Also, the general form of renewal processes requires the possibility that the first occurrence PDF be different from the next occurrence PDF.

Next Occurrence PDF: $F(x)$

One of the important factors that governs information system performance is the ordering of files. A file can be ordered in many different ways using various combinations of attributes as the sort keys. However, the ordering in the logical name (ordering) space need not be the same as the logical address space. This depends on the organization method employed. These

Methodology

storage structures can be viewed as different ways of locating the objects so that objects with the same attribute can be retrieved more efficiently. However, the methodology only deals with the file's logical record space. The next occurrence PDF is used to characterize the distribution of objects which have the same attributes in this space. It is based on an ordering. Therefore, if the ordering is altered by changing the sort keys, there generally is a new F(x) required. Suppose object O(i) contains an attribute t. The probability that object O(i + n) is the next object with attribute t is defined as follows:

F(x) = nx/t/(m GIVEN i) = PR(t ELM-OF O(i+m)

t N-ELM-OF O(k) F-ALL O(i)<O(k)<O(i+m)

$$\text{Given t ELM-OF O(i))}$$

The above PDF states the probability that:

a. given that attribute t is in object O(i), then
b. attribute t is in object O(i+m), and
c. attribute t is not in any object O(k), where O(k) is between O(i) and O(i+m).

Suppose that the probability of the next occurrence of an attribute is independent of the current occurrence. That is, if the above probability is independent of the value of i, then the above definition becomes:

nx/t/(m) = Pr (t ELM-OF O(i), O(i+m)

and

t N-ELM-OF O(k) F-ALL O(i) < O(k) < O(i+m))

The Next Occurrence PDF nx/t/(m) is defined as the probability that an attribute t reoccurs after less than or equal to m objects.

NX/t/(m) = nx/t/(1) + nx/t/(2) ...... nx/t/(m)

The next occurrence PDF is used to locate records that satisfied the Boolean queries generated as a result of the query transformation process.

Last Occurrence PDF: $L(x)$

In retrieving objects with the same attribute, the last object that contains the attribute marks the logical end of the search process. The probability that object O(m) is the last object that contains attribute t is defined below.

$$L(x) = ls/t/(m) = Pr(t \text{ ELM-OF } O(m))$$

and

$$t \text{ N-ELM-OF } O(k) \text{ F-ALL } O(k) > O(m))$$

The last occurrence PDF, LS/t/(m), gives the probability that the last occurrence of the attribute t is in or before object O(m).

$$LS/t/(m) = ls/t/(1) + ls/t/(2) + \ldots + ls/t/(m)$$

Given the first occurrence PDF and the next occurrence PDF, the logical end of the search for objects with the same attribute can be determined by either the number of occurrences PDF or the last occurrence PDF. That is, only one of the two PDF's is needed to characterize the distribution of an attribute.

Number of Occurrences PDF: $N(x)$

In a file, the number of objects with the same attribute is an important factor governing the access efficiency. The probability that a file F has m objects with attribute t is defined as follows:

$$N(x) = no/t/(m) = Pr \text{ (the cardinality of the set } O \text{ \{where t ELM-OF}$$
$$O \text{ and } O \text{ ELM-OF } F\} = m).$$

The number of occurrences PDF gives the probability that in file F there are m or less objects with attribute t.

$$NO/t/(m) = no/t/(1) + no/t/(2) + \ldots + no/t/(m)$$

The last occurrence and number of occurrences PDF's determine the number of records that have to be retrieved. These records form part of the user workload.

Value PDF

Associated with each attribute t is a set of possible values for the attribute V(t). For example, the attribute WEEKDAY has a set of possible values: V(WEEKDAY) = {monday, tuesday, wednesday, thursday, friday}. If the attribute t is in object O then the value PDF, VL(x GIVEN t), characterizes the distribution of values for the attribute.

VL(x GIVEN t) = Pr((t,x) ELM-OF O GIVEN t ELM-OF O)

The value PDF is used to determine if an object satisfies the value conditions of Boolean queries.

Search Key

One of the basic functions of an information system is to retrieve objects in response to a user generated query. In order to retrieve the desired objects, a user indicates in the query the criteria for selecting these objects. The selection criteria are expressed in 'search keys'. A search key, SK, is the basic unit of user request. If SK is a search key, then SK is associated with an ordered triple (t,v,c) called the search criterion such that: t is an attribute, v is a value, and c is a condition function that maps ordered pairs of values (x,y), where x, y ELM-OF V(t), into the set {TRUE, FALSE}. Having defined the search criterion, the search key, SK, can be defined as a function that maps objects into the set {TRUE, FALSE}.

SK(O) = TRUE if ∃ (t1, v1) ELM=OF O such that t1 = t and

c(v1,v) = TRUE, FALSE otherwise

For example, let (YEAR, 1979, LT) be the search criterion for search key SK. The condition function LT is defined as follows:

LT(x,1979) =   TRUE if x < 1979, FALSE otherwise

The above search key represents a request for objects with the attribute YEAR having a value of less than 1979. For simplicity, the above search key is also denoted as YEAR < 1979.

Query

A user request for information is called a query. Since a search key is a fundamental unit of information request, a query is made up of search keys connected by the logical operators AND, OR, NOT. The following is a recursive definition of a query:

a) if SK is a search key then SK is a query,
b) if Q is a query then NOT Q is a query,
c) if Q1, Q2 are queries, then Q1 and Q2, Q1 and Q2 are queries, and
d) Q is a query if and only if it is formed by a finite number of applications of rules (a), (b), and (c).

For example, the following is a query:

YEAR < 1970 AND NOT YEAR < 1960 OR YEAR = 1975

The above query requests for objects with the YEAR attribute having either a value between 1960 and 1969 or a value equal to 1975.

System Loading

The workload on an information system is called the system loading. The system loading is a series of user queries and is defined as follows: The system loading, LD, is a stochastic counting process. $LD = CT/t/(x), t \geq 0$, where $CT/t/$ is a random variable that gives the total number of queries that have occurred between time = 0 to time = t. If $t(1), t(2), \ldots$ are the times where queries have occurred and $0 < t(1) < t(2) \ldots$, then the random variables $T(1) = t(1)$, $T(2) = t(2) - t(1), \ldots, T(n) = t(n) - t(n-1), \ldots$ are called successive inter-arrival times.
    This completes the definition of the methodological components. In the next section, components will then be used to transform the user input stream into the user workload.

Transformations

As was shown in figure 4.2, the data base workload definition process is represented by two transformations: query decomposition, which transforms each query into a series of references to the data base files based on the search key, and data base workload definition which transforms the file search instances into a list of file objects that satisfy the user queries.

Query Transformation

The query transformation process accepts input in the form of high-level user queries such as relational calculus commands. The user queries which may access multiple files are translated to Boolean queries that access individual files.

Since the system loading is a stochastic process, the occurrences of user requests between time = 0 to time = t can be represented by a series of time instances t(1), t(2), ..., t(n). If Q(1), Q(2), ..., Q(x) is the set of possible queries, then query transformation functions, TR, give the probability of the above queries occurring at the given time instances.

TR (Q(i), F(j)) = Pr (query, Q(i), is used to search file F(j) at any one

of the time instances of the system loading process).

The above probability function is usually estimated based on benchmarks or user query statistics. User queries can access multiple files. It is necessary to transform these expressions into simple subqueries defined by one or more search keys over a single data base file (relation).

In relational calculus, the DML operations may access several relations. The following algorithm shows how query transformation can be performed to generate single relation requests in the form of Boolean expressions.

    a. Projection
   Let R (d(1), d(2), ..., d(n)) denote a relation R with domains d(1), d(2), ..., d(n). The projection of R on domains $d(x_1)$, $d(x_2)$, ..., $d(x_k)$ can be represented by the following query: $d(x_1)$ AND $d(x_2)$ AND ... AND $d(x_k)$.

    b. Joint
   Let A $(z_1, a_2, ..., a_n)$ and B $(b_1, b_2, ..., b_n)$ be two relations. The joint relations A and B on domain a_n and b_1 to form relation C is represented by the following sequence of queries.

   Step 1: Get a new tuple $((a_1, va_1), ..., (a_n, va_n))$ using query $(a_1$ AND $a_2, ...,$ AND $a_n)$ on relation A.
   Step 2: Get a new tuple $((b_1, vb_1), ..., (b_n, vb_n))$ using query $(b_1 = va_n$ AND b_2 AND b_3 ... AND $b_n)$ on relation B.
   Step 3: Concatenate the tuples retrieved in Step 1 and Step 2 to form a tuple of relation C: $((a_1, va_1), ..., (a_n, va_n), (b_2, vb_2), ..., (b_n, vb_n))$.
   Step 4: Repeat Step 2 and Step 3 until all valid tuples in B (using query in Step 2) are retrieved.
   Step 5: Repeat Step 1 through Step 3 until all valid tuples in A (using query in Step 1) are retrieved.

72   Methodology

c. Division
Let A (a_1, a_2) and B (b_1) be two relations. The division of relation A by relation B on domain d_2 to form relation C is represented by the following sequence of queries.

Step 1: Get all tuples of relation B using query (b_1).
Step 2: From the tuples retrieved, assemble a list of possible values for domain b_1: $(v(1), \ldots, v(n))$.
Step 3: Get a new tuple $((a_1, va_1), (a_2, va_2))$ using query $(a_1$ AND $a_2 = v(1))$, on relation A.
Step 4: Repeat for $j = 2$ to n. (Get a new tuple using query $(a_1 = va_1$ AND $a_2 = v(j))$ on relation A, if no such tuple exists then exit to Step 6.
Step 5: Store tuple (a_1, va_1) in relation C.
Step 6: Repeat Step 3 through Step 5 until all valid tuples from A (using query in Step 3) are retrieved.

Data Base Workload Transformation (Attribute Transformation)

The transformation of Boolean queries to object identifiers is called the data base workload transformation. Each query is transformed into a list of objects that satisfies the query instance.

Let Q be a Boolean query that searches file F, where

$Q =$ (SK(1,1) AND ... AND SK(1,n1)) OR
(SK(2,1) AND ... AND SK(2,n2) OR
.
.
.
SK(k,1) AND ... AND SK(k,nk)).

The data base workload transformation generates a list of objects, L, defined as follows:

$L =$ (O_x such that T-EXT O_x ELM-OF F and the expression
(SK(1,1) (O_x) AND ... AND SK(1,n1) (O_x)) OR
(SK(2,1) (O_x) AND ... AND SK(2,n2) (O_x)) OR
.
.
.
(SK(K,1)(O_x) AND ... AND SK(k,nk) (O_x)) has
the value: TRUE).

The list of objects, L, that satisfied the query, Q, can be characterized again by four distribution functions. These PDF's are similar to those defined for attributes and are defined as follows:

(a) First Query Occurrence PDF: TT/Q/(t) = Pr (object O(x) is the first object that satisfied query, Q, where x .LE. t)
(b) Next Query Occurrence PDF: RR/Q/(t) = Pr (object O(x+j), satisfied query Q, given that object O(j) satisfied query Q and x .LE. t)
(c) Number of Query Occurrences PDF: NN/Q/(t) = Pr (total number of objects that satisfied query Q is less than or equal to t).
(d) Last Query Occurrence PDF: LL/Q/(t) = Pr (the last object that satisfied query Q occurred before object O(x) where x.LE.t).

The above algorithm shows how the basic attribute and values PDF's can be used to compute the distribution of objects that satisfied various Boolean queries.

Although the above PDF's can be expressed in terms of the attribute and value PDF's defined as part of the methodological components, in general the mathematical equations used to express the above PDF's are very complex. The following shows how these equations can be computed under certain special conditions.

Let (a(i,j), v(i,j), c(i,j)) be the search criterion associated with search key SK(i,j) in query Q. Assume c/i,j/ (x, v(i,j)) = TRUE F-ALL x ELM-OF V(a(i,j)). That is, the search criterion is independent of the values. Suppose the first and next occurrences probability functions for all the attributes a(i,j) have the same distribution, that is, r/i,j/(x). Also suppose all the attributes a(i,j) in query Q are distinct. That is, a(i,j) .NE. a(ℓ,k) for all i .NE. ℓ or j .NE. k. Let r*/i,j/(y) be the probability function that gives the probability of attribute a(i,j) reoccuring in object O(d+y) after it occurs in object O(d) for some O(d) in file F. Then r*/i,j/(y) can be expressed in terms of r/i,j/(y).

Equation R1

r*/i,j/(y) = SUM (r/i,j/(x_1))(r/i,j/(x_2)) ... (r/i,j/(x_n)) for all
$x_1, x_2, \ldots, x_n$ such that
$x_1 + x_2 \ldots + x_n$ = y and $x_1, x_2, \ldots, x_n$ .GE. 1.

Let P/Q/(y) = Pr (object O(y+j) satisfied query Q given that object O(j) satisfied query Q).
Then P/Q/(y) can be computed as follows:

Methodology

Equation R2

$$
\begin{aligned}
P/Q/(y) = \ & (r*/1,1/(y))\,(r*/1,2/(y)) \ldots (r*/i,n1/(y)) \\
+\ & (r*/2,1/(y))\,(r*/2,2/(y)) \ldots (r*/2,n2/(y)) \\
+\ & \ldots \\
+\ & /r*/k,1/(y))\,(r*/k,2/(y)) \ldots (r*/k,nk/(y))
\end{aligned}
$$

The next query occurrence probability function, $rr/Q/(t)$ gives the probability that object $O(t+j)$ is the next object that satisfied query Q given that object $O(j)$ satisfied query Q. This probability function can be computed as follows:

Equation R3

$$rr/Q/(t) = (P/Q/(j))$$

$$(1 - P/Q/(j+1))\ldots(1 - P/Q/(j+t-1))(P/Q/(j+t))$$

The next query occurrence PDF can be computed as follows:

Equation R4

$$RR/Q/(t) = rr/Q/(1) + rr/Q/(2) + \ldots + rr/Q/(t)$$

Substituting equations R3, R2, and R1 in equation R4 gives an equation of Next Query Occurrence PDF in terms of the attribute PDF's. Similarly, the First and Last Query Occurrence PDF's can be computed in terms of the attribute PDF's.

The above equations can be used to directly compute the location of records, i.e., the workload required to satisfy the user queries. Since the analytic equations for the transformation are very complex, a simulation algorithm has been developed to model these transformations. This simulation model is described in the next chapter.

Methodology   75

Date Base Workload Measures

One of the basic tasks of an information system analyst or designer is to make sure that the information system's performance is at an acceptable level. In this section, workload equations will be developed to show the dependence of system performance on the methodological components and the transformations defined earlier in this chapter.

System workload is measured in terms of effort. The unit of effort is not defined in the mathematical model, but instead two functions are used to characterize the work associated with accessing data. These work functions are defined as follows:

(a) Object Retrieval Work Function $CO(F_i)$
Associated with each file, F_i, the object retrieval work function $CO(F_i)$ measures the work of retrieving an object in the file. For example, this work function may measure work in terms of the amount of data transferred in each object retrieval or in terms of the amount of central processor time involved in each object retrieval.

(b) File Traversal Work Function $CI(t, F_i)$
The file traversal work function measures the work associated with search operations in a file. Let object $O(x)$ and $O(x+t)$ be two consecutive objects that satisfied a query Q. Then t is called the inter-object distance. The file traversal function $CI(t, F_i)$ measures the work of traversing a distance of t in file F_i. For example, this work function may measure the device controller time involved in moving the access mechanism from object $O(x)$ to object $O(x+t)$.

The work functions can be viewed as a mathematical abstraction of the transformations T_2 through T_7 in figure 18. In general, the computation of these functions is a complex process and is dependent on how data is organized and stored.

The expected work in finding the objects in file F_j that satisfied query Q_i can be divided into two parts: (a) the expected work of retrieving the objects, and (b) the expected work in searching for the objects. Using the work functions just defined, these expected costs can be computed as follows.

Let $ER(Q_i, F_j)$ be the expected work in retrieving from file F_j, using query Q_i. Then,

Methodology

$$ER(Q_i, F_j) = \text{Expected Number of Objects} \times \text{Object Retrieval Work}$$

$$= E(NN/Q_i/(t))\,(CO(F_j))$$

$$= CO(F_j)\,SUMt\,((t)\,(NN/Q_i/(t))).$$

where $E(x)$ means the expected value of random variable x.

$NN/Q_i/(t)$ is the number of query occurrences PDF defined in the previous section. Let $ET(Q_i, F_j)$ be the expected work in traversing file F_j for objects that satisfied query Q_i. Then,

$$ET(Q_i, F_j) = E(\text{file traversal work} \times \text{inter-object distance})$$

$$= E(CI(t, F_j)\,(rr/Q_i/(t)))$$

$$= SUMt(CI(t, F_j)\,(rr/Q_i/(t)))$$

where $rr/Q/(t)$ is the next query occurrence probability function described in the previous section.

Combining the above expected work gives the expected work of processing query Q_i on file F_j as follows:

Equation P1

$$EC(Q_i, F_j) = ER(Q_i, F_j) + ET(Q_i, F_j)$$

$$= CO(F_j)\,SUMt\,((t)(NN/Q_i/(t)) + SUMt\,(CI(t, F_j)$$

$$(rr/Q_i/(t))))$$

When a query arrives at the information system, the probability that the query is Q_i and searches file F_j is given by the query transformation function $TR(Q_i, F_j)$ defined earlier in this chapter. Therefore, the expected work per query, EQC, can be computed as follows:

Equation P2

$$EQC = SUM_{ij}\,(EC(Q_i, F_j)\,TR(Q_i, F_j))$$

Since the total number of queries at time t is given by the system loading process $(CT/t/(x), t\ .GE.\ O)$, the expected processing work at time t can be computed as follows:

Equation P3

$EPC(t)$ = expected work per query × expected number of queries

$= (EQC) \, E(CT/t/(x))$

$= SUM_{ij} \, (EC(Q_i, F_j) \, TR(Q_iF_j)) \, SUMx \, (CT/t/(x))$.

Substituting equation P1 in equations P2 and P3 and substituting the query occurrence PDF's derived earlier, the expected work per query and the expected work at time t can be expressed in terms of the following system parameters:

(S-1) system loading process (input stream) $(CT/t/(x), t \, .GE. \, O)$
(S-2) query transformation function $(TR(Q_i,F_j))$
(S-3) object retrieval work function $(CO(F_j))$
(S-4) file traversal work function $(CI(Q_i,F_j))$
(S-5) first attribute occurrence PDF $(FR/a/(m))$
(S-6) next attribute occurrence PDF $(NX/a/(m))$
(S-7) number of attribute occurrence PDF $(NO/a/(m))$
(S-8) last attribute occurrence PDF $(LS/a/(m))$
(S-9) value PDF $(VL(x \, GIVEN \, a))$.

The expected work per query, EQC, and the expected processing cost at time t, EPC(t), are called the system performance measures. By varying the system parameters above, the system analyst can compare performance measurements for different system architectures. The mathematical model can be used to analyze information system performance. For example: (a) by varying parameters (S-1) and (S-2), the effect on system performance of change in user request pattern can be evaluated, (b) by varying parameters (S-3) and (S-4), the effect on system performance of change in hardware or physical storage methods can be evaluated, and (c) by varying parameters (S-5) through (S-9), the effect on system performance of change in information structure or logical storage organizations can be evaluated.

In general, the mathematical model for workload measurement does not usually yield simple analytical solutions. That is, workloads based on the methodological model are usually too complex to be derived or computed. Simulation facilities based on the methodological model have been developed. Special simulation facilities have been built to model each of the system parameters mentioned above. A discussion of these simulation facilities is given in the next chapter.

5
Verification of the Methodology

The previous chapter presented a methodology for the definition and analysis of information system data base workload. This methodology is realized as a simulation language called IPSS/REL (for Information Processing System Simulator Relational Extensions). This language has been implemented as a discrete event simulator, the execution facility for IPSS/REL.

IPSS/REL is an extension of the Information Processing System Simulator (IPSS). The lower level views of an information system which correspond to transformations T_2 through T_7 in figure 19 are already modeled by the IPSS Modeling and Executional Facilities. The higher level or user view of an information system, which corresponds to transformation T_1 in figure 19, is modeled by IPSS/REL, the relational extensions. This user view includes the information structure of the data base and the user query stream. IPSS/REL allows the analyst to model his system at various levels of detail. He can model any number of transformations (T_1 to T_7) given in figure 19. For example, he can model the user level view of an information system by utilizing only those features in the relational extension. He can also model an information system in which the user view of the data base is relational but the physical organization of the data is a network by using IPSS [DELU77] and the relational extensions in conjunction. In this chapter, the relational extensions to the IPSS Modeling Facility are discussed. The testing and verification of these extensions are also described.

IPSS/REL Design

The relational extensions provide the following modeling features: a data definition language for defining the information structure of a data base, a data manipulation language for defining the user query stream, and a simulation driver and monitor that directs the execution and statistics collected. Figure 21 gives the structure of an IPSS/REL model. As in IPSS, each

80 Verification of the Methodology

extension facility has its own language parser written in PL/1. The code generated by the parsers and the system routines is written in FORTRAN. The request stream component and the storage structure component remain basically unchanged in the extensions. In the system resources component, facilities for defining query structure and information structure are added. In the model director component, transformation routines are added to simulate the execution of data manipulation commands. In addition to the standard statistics outputted by IPSS, retrieval performance statistics are added. In chapter 4, the following methodological components were specified: data base, file, object, attribute, value, occurrence functions, query, search key, system loading, query transformation, attribute transformation, and system performance cost functions. These components are modeled using IPSS/REL statements in conjunction with existing IPSS statements. The new IPSS statements are: ATTRIBUTE, PDF, QUERY, SEARCH KEY, CREATE QUERY COMMAND, DESTROY QUERY COMMAND, FIND NEXT RECORD COMMAND, GET LIST LENGTH COMMAND. Table 2 shows the relationship between the methodological components and the IPSS/REL language statements. Using these statements, information systems described by the methodological model in chapter 4 can be modeled. The following is a discussion of these language statements and the procedures used for verification.

Testing and Verification

The PL/1 parsers for the relational extensions were tested and verified by examining the FORTRAN code and internal tables generated. These code and internal tables are produced as part of the call to the library listing facilities of IPSS/REL. The individual FORTRAN system routines used by the modeler driver were tested and verified. In addition to these tests, a series of models with various combinations of the extension facilities were tested. Also, a basic model that included all of the extension facilities was built. A series of tests was conducted by varying the values of parameters associated with different facilities in the model. The facility definition tables generated by the language parsers, the internal system tables generated by the transformation algorithms, and the query statistics tables were examined. The values from these tables verified the accuracy of the relational extension. A sample computer run of this model is included in Appendix B. In addition to running the above test, a large simulation model that ran on IPSS was rerun using IPSS/REL to ensure that the extension had no adverse effect on the rest of IPSS. The model used was a model of the OCLC information system [DELU77b, DELU79]. This model utilizes many of the IPSS facilities. The simulation statistics of this model running on IPSS/REL were

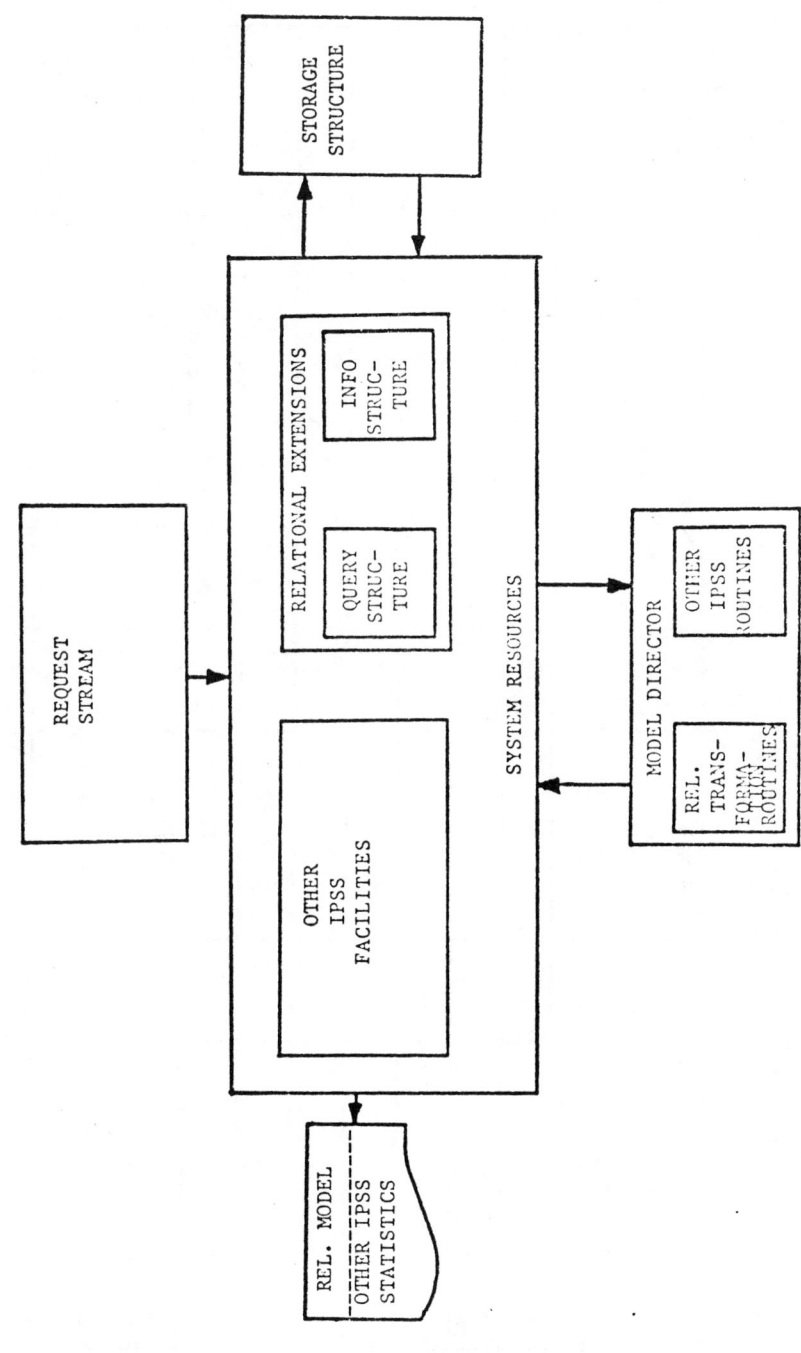

Figure 21. Structure of an IPSS/REL Model

Table 2. IPSS/REL Implementation of Methodological Model

IPSS/REL FACILITIES METHODOLOGICAL COMPONENTS/ALGORITHMS	ATTRI-BUTE	PDF	QUERY	SEARCH KEY	CREATE QUERY	DESTROY QUERY	FIND NEXT RECORD	FIND LIST LENGTH	ENDO* SERVICE	EXO* SERVICE
DATA BASE	X									
FILE	X									
OBJECT	X									
ATTRIBUTE	X	X								
VALUES	X	X								
DISTRIBUTIONS	X	X								
QUERY			X		X	X				
SEARCH KEY	X			X						
QUERY TRANSFORMATION			X	X	X	X	X	X	X	
ATTRIBUTE TRANSFORMATION					X	X	X	X		
SYSTEM LOADING										X
PERFORMANCE COST FUNCTIONS									X	

* currently exist in IPSS

compared with the statistics of the model running on IPSS. The statistics were identical and thus verified that the extensions did not interfer with the operations of other IPSS facilities.

A set of debugging aids have been added to IPSS to facilitate the above testing procedure. Several specialized system utility routines have been programmed to print out internal system tables used in the query and attribute transformation process. The library listing routines of IPSS have been modified to allow the printing of facility definition tables associated with the relational extensions. The debugging aids were found to be extremely useful in testing the language parsers and the system routines.

IPSS/REL Language Statements

PDF Statement

The information structure allows the modeler to characterize the information content of the data base. The information structure is represented by a set of distribution functions that specify the occurrences of attributes and values. That is, the information structure defines the logical clustering of attribute and values. Two facilities are available for defining the information structure: the PDF facility and the attribute facility.

The PDF facility allows the modeler to define probability distribution functions in the form of a table. Distribution functions used in simulation models are often based on statistics collected in terms of a frequency table. For example, the frequency of occurrences of different attributes in a data base is often presented as a cumulative frequency table [MEAD67]. The PDF facility is defined as a table of two columns (table 3). In the first column, values of the random variable for the PDF are defined. The second column includes the corresponding cumulation probabilities. This table can be used to represent either a discrete probability distribution function or a continuous probability distribution function. Each PDF facility is translated by the language parsers to a FORTRAN procedure. A call to this procedure will return a random variable value. For example, in using a bibliographical file, the random variable: "year of publication" may be defined as a discrete PDF facility (figure 22). Each calls the PDF procedure and will return an integer value between 1974 and 1979. The following IPSS/REL statement defines the above distribution:

Example 5a

    DEFINE PDF: *ID* = YR PUB,
                          MODE = DISCRETE,
                          TABLE = ((1974, 0.1), (1975, 0.3), (1976, 0.6),
                                        (1977, 0.8), (1978, 0.9), (1979, 1.0));

Table 3. Definition of PDF

VALUE OF RANDOM VARIABLE	CUMULATIVE PROBABILITY
V(1)	P(1)
V(2)	P(2)
V(3)	P(3)
⋮	⋮
V(n)	P(n)

$\underbrace{}$
search argument for
u, $u \in U$

Figure 22. Example of a PDF

YEAR OF PUBLICATION	CUMULATIVE PROBABILITY
1974	0.1
1975	0.3
1976	0.6
1977	0.8
1978	0.9
1979	1.0

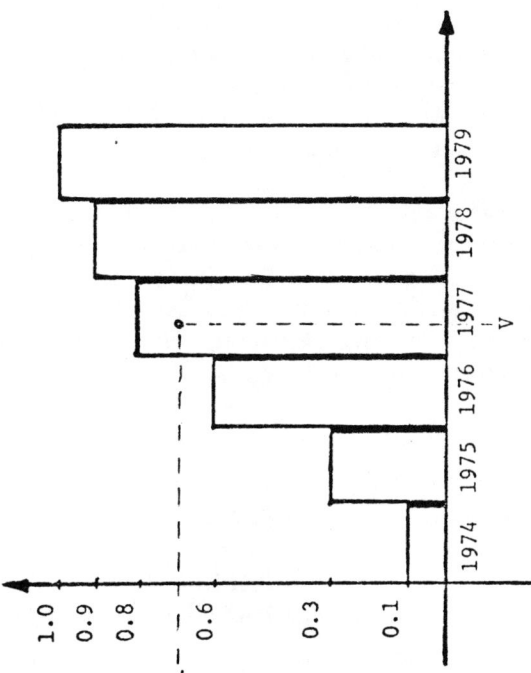

Attribute Statement

The Attribute facility is used to describe the distribution of one or more attributes in the information system data base. A set of attribute definitions is used to characterize the presence of multiple secondary keys (or attributes) within individual data base files. However, the association of an attribute with a file is not established until the IPSS/REL simulation model is executed. Thus, the same definition can be used with many files. The attribute facility defines the following distributions: first occurrence distribution, next occurrence distribution, number of occurrences distribution and values distribution. These distributions give the location of successive records that contain the given attribute. The values distribution describes the possible values of the attribute.

Example 5b

  ATTRIBUTE: ID = PLANG,
        DISTRIBUTION = (FIRST = 1200,
               NEXT = PDF (BIN5),
               LAST = 2000,
               VALUES = PDF (VDIST));

where BIN5 and VDIST are distributions defined as follows:

  DEFINE PDF: ID = BIN5,
        MODE = DISCRETE,
        TABLE = ((1, 0.0625), (2, 0.3125),
             (3, 0.6875), (4, 0.9375),
             (5, 1.0));

  DEFINE PDF: ID = VDIST,
        MODE = DISCRETE,
        TABLE = ((1, 0.4), (2, 0.6),
             (3, 0.8), (4, 0.4),
             (5, 1.0));

This example specified PLANG (programming language) as the attribute. The first occurrence of this attribute is at record 1200. Starting from this record, the inter-record distances are distributed according to the binomial distribution defined by the PDF BIN5. The last record with the PLANG attribute is at record 2000. Figure 23 of inter-record distances for records that contain the same attribute. The last occurrence distribution gives the

Figure 23. Example of an Attribute Definition

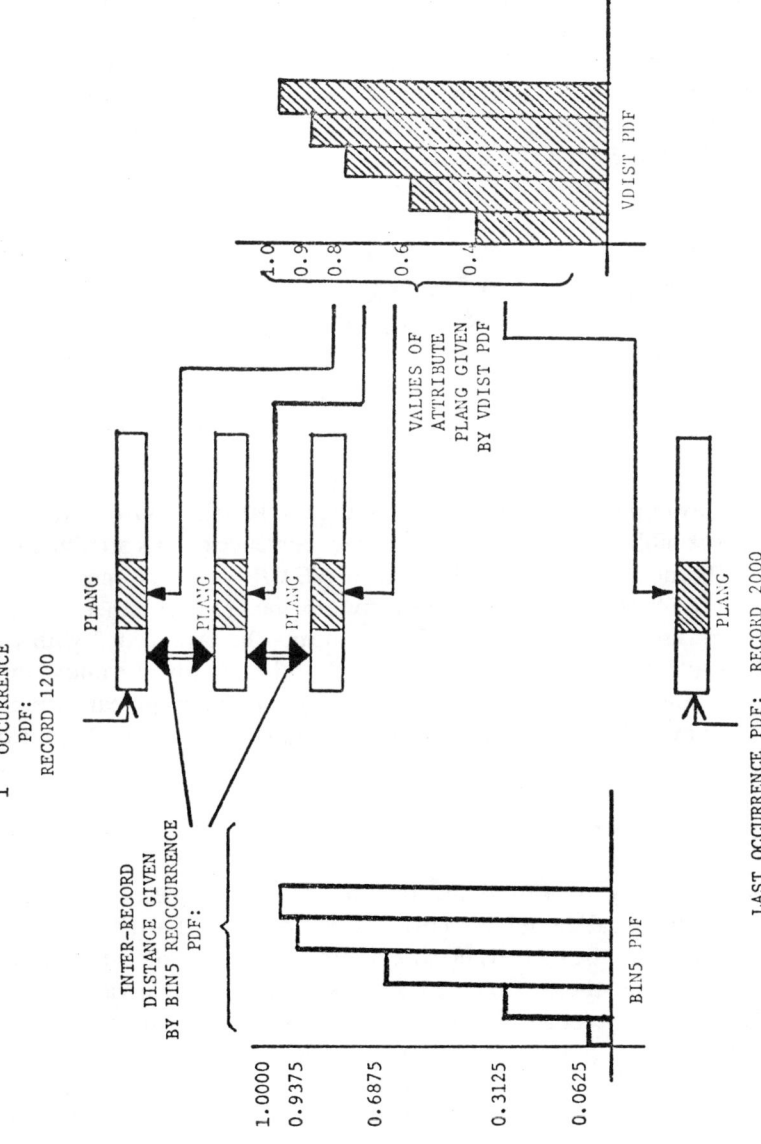

88   Verification of the Methodology

location of the last record that contains the given attribute. The number of occurrences distribution gives the number of records in the file that contain the given attribute. The values distribution describes the distribution of possible values for the given attribute. For example, let "PROGRAMMING LANGUAGES" be an attribute of a bibliographical file. That is, a bibliographical record has this attribute if the record describes a document that relates to programming languages. Suppose the possible values of this attribute are coded as 1 for COBOL, 2 for FORTRAN, 3 for PL/1, 4 for BASIC and 5 for OTHERS.

Example 5c

> *ATTRIBUTE: ID* = YEAR,
> *DISTRIBUTION* = (*FIRST* = 1,
> *NEXT* = NEXT,
> *LAST* = LAST,
> *VALUE* = PDF (YRPUB));

This example defines the "YEAR OF PUBLICATION" attribute YEAR for the bibliographical file. The first occurrence of this attribute is at record 1. The next occurrence distribution *NEXT* = NEXT means that records with the YEAR attribute are sequentially next to each other. The last occurrence distribution *LAST* = LAST means the last record with the YEAR attribute is the last record of the file. In other words, the above distribution functions specifies that every record of the bibliographical file contains the attribute YEAR. The values of this attribute are distributed according to the PDF definition on p. 83.

Search Key Statement

A search key is a fundamental unit of user request. As defined in the methodological model, a record consists of a set of attribute-value pairs. A user specifies the records he wants through the use of search keys. A search key describes the attribute together with the possible values that must be present in the record. The search key facility allows the modeler to describe the basic user request in one of the following forms:

(1) A search key represents a request for all records with a given attribute. Using example 5b, a request for all bibliographical records that relates to programming language documents is specified by the search key PLSRCH.

Example 5d

> SEARCH KEY: ID = PLSRCH,
> ATTRIBUTE = PLANG;

(2) A search key represents a request for all records with a given attribute and value. Using example 5b, a request for all bibliographical records that contain the programming language attribute with a value of FORTRAN (coded as 2) is specified by the search key FORT.

Example 5e

> SEARCH KEY: ID = FORT,
> ATTRIBUTE = ATTR,
> VALUE = 2;

where ATTR is a FORTRAN variable.

(3) A search key represents a request for all records with a given attribute and a value that is within a given range of values. Using example 5c, a request for all bibliographical records that describe documents published between 1976 and 1979 is specified by the search key YR7679.

Example 5f

> SEARCH KEY: ID = YR7679,
> ATTRIBUTE = YEAR,
> VALUE = RANGE (1976, 1979);

(4) A search key represents a request for all records with a given attribute and a given set of possible values. Using example 5b, a request for all bibliographical records that describe COBOL (coded as 1), for PL/1 (coded as 3), programming language documents is specified by the search key COBPL1.

Example 5g

> SEARCH KEY: ID = COBPL1,
> ATTRIBUTE = PLANG,
> VALUE = LIST(1,3);

(5) A search key represents a request for all records with a given attribute and a value which satisfies a comparison operation (such as equal, less than, or greater than). Using example 5c, a request for all biblio-

graphical records that describe documents published on or before the year 1976 is specified by the search key, YRLE76.

Example 5h

    SEARCH KEY: ID = YRLE76,
                         ATTRIBUTE = YEAR,
                         VALUE = (LE, 1976);

Query Statement

The query facility allows the modeler to characterize the user queries with a series of relational calculus-like expressions. These logical expressions consist of a set of search keys connected by logical operations. The logical operators are AND, OR, and NOT. For each record in the file being searched, the search keys yield a set of truth values. These truth values are combined by the logical operators to give a truth value for the record. The record satisfies the query if the truth value is TRUE. In other words, the logical expression specifies the conditions that a record has to satisfy before it is retrieved. Using the bibliographical file example, a request for all bibliographical records of COBOL or PL/1 documents published between 1976 and 1979 or FORTRAN documents published on or before 1976 is specified by the query SRCH1.

Example 5i

    QUERY: ID = SRCH1,
                EXPRESSION = COBPL1 .AND. YR7679
                                    .OR.
                         FORT   .AND. YRLE76;

The search keys: COBPL1, YR7679, FORT, and YRLE76 are defined in examples 5e, 5f, 5g, and 5h.

Create Query Facility

The create query system routine allocates and initializes special IPSS/REL internal storage areas which are necessary for the execution of the specified query. Once a query is created, it can be used to direct the retrieval or records. Since each created query represents a type of user request, simultaneous occurrences of the same type of user request can be simulated by creating multiple copies of the same query. Each copy of these queries is differentiated by specifying different indices in the CREATE QUERY statement. The CREATE QUERY statement also allows the modeler to specify the data set/file or schema/record type to be accessed. The same file can be used to access different data organizations at different times. A copy of the query in example 5i can be created by the following statement:

Example 5j

  CREATE QUERY: *QUERY ID* = SRCH1,
         INDEX = 1,
         DATA SET = MAINDB,
         FILE = 5;

Destroy Query Facility

The DESTROY QUERY statement deallocates the IPSS/REL internal storage areas associated with the specified query. Cumulative statistics for the query are updated.

Example 5k

  DESTROY QUERY: *QUERY ID* = SRCH1,
          INDEX = 1;

The above statement deallocates the internal storage areas allocated by example 5j.

Find Next Record(s) Facility

The FIND NEXT RECORD (singular) statement computes the location of the next record that satisfies the given query. The FIND NEXT RECORDS (plural) statement computes the locations of the next n records that satisfies the given query. The number, n, is a parameter of the FIND NEXT RECORDS statement. The FIND NEXT RECORD(S) system routine keeps a currency pointer for each query. This pointer contains the address of the current record that satisfies the user query. This pointer is built and initialized to zero by the CREATE QUERY statement. Each execution of the FIND NEXT RECORD(S) statement updates the corresponding current pointer. The address(es) of the next record(s) are returned in an address variable or array. If no more records satisfy the query, negative values are stored in the address variable or corresponding entries of the array. The FIND NEXT RECORD(S) statement makes use of the distribution functions defined for the query to compute the next record addresses. In the following example, the FIND NEXT RECORDS statement will return the

92 Verification of the Methodology

record IDs of the next ten records that satisfy the query defined in example 5i. These record IDs are stored in the address array named RECLST.

Example 5l

    FIND NEXT RECORDS: *QUERY ID* = SRCH1,
                                              INDEX = 1,
                                              NUMBER OF RECORDS = 10,
                                              ADDRESS = RECLST;

Find List Length Facility

Associated with each copy of a query is a counter that counts the number of records that have been accessed since the creation of the query. This counter is built and initialized to zero by the CREATE QUERY statement. This counter is updated whenever the FIND NEXT RECORD(S) statement is executed. The FIND LIST LENGTH system routine returns the counter value in a modeler-specified variable. In the following example, the number of records retrieved by the query SRCH1 is returned in the variable CURLEN.

Example 5m

    FIND LIST LENGTH: *QUERY ID* = SRCH1,
                                        INDEX = 1,
                                        LENGTH = CURLEN;

Transformations

In chapter 4, two transformations were discussed: the query transformation and the workload transformation. The query transformation is simulated by the endogenous services and exogenous services of IPSS. An algorithm for performing the query transformation for relational algebra is given in chapter 4. The workload transformation is automatically performed by IPSS/REL. The following is a description of this algorithm.

    The modeler director component directs the execution of an IPSS/REL model through the use of discrete event simulation. For the relational extensions, a set of query and attribute transformation routines are added. These routines are written in FORTRAN. One of the basic functions of these routines is to generate a list of record ID's that can be used to drive either the storage structure component or the DBMS component of the simulator. This transformation process is illustrated in figure 24.

    When a query is created, the associated query and search key defin-

Figure 24. Transformation of Query to Record Addresses

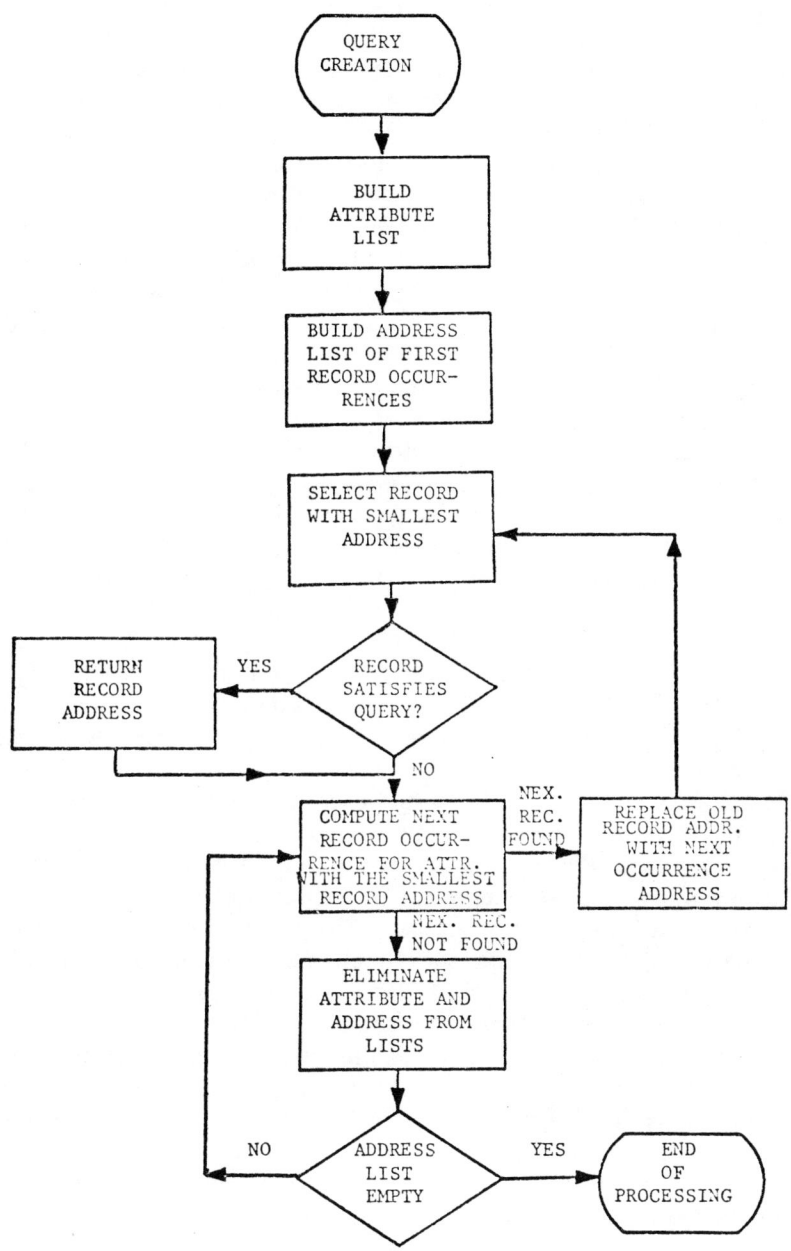

itions are examined to identify a list of attributes. This list consists of all attributes that are specified by the query's search criteria. Using this list of attributes, a corresponding list of record addresses is computed. For each attribute, the first occurrence distribution is used to compute and record the address. From this list of record addresses, the record with the smallest record address is selected. This record is tested against the query's search criteria. If the attributes and values of the record satisfy the query, the record address is returned to the routine that initiated the transformation process. After testing the record against the search criteria, the next record occurrence for the attribute is computed using the next occurrence distribution. This new address replaces the old record address in the address list. The address list is used again to find the next record that satisfies the query. If there are no more records that contain the attribute, the record address associated with the attribute is eliminated from the address list. Whether there are any more records that contain the attribute is determined by the next or last occurrence distributions. The above record search key process continues until all entries in the address list are eliminated.

In addition to directing the execution of the simulation model, the model director also keeps simulation statistics. The following section discusses the statistics for the relational extensions.

Statistics

In addition to statistics generated by IPSS, the relational extensions generate a new set of model statistics specific to data base workloads. These statistics evaluate the logical retrieval efficiency of the queries. At the end of a simulation run, statistics are printed for all queries that are still active, that is, for all queries that have not been destroyed by the DESTROY QUERY statement. For each of these active queries, the total number of records retrieved, the record number of the last record retrieved, a frequency table, and a histogram of inter-record distances are printed. Figures 25 and 26 show an example of these statistics. Besides the active query statistics, cumulative statistics for all queries that have been processed are also printed. For each query, the total number of times of query execution, mean number of records retrieved per execution, a cumulative inter-record frequency table, and a cumulative inter-record histogram are printed. Figure 26 shows an example of the cumulative query statistics. Both the active and cumulative query statistics are measures of logical clustering efficiency. If records with similar attributes are clustered together in the logical record space, then the query statistics should indicate a predominance of small inter-record distances.

Summary

The relational extensions of IPSS have been implemented. These extensions allow the modeler to evaluate the effects of the data base information structure and the user query stream characterizations on the information system's performance. Using these extensions, the modeler can evaluate various scenarios of data base organizations and query language designs. The model's relational extensions can be run without using any of the other special facilities of IPSS to generate statistics about the logical data base access pattern. The relational extensions can be used together with other facilities of IPSS to generate the hardware and software utilization statistics. These statistics can be used to evaluate both the logical and physical designs of an information system. In appendix A, the formal syntax and internal tables of the relational extensions are given.

Figure 25. Active Query Statistics

```
INFORMATION PROCESSING SYSTEM SIMULATOR
         MODEL SIMULATION PHASE
         POST SIMULATION STATISTICS
     PART G1 - ACTIVE QUERY STATISTICS

QUERY NAME    Q4567            QUERY INDEX   1

CURRENT RECORD NUMBER       =    100
TOTAL NUMBER OF RECORDS     =     70
MIN. INTER-RECORD DISTANCE  =  1.000
MAX. INTER-RECORD DISTANCE  =  3.000
MEAN INTER-RECORD DISTANCE  =  1.406
STD. INTER-RECORD DISTANCE  =  0.709

INTER-RECORD DISTANCE FREQUENCY TABLE

FREQ.   INTERVAL   INTERVAL   INTERVAL   FREQ.
CLASS   START      MEAN       END
  1      0.50       1.00       1.50        50
  2      1.50       2.00       2.50        10
  3      2.50       3.00       3.50         9
  4      3.50       4.00       4.50         0
  5      4.50       5.00       5.50         0
  6      5.50       6.00       6.50         0
  7      6.50       7.00       7.50         0
  8      7.50       8.00       8.50         0
  9      8.50       9.00       9.50         0
 10      9.50      10.00      10.50         0
```

INFORMATION PROCESSING SYSTEM SIMULATOR
MODEL SIMULATION PHASE
POST SIMULATION STATISTICS
PART.G1 - ACTIVE QUERY STATISTICS
INTER-RECORD DISTANCE HISTOGRAM

```
FREQUENCY  50   10   9    0    0    0    0    0    0    0    0
EACH * EQUALS 2 POINTS
   50       *
   48       *
   46       *
   44       *
   42       *
   40       *
   38       *
   36       *
   34       *
   32       *
   30       *
   28       *
   26       *
   24       *
   22       *
   20       *
   18       *
   16       *
   14       *
   12       *     *
   10       *     *
    8       *     *     *
    6       *     *     *
    4       *     *     *
    2       *     *     *
           ---------------------------------------------------
INTERVAL    1    2    3    4    5    6    7    8    9   10
CLASS
```

PAGE 31

Figure 26. Cumulative Query Statistics

```
                    INFORMATION PROCESSING SYSTEM SIMULATOR                PAGE  50

                              MODEL SIMULATION PHASE

                            POST SIMULATION STATISTICS

                       PART G2 - CUMULATIVE QUERY STATISTICS

QUERY NAME       QRY5

TOTAL NUMBER OF QUERIES      =      1.000
MEAN NO. OF REC. PER QUERY   =     30.000
STD. NO. OF REC. PER QUERY   =      0.0
MIN. INTER-RECORD DISTANCE   =      2.000
MAX. INTER-RECORD DISTANCE   =      5.000
MEAN INTER-RECORD DISTANCE   =      3.276
STD. INTER-RECORD DISTANCE   =      1.229

INTER-RECORD DISTANCE FREQUENCY TABLE

-------------------------------------------------------------------
FREQ.  | INTERVAL | INTERVAL | INTERVAL | FREQ.
CLASS  | START    | MEAN     | END      |
-------------------------------------------------------------------
  1    |   1.50   |   2.00   |   2.50   |  10
  2    |   2.50   |   3.00   |   3.50   |  10
  3    |   3.50   |   4.00   |   4.50   |   0
  4    |   4.50   |   5.00   |   5.50   |   9
  5    |   5.50   |   6.00   |   6.50   |   0
  6    |   6.50   |   7.00   |   7.50   |   0
  7    |   7.50   |   8.00   |   8.50   |   0
  8    |   8.50   |   9.00   |   9.50   |   0
  9    |   9.50   |  10.00   |  10.50   |   0
 10    |  10.50   |  11.00   |  11.50   |   0
-------------------------------------------------------------------
```

INFORMATION PROCESSING SYSTEM SIMULATOR

MODEL SIMULATION PHASE

POST SIMULATION STATISTICS

PART G2 - CUMULATIVE QUERY STATISTICS

INTER-RECORD DISTANCE HISTOGRAM

```
FREQUENCY  10   10   0    9    0    0    0    0    0    0
          -|----|----|----|----|----|----|----|----|----|----|
       10  |****                                              
        9  |*******                                           
        8  |*******                                           
        7  |*******                                           
        6  |*******                                           
        5  |*******                                           
        4  |*****                                             
        3  |***                                               
        2  |**                                                
        1  |*                                                 
          -|----|----|----|----|----|----|----|----|----|----|
INTERVAL   1    2    3    4    5    6    7    8    9    10
CLASS
```

6
Conclusions and Recommendations

Advances in computer hardware and software technologies have facilitated the building of powerful information systems. Many government and industrial organizations are highly dependent upon these information systems. A large number of these systems are on-line or real-time and use large data bases. The system's data base contributes substantially to the costs of designing, implementing, and maintaining these complex systems. Therefore, poor performance due to bad data design cannot be accepted. One requirement for good design is an accurate definition of the data base workload. Chapter 2 discussed design and evaluation tools applicable to this problem. However, these tools are restrictive and can only be applied to special classes of the problem. It is difficult to use them to evaluate data base workload based on data base access patterns and the data base information content.

The goal of this research is to provide a general methodology for workload definition to support the design and evaluation of information systems. This methodology allows the analyst to view his system from the highest level of transformation. The information system is viewed as a user workload in the form of high-level queries interacting with the data base information structure.

Since the pattern of user queries and the information structure of an information system directly affects the processing efficiency of the system, a methodology has been developed to characterize and evaluate these factors. The methodology was discussed in detail in chapter 4. Chapter 5 described the extensions to IPSS based on this methodology. This activity also verified the feasibility of the methodological concepts by translating them into language constructs and associated semantics. The major facets of the research are as follows:

1. Development of a method for characterizing the data base information structure,
2. Development of a method for characterizing the user queries,

102 Conclusions and Recommendations

3. Development of a methodological model that describes the interactions of the various components of an information system including the information structure and user workload components to derive workload definitions,
4. Development of language constructs based on the methodology, and
5. Implementation of the language as an extension to the IPSS Executional Facility.

The data base information structure has been characterized by sets of probability distribution functions. These functions describe how attributes and values are distributed throughout the files of an information system. Attributes were assumed to be independent of each other. However, characterization assuming interdependencies of attributes may provide even better models of information structure.

The user input stream has been characterized by a stream of multi-attributed queries in the form of Boolean expressions. This user input stream characterization allows the modeler to simulate the system at a high level as compared to user workloads that are at the physical I/O request level. This type of input stream can be constructed from a daily log of user query and inputted into the simulation model.

Transformation algorithms developed as part of the methodological model utilize the query and information structure characteristics to produce the system's workload definition for a query. The aggregate response for all queries is the system's data base workload definition. This model is general and is capable of describing a wide range of information systems including relational data base management systems.

The methodology was verified by developing a language syntax and semantics. To show its feasibility, a subset of this language was implemented as part of the IPSS Executional Facility. The facilities in the extensions have been tested and the results verified the accuracy of the implementation. A powerful query transformation algorithm has been developed as part of the implementation of the FIND NEXT RECORD system routine. This algorithm transform high-level user queries in the form of relational calculus expressions into file and record ID's. Using these file and record ID's the modeler can use the GET RECORD ADDRESS system routine of basic IPSS to transform the file and record ID's into physical record numbers, track numbers, cylinder numbers, and disk pack numbers. Thus, in two statements the simulator transforms a high-level user query ($A < 10$ and $B > 5$ OR $C = 100$) into a set of physical addresses (e.g., record 4 on track 5 of cylinder 10 in disk pack 6).

Recommendations for Extension of the Methodology

The type of user queries described in the methodology access files one at a time. This type of query corresponds to the level of propositional calculus in symbolic logic. A more powerful type of query allows the accessing of several files simultaneously. This type of query corresponds to the level of predicate calculus in symbolic logic. Extension of the current methodology to handle queries that have the existential quantifier ("THERE EXISTS") and the universal quantifier ("FOR ALL") will adequately model this type of query.

In the current methodology, the structure of a user query is static and cannot be altered during the execution of a model. It is desirable to have an extension that allows the dynamic construction of queries.

The information structure is defined in terms of a set of distribution functions. These distribution functions can be obtained through the analysis of actual data collections [DELU68]. Since the data collections may be very large, a better approach is to take a sample of the data collections to derive the distribution functions. Further research is needed to provide guidelines or formulas for the selection of samples.

In this methodology, the information structure is mapped onto the physical file organization. Currently, the file organizations have to be defined by the modeler. As an extension to the methodology, file organizations such as hashing, linked lists, and binary trees can be provided as file structure definition facilities.

Relational data base management systems are becoming increasingly popular in the implementation of information systems. Many modern data base management systems such as Query-By-Example [ZLOO77] and System R [SYSR79] are relational. The design and evaluation of these systems is difficult due to the high-level data independence between the logical data model and the physical storage organization. Although the current methodology provides sufficient facilities to model relational DBMS's, more facilities that deal specifically with relational DBMS will facilitate the modeling of these systems. The following extensions are recommended: Develop facilities for defining storage structures for relations, and develop facilities for defining the relational algebraic operations such as joint, project, and division.

Traditionally, two measures: precision and recall, are used to judge the system performance based on a given user workload. Both of these measures are subjective measures since they are based on the relevance of documents to users. The recall ration is defined as:

104   Conclusions and Recommendations

$$\text{recall ratio} = \frac{\text{number of relevant documents retrieved}}{\text{number of relevant documents present in the data base}}$$

The precision ratio is defined as:

$$\text{precision ratio} = \frac{\text{number of relevant documents retrieved}}{\text{total number of documents retrieved}}$$

A high level of retrieval efficiency is indicated by having both the average recall and precision ratios close to unity. These measures are dependent on what the users consider as relevant information to their queries. Unfortunately, relevance is a very subjective measure. Even for the same user, the relevance of a document may change over time. Therefore, both of the above measures are not objective estimates of system performance.

In this research, a set of inter-record distance statistics are used as objective measures of the user workload. In addition to these statistics, the following three measures of workload retrieval efficiency are suggested for future implementation. All three are based on the idea of a logical record. A logical record is the smallest unit of information that can be stored or retrieved by the users. A logical record is actually a more computer oriented term for a document descriptor.

Logical Retrieval Efficiency. This is a measure of the work effort in terms of the logical records referenced. In retrieving the logical records that satisfy a query, a system usually has to retrieve many other logical records, due to the need to search indexes and/or retrieve architectural constraints on data base records, before retrieving the desired records. The Logical Retrieval Efficiency (RD) is defined as follows:

$$RD = \frac{\text{Number of records that satisfy a user query}}{\text{total number of records referenced}}$$

The average record retrieval efficiency is dependent on the data base organization. A high level of record retrieval efficiency is indicated by an RD close to unity. For example, if 10 records satisfy a user query but the system has to retrieve 5 index records before retrieving the 10 records, then the record efficiency ratio is $10/15 = 0.67$.

Physical Retrieval Efficiency. This is a measure of the work effort in terms of the physical records referenced. The volume of I/O operations performed is an important factor in information system performance. Very often, I/O is the major cause of bottle-necks in information systems. Therefore, it is desirable to organize records in such a way that the number of I/O operations is minimized. One way of accomplishing this is to combine logical records in the physical records. A physical record or block can contain many logical records. Since the number of I/O operations performed in response to a query is proportional to the number of blocks retrieved, blocking the logical records will reduce the amount of I/O operations. The Physical Retrieval Efficiency (OP) is defined as follows:

$$OP = 1 - \frac{\text{total number of physical records accessed}}{\text{total number of records that satisfy a user query}}$$

A high level of physical retrieval efficiency is indicated by an OP close to unity, while a low level of operations retrieval efficiency is indicated by an OP close to zero. For example, if only 3 blocks are required in order to retrieve 15 records for a user, then the Operations Retrieval Efficiency is $1 - 3/15 = 0.8$.

Data Retrieval Efficiency. This is a measure of work effort in terms of the total amount of data referenced. Often, in retrieving information for a user, not only do unnecessary records have to be retrieved because of the way the data is organized, but a large portion of the data in the desired blocks also proves inapplicable to the user query. A way to reduce the amount of unwanted data is to use a clustering technique, so that records that are likely to be retrieved together are stored in the same block. The Data Retrieval Efficiency (DA) is a measure of how well these similar logical records are blocked together and is defined as follows:

$$DA = \frac{\text{actual number of characters or bits that satisfy a user query}}{\text{total number of characters or bits accessed}}$$

The Data Retrieval Efficiency measure evaluates how much unnecessary data is retrieved. A high level of data retrieval efficiency is indicated by a DA close to unity and a low level of data retrieval efficiency is indicated by a DA close to zero. For example, if the information that satisfies a given user query is stored in 10 logical records of 15 characters and the information system actually retrieved 3 blocks of 100 characters, then the data retrieval efficiency is $(10 \times 15)/(3 \times 100) = 0.5$.

The above discussion only illustrates some of the user workload related measures. More research has to be done in this area to develop a comprehensive set of measures for characterizing different types of user workload.

Conclusions and Recommendations

Summary

The objective of this research was to develop a methodology to more accurately define data base workload in contemporary systems. Various tools that evaluate system performance as a function of workload were examined. It was found that all of these tools lack sufficient constructs to model the user workload of an information system. A methodology was developed to attack this problem. This methodology was based on three underlying methodologies: relational data model, attribute analysis, and IPSS. The relational data model was selected because it can model a wide range of data base systems. It was shown that the relational data model was capable of describing both the hierarchical and network data models. Attribute analysis was used to characterize the data base information structure. This information structure consists of distribution functions that describe the reoccurrence of attributes throughout the data base. The IPSS methodology allows the system designer to view his information system as a series of transformations: a) information system level transformation, b) application level transformation, c) DBMS level transformation, d) file management level transformation, and e) secondary storage level transformation. All the above transformations, except the application level transformation, have been characterized and facilities for modeling these transformations have been implemented. In this research, the IPSS methodology has been expanded to model the application level transformation. The input to this transformation consists of a stream of user queries in some query language. The output of this transformation is the data base workload. This data base workload consists of a list of the file and record identifiers required to satisfy the user queries. The system level transformation is divided into two sub-transformations: the query transformation and the workload transformation. The query transformation accepts user queries which may reference multiple files or relations. These queries are converted to a series of single file or relation queries in the form of Boolean expressions. These Boolean expressions are made up of arbitrary numbers of attributes and value conditions (i.e., attribute, comparison operator, value), triplets, connected by the logical operators AND, OR, and NOT. The Boolean expressions are inputted to the data base workload transformation. Each Boolean expression is processed against the individual files of the data base. The data base workload transformation locates the records that satisfied the Boolean expressions by utilizing the information structure defined for the data base. A procedure for deriving equations that describe the user workload and user workload measures as a function of the following parameters: system loading process, query transformation function, object retrieval work function, file traversal work function, first attribute occurrence PDF, next attribute occurrence PDF, number of occurrences PDF, last attribute occurrence PDF, and value PDF has been developed. Although these equations describe the system level transformation at the conceptual level, in general they are very difficult to derive or compute. Therefore, simulation facilities were defined and implemented to model the conceptual model components and transformations. The syntax and semantics of IPSS statements necessary for the modeling of the system level transformation was defined. Parsers for translating these statements into FORTRAN were developed. System routines that are needed to support the transformation process were also developed. Special routines that compute workload statistics were added to the standard IPSS statistics package. The IPSS model director was modified to accomodate the new extensions. All the extended IPSS facilities have been tested.

A methodology for modeling the data base workload for large multi-attributed data bases and complex Boolean type queries has been developed. A methodological model that describes the workload as a function of the interactions of the various system components has been completed. This methodological model has been implemented as an extension to the IPSS simulation language. The simulation facilities have been tested and validated. It was found that the methodology is applicable to both conventional information storage and retrieval systems and relational data base management systems.

APPENDIX A

Syntax and Semantics for

the Relational Extentions to IPSS

1.0 Introduction

The purpose of this appendix is to present the syntax and semantics for the IPSS statements comprising the Relational Extensions. Two collections of IPSS language statements are presented. The first collection are those statements which extend the IPSS Executional Facility, i.e., they are currently executable. The second collection are those statements which extend the IPSS Modeling Facility, i.e., the hypothetical language based on the IPSS Methodology that is used as the IPSS publication language.

The IPSS methodology is based on a sequence of successive transformations of an external request for system services to performance measures. The Implementation of this methodology proceeded from the bottom, i.e., most detailed system transformations upward. IPSS/BASIC focused on the file organization, physical storage, and support facilities oriented transformations. IPSS/DBS continued the upward focus to the application and database management level transformations. The Relational Extensions focus on the system level Transformations. The relational extensions facilitate the analysis of information processing systems based on multi attributed query processing. They can be used in either the System's Resources Component (IPSS/BASIC) and the Data Access Component (IPSS/DBS).

2.0 Information Structure Characterization By Attribute Analysis

The way information is distributed in a data base largely determines the performance of an information system. Attribute Analysis is a method for characterizing this information structure. In attribute analysis, a data base is defined as a set of flat files. Each file is a collection of records sequentially ordered via the concatenation of one or more keys present in every record. For the purpose of this dicussion, the records are assumed to be ordered by accession number, i.e., FIFO. The information in a record is characterized by attributes and their associated values (attribute-value pairs). The distributions of a file's attribute-value pairs are characterized by probability distribution functions (pdf). Five pdf's are used to completely characterize the attribute-value pair occurrence, these are: (a) first occurrence pdf, (b) next occurrence pdf, (c) number of occurrences pdf, (d) last occurrence pdf and (e) attribute value pdf. Information system workload is characterized by the occurrences of multi-attributed queries. Each query is comprised of one or more search keys connected by the logical operators: AND, OR and NOT. Each search key consists of an attribute, a value and a comparision operator. The comparsion operators are:

less-than, less-than-or-equal, equal, greater-than-or-equal, greater-than, and not-equal. Using these attribute and query characterizations, the information system level transformation can be realized. Table A-1 identifies the statements that comprise the relational extensions to IPSS.

Table A-1.
IPSS Statements and Functions for
Multi-Attribute Analysis

IPSS Statement	Form [:Type/Class]*	Execution Facility	Modeling Facility
ATTRIBUTE	Definitional: Attribute/Static	4.1	5.1
PDF	Definitional: Attribute/Static	4.2	
DISTRIBUTION FUNCTION	Definitional: Attribute/Static		5.2
CREATE QUERY DESTROY	Procedural	4.5	5.5
FIND NEXT RECORD	Procedural	4.6	5.6
QUERY	Definitional: Entity/Static	4.4	5.4
FIND LIST LENGTH	Procedural	4.7	
QUERY LIST LENGTH	Procedural		5.7
SEARCH KEY	Definitional: Attribute/Static	4.3	5.3
DEFINE QUERY STATISTICS	Definitional: Attribute/Static		5.8

* Definitional means that the statement is used to define an
IPSS facility. Statistics are gathered for entity type
facilities. Attribute type facilities supply additional
characterization data for entities. A static class facility is one in which the statement defines parameters to
a generalized IPSS software procedure. A dynamic class
facility is one in which the modeler defines the procedure
to be used.

Procedural means that the statement is an IPSS Built-in
Procedure available to the modeler. The statement is
translated into a sequence of Fortran statements which
invoked the named Built-in Procedure.

3.0 IPSS Meta Language

In this appendix, basic formats are prescribed for various elements of IPSS. These generalized descriptions (metasymbols) are intended to guide the reader to better understanding of the syntax of the IPSS statements. The rules of the notation follow.

(a) Keywords: All words printed entirely in capital letters represent actual occurrences of those words, e.g., ATTRIBUTE.

(b) Special Characters: All special characters including colon [:], equal [], left parenthesis [(], right parenthesis [)], period [.], comma [,], and semicolon [;] represent the actual occurrences of those characters.

(c) Lower Case Words and Phrases: Words or phrases printed in lower case letters and not delineated by < and > describe information to be supplied by the modeler.

(d) Square Brackets ([]): Square brackets are used to indicate that the enclosed syntactic unit(s) are optional.

(e) Braces [ ]: Braces enclose vertically stacked items and indicate that one of the enclosed units is required.

(f) Ellipsis [...]: The ellipsis indicates that the immediately preceeding syntactic unit may recur one or more times in succession with each unit separated by a comma [,].

(g) Metavariables: A metabariable is a string of upper and lower case letters, digits and embedded hyphens delineated by < and > used to name a class of options available as statement parameter values.

(h) Modeler-Specified Identifiers: Modeler-specified identifiers can be any valid Fortran vairiable name with the restriction that these names do not begin with "$".

4.0 Execution Facilites

The IPSS/REL execution facilities consists of the following statements.

* Attribute
* PDF
* Search Key
* Query
* Create/Destroy Query
* Find Next Record
* Find List Length

4.1 The ATTRIBUTE Statement

A. PURPOSE

The ATTRIBUTE statement defines one or more attribute facilities. The distribution of attribute and values within the logical record address space of a file is defined by the attribute facility. These distributions are used in a search procedure during model execution to locate the logical records that contain the given attribute.

B. SYNTAX

```
ATTRIBUTE:
     ⎧ <identifier>                              ⎫
ID = ⎨                                           ⎬
     ⎩ <identifier>, [NUMBER=] <integer>         ⎭
,DISTRIBUTION=
                    ⎧ <value-1>           ⎫
     (FIRST  =      ⎨ PDF((<PDF-id-1>)    ⎬
                    ⎩ PROC((<PROC-ref-1>) ⎭

                    ⎧ <value-2>           ⎫
     ,NEXT   =      ⎨ PDF((<PDF-id-2>)    ⎬
                    ⎩ PROC((<PROC-ref-2>) ⎭

                    ⎧ <value-3>           ⎫
     ,LAST   =      ⎨ PDF((<PDF-id-3>)    ⎬
                    ⎩ PROC((<PROC-ref-3>) ⎭

                    ⎧ <value-4>           ⎫
     ,NUMBER=       ⎨ PDF((<PDF-id-4>)    ⎬
                    ⎩ PROC((<PROC-ref-4>) ⎭

                    ⎧ <value-5>                        ⎫
     [,VALUES=      ⎨ PDF((<PDF-id-5>)                 ⎬ ] ) ];
                    ⎪ PROC((<PROC-ref-5>)              ⎪
                    ⎩ UNIFORM(<value-6>, <value-7>)    ⎭
```

C. SEMANTICS

The parameters associated with the ATTRIBUTE statement have the following meanings.

1. ID: Specifies the external identifier(s) of the attribute(s).
2. DISTRIBUTION: Specifies the three distributions associated with an attribute. The subparameters have the following meanings:
   a. FIRST: identifies the first occurrence probability distribution function value, Fx(.), for the attribute. During model execution, this pdf is used to locate the first file record that contains the given attribute. The availabe options are:
      i.   <value-1> states that the record number given by <value-1> is the first record that contains the attribute, i.e.,
      $$Fx(.) = \begin{cases} 0 \text{ if } x < \text{value}(1) \\ 1 \text{ if } x >= \text{value}(1) \end{cases}$$
      ii. PDF(<PDF-id-1>) states that the named PDF facility is used to define the first occurrence value.
      iii. PROC(<PROC-ref-1>) states that the named Procedure facility is used to define the first occurrence value.
   b. NEXT: states by what means the next occurrence pdf values, Rx(.), associated with the attribute are to be generated. During model execution this pdf is used to compute inter-record distances. The

available options are:

i. <value-2> states that the next record to contain the same attribute is always equal to the current record location plus the current value found in <value-2>, i.e.,

$$Rx(.) = \begin{cases} 0 \text{ if } x < \text{value}(2) \\ 1 \text{ if } x >= \text{value}(2) \end{cases}$$

ii. PDF(<PDF-id-2>) states that a PDF facility is used to generate the next occurrence values.

iii. PROC(<PROC-ref-2>) states that an IPSS Procedure facility is used to define the next occurrence values.

C. LAST: identifies the last occurrence pdf, Lx(.), for the attribute. During model execution, the last occurrence pdf is used to locate the last record that contains the given attribute.

i. <value-3> states that the record number given by <value-3> is the last record that contains the attribute, i.e.,

$$Lx(.) = \begin{cases} 0 \text{ if } x < \text{value}(3) \\ 1 \text{ if } x >= \text{value}(3) \end{cases}$$

ii. PDF(<PDF-id-3>) states that a PDF facility is used to define the last occurrence pdf.

iii. PROC(<PROC-ref-3>) states that an IPSS facility

is used to define the last occurrence pdf.

D. NUMBER: specifies the number of occurrences pdf, $Nx(.)$, for the attribute. During model execution, the number of occurrences pdf is used to compute the number of records that contain the given attribute. The abailable options are:

i. <value-4> specifies that the number of records containing the attribute is equal to <value-4>, i.e.,
$$Nx(.) = \begin{cases} 0 \text{ if } x < \text{value}(4) \\ 1 \text{ if } x >= \text{value}(4) \end{cases}$$

ii. PDF(<PDF-id-4>) states that a PDF facility is used to define the number of occurrences pdf.

iii. PROC(<PROC-ref-4>) states that an IPSS procedure is used to define the number of occurrences pdf.

3. VALUES: Specifies the distribution of possible values for the attribute. During model execution, the value pdf, $Vx(.)$, is used to compute values for the given attribute. The subparameters have the following meanings:

a. <value-5> states that that the only possible value for the attribute is <value-5>, i.e.,
$$Vx(.) = \begin{cases} 0 \text{ if } x < \text{value}(5) \\ 1 \text{ if } x >= \text{value}(5) \end{cases}$$

b. PDF(<PDF-id-5>) states that a PDF facility is used to define the value pdf.

c. PROC(<PROC-ref-5>) states that an IPSS procedure is

used to define the value pdf.

d. UNIFORM states that the values of the attribute
are uniformly distributed between the minimum value
<value-6> and the maximum value <value-7>. The
available options are:

   i. DISCRETE states that the distribution is
   a discrete uniform distribution, i.e.,
   $$Vx(.) = \begin{cases} 0 & \text{if } x < value(6) \\ (x-value(6)+1)/(value(7)-value(6)+1) & \text{if } value(6) <= x <= value(7) \\ 0 & \text{if } x > value(7) \end{cases}$$

   ii. CONTINUOUS specifies that the distribution is
   a continuous uniform distribution, i.e.,
   $$Vx(.) = \begin{cases} 0 & \text{if } x <= value(6) \\ (x-value(6))/(value(7)-value(6)) & \text{if } value(6) < x < value(7) \\ 0 & \text{if } x >= value(7) \end{cases}$$

The default is no value pdf. That is the attribute has
a null value.

The $COMM conventions to be observed are shown in table A-2.

Table A-2.
$COMM conventions for ATTRIBUTE statement

ATTRIBUTE Statement	$COMM Location	Value		when called
		Dimension	Data Type	
FIRST	1	logical records	real	A
NEXT	1	logical records	real	B
LAST	1	logical records	real	A
NUMBER	1	logical records	real	A
VALUES	1	mode of attr.	real	B

A - Invoked each time attribute facility is referenced through the CREATE QUERY statement during execution time.

B - Invoked each time attribute facility is referenced through the FIND NEXT RECORD statement during execution time.

4.2 The PDF Statement

A. PURPOSE

The PDF statement is used to define cumulative probability distribution functions. When a PDF is referenced during execution time, an occurrence of the associated random variate is generated.

B. SYNTAX

PDF:

ID= <identifier>

[, MODE = $\begin{Bmatrix} DISCRETE \\ CONTINUOUS \end{Bmatrix}$]

, TABLE = ((<value-1>, <prob-1>)
            [,(<value-2>, <prob-2>)] ...);

C. SEMANTICS

The parameters associated with the PDF statement have the following meanings.

1. ID: Specifies the external identifier of the PDF.
2. MODE: Specifies the mode of the PDF. The available options are:
   a. DISCRETE: Specifies that the PDF is a discrete distribution.
   b. CONTINUOUS: Specifies that the PDF is a continuous distribution.
3. TABLE: Specifies the possible values for the random variate and the corresponding probabilities. The table consists of a list of value elements. Each value element is composed of a random variate element

<value-i> and a function element <prob-i>. The
random variate element gives a possible value of the
the random variable and the function element gives
the corresponding cumulatiave probability. Let x be
the random variate, Fx(.) be the distribution
function and suppose there are n value elements in
the form of (V(1), P(1), V(2), P(2),...,V(n),P(n)).
If the PDF is discrete, then the following formulae
applies:

$$Fx(.) = \begin{cases} P(1) & \text{if } x \leq V(1) \\ P(2) & \text{if } V(1) < x \leq V(2) \\ \cdot \\ \cdot \\ \cdot \\ P(n) & \text{if } V(n-1) < x \leq V(n). \end{cases}$$

This PDF is illustrated in figure 27. If the
PDF is continuous, then the following formulae
applies:

$$Fx(.) = \begin{cases} 0 & \text{if } x \leq V(1) \\ P(k+1) + \dfrac{(x-V(k-1))(P(k)-P(k-1))}{(V(k)-V(k-1))} \\ \quad \text{if } V(k-1) < x \leq V(k) \\ \quad \text{for } k=2,3,...,n-1 \\ 1 & \text{if } x > V(n) \end{cases}$$

This PDF is illustrated in figure 28.

The $COMM conventions to be observed when a PDF
is referenced is given in Table A-3 .

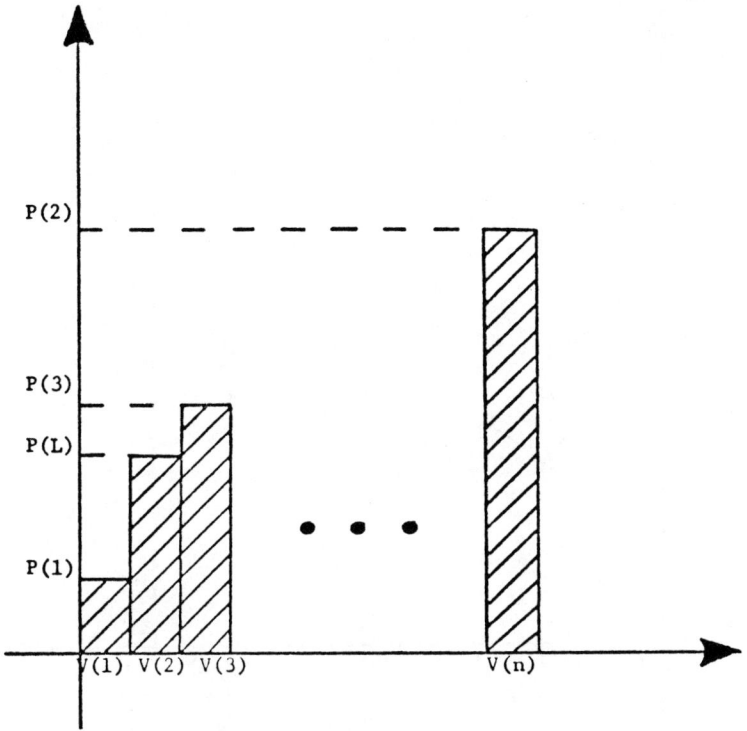

$F_X(x) = P(i)$ if $v(i-1) < x \leq v(i)$

Figure 27

DISCRETE PDF: $F_X(\cdot)$

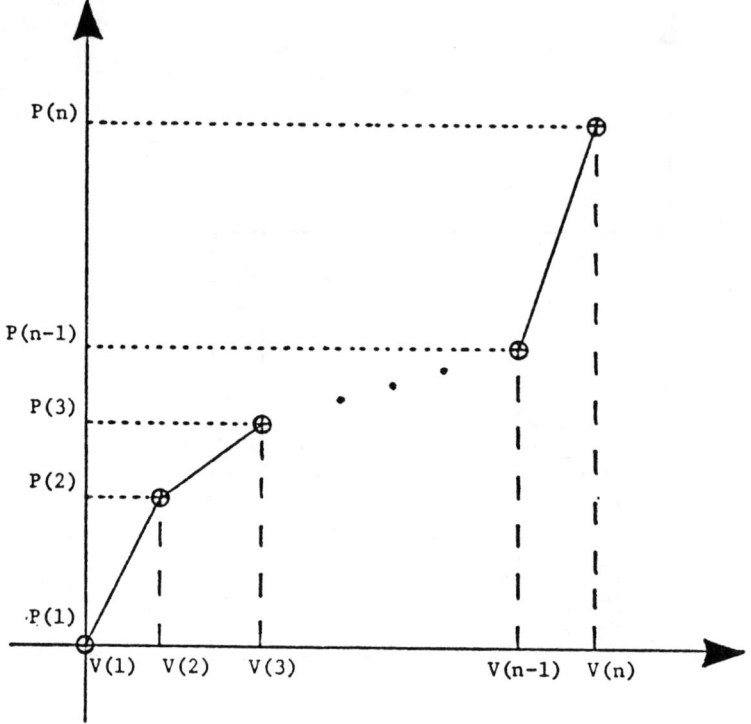

$$F_X(x) = P(k-1) + \frac{(x-V(k-1))\ (P(k) - P(k-1)}{(V(k) - V(k-1))}$$

Figure 28

CONTINUOUS PDF: $F_X(\cdot)$

Table A-3
$COMM conventions for PDF statement

PDF Statement	$COMM Location	Value	
		Dimension	Data Type
RANDOM VARIATE	1	random variate type	real

4.3 The SEARCH KEY Statement

A. PURPOSE

The SEARCH KEY statement is used to identify the search requirements relating to an attribute. A search key is defined as an attribute and a set of conditions on the values of the attribute. Search keys are combined to form queries in the QUERY statement.

B. SYNTAX
SEARCH KEY:

ID = \<identifier\>

,ATTRIBUTE = \<ATTR-id\>

[,VALUES= $\left\{ \begin{array}{l} \text{<value-1>} \\ \text{ALL} \\ (\text{<condition>}, \begin{array}{l} \text{<value-2>} \\ \text{PROC(<proc-ref>)} \\ \text{PDF(<PDF-ret>)} \end{array}) \\ \text{LIST(<value-3> [,<value-4>] ...)} \\ \text{RANGE(<value-5>, <value-6>)} \end{array} \right\}$] ;

where

\<condition\> = $\left\{ \begin{array}{l} \text{LT} \\ \text{LE} \\ \text{EQ} \\ \text{GE} \\ \text{GT} \\ \text{NE} \end{array} \right\}$

C. SEMANTICS

The parameters associated with the SEARCH KEY statement have the following meanings.

1. ID: Specifies the external identifier of the search key.

2. ATTRIBUTE: Specifies an attribute name. This name links the search key with a corresponding attribute

defined using the ATTRIBUTE statement.
3. VALUES: Specifies the conditions on the values of
   the attribute. The available options are:
   a. <value-1> states that the attribute must have
      a value equal to <value-1>.
   b. ALL: states that the attribute can take on all
      possible values.
   c. (<condition>, <value-2> or PROC or PDF) states
      a condition on the attribute. The options LT,
      LE, EQ, GE, GT and NE specifies that the value
      of the attribute must be "less than", "less than
      or equal", "equal", "greater than or equal",
      "greater than" or "not equal" to the value
      represented by <value-2> or PROC or PDF.
   d. LIST(<value-3> [,<value-4>]...) states that the
      attribute can have any of the values given in
      the list.
   e. RANGE(<value-5>,<value-6>) states that the attribute
      can have any value between the minimum <value-5>
      and the maximum value <value-6>.
   The default for the VALUES parameter is ALL. That is
   any attribute value will satisfy the search key.

Table A-4 identifies the $COMM communication
conventions to be followed if a Procedure or PDF is used
to supply a conditional comparison value.

Table A-4
$COMM conventions for SEARCH KEY statement

SEARCH KEY Statement	$COMM Location	Value		when called
		Dimension	Data Type	
VALUES	1	attr. type	real	*

* - Invoked each time search key facility is referenced during execution.

4.4 The QUERY Statement

A. PURPOSE

The QUERY statement is used to identify the search keys and logical operators ('AND', 'OR', 'NOT') used to build a query. This statement can define any query expressable as a boolean expression (propositional calculus expression).

B. SYNTAX

QUERY:

ID = <identifier>,

EXPRESSION = (<sub-expr-1>, [.OR. <sub-expr-2>]...);

where

<sub-expr> = [.not.] <SK-id-1> [.and.[.not.]<SK-id-2>]...

C. SEMANTICS

The parameters associated with the QUERY statement have the following meanings.

1. ID: Specifies the external identifier of the query.
2. EXPRESSION: Specifies one or more sub-expressions connected by the logical operator '.OR.'. Each sub-expression consists of one or more search keys, <SK-id>, connected by the logical operator '.AND.'. Each search key can optionally have the logical operator '.NOT.' in front of it.

4.5 CREATE and DESTROY QUERY Statement

A. SYNTAX

```
CREATE     QUERY:
DESTROY

QUERY ID = <QRY-ref> [,INDEX = <integer>]

  [,DATA SET = <DS-ref> [,FILE = <FILE-ref> ] ]
                                     PRIME
  [,SCHEMA = <SCH-ref> [,REC TYPE = <RT-ref>] ]

                      ⎧  <label>        ⎫
  [,ERROR EXIT =      ⎨  STOP SIMULATION ⎬  ];
                      ⎩  CONTINUE       ⎭
```

B. FUNCTION

The purpose of the CREATE QUERY procedure is to create for the named QUERY facility a copy of its associated query structure definition. The copy is placed in a pre-defined area of the model's transaction array ($TRANS). Once copied, simulation functions involving the Query facility can occur. The definition remains valid until the issuing of a DESTROY QUERY statement for the same query facility.

C. PARAMETERS

1. QUERY ID: Names the Query facility which is to be created or destroyed. An error condition occurrs if a non-Query facility is referenced.

2. INDEX: Each copy of the query facility is given an index number. This number is specified by the user. The default index is 1. If the index references an already created query, the old copy of the query is destroyed.

3. DATA SET: Specifies the data set associated with the

query.

4. FILE: Specifies the file asociated with the query.
The available options are:
   a. <FILE-ref>: states the file number as an integer between 1 and 8.
   b. PRIME: states thate only the PRIME file of the data set is used.
5. SCHEMA: Specfies the schema facility associated with the query if IPSS/DBS is being used.
6. REC TYPE: Specifies the record type associated with the query if IPSS/DBS is being used.
7. ERROR EXIT: Specifies the processing to be performed when an error is detected during execution of the CREATE or DESTROY QUERY Built-in procedures. The available options are:
   a. <label> states the next statement to be executed.
   b. STOP SIMULATION means that the simulation is aborted when control returns to the nucleus.
   c. CONTINUE results in execution to proceed as though no error had occurred.

   CONTINUE is the default option.

D. IPSS TRANSLATION

CALL CFSQRY(P1, P2, P3, P4, P5, P6, P7, P8 [,P9])

where
P1 = <QRY-ref>

P2 = $\begin{cases} 1 & \text{if index is not specified} \\ \text{<integer>} & \text{if index is specified} \end{cases}$

$$P3 = \begin{cases} 0 & \text{if DATA SET is not specified} \\ \text{<DS-ref>} & \text{if DATA SET is specified} \end{cases}$$

$$P4 = \begin{cases} 0 & \text{if FILE is not specified} \\ 1 & \text{if PRIME is specified} \\ \text{<FILE-ref>} & \text{if file number is specified} \end{cases}$$

$$P5 = \begin{cases} 0 & \text{if SCHEMA is not specified} \\ \text{<SCH-ref>} & \text{if SCHEMA is specified} \end{cases}$$

$$P6 = \begin{cases} 0 & \text{if REC TYPE is not specified} \\ \text{<RT-ref>} & \text{if REC TYPE is specified} \end{cases}$$

$$P7 = \begin{cases} 1 & \text{if ERROR EXIT is a label} \\ 2 & \text{if ERROR EXIT is STOP SIMULATION} \\ 3 & \text{if ERROR EXIT is CONTINUE or ERROR EXIT is not specified} \end{cases}$$

$$P8 = \begin{cases} 1 & \text{if CREATE QUERY} \\ 2 & \text{if DESTROY QUERY} \end{cases}$$

P9 = &<label>   if <label> is specified.

E. EXAMPLES

Example 1:

IPSS Source --

CREATE QUERY: QUERY ID = QRYX,

            INDEX = ID,

            DATA SET = D21,

            FILE = 3,

            ERROR EXIT = 1414;

Fortran Source -

CALL CF$QRY(QRYX,ID,DS21,3,0,0,1,1,&1414)

Example 2:

IPSS Source -

DESTROY QUERY: QUERY ID = QRYZ,

DATA SET = DS21;

Fortran Source -

CALL CF$QRY(QRYZ,1,DS21,0,0,0,0,3)

4.6 FIND NEXT RECORD Statement

A. SYNTAX
FIND NEXT RECORD[S]:

QUERY ID = <QRY-ref>

[, INDEX = <value-1>]

[, NUMBER OF RECORDS = <value-2>]

[, INTERVAL = <value-3>]

, ADDRESS = $\begin{Bmatrix} \text{<variable>} \\ \text{<array name>} \end{Bmatrix}$

[, ERROR EXIT = $\begin{Bmatrix} \text{<label>} \\ \text{STOP SIMULATION} \\ \text{CONTINUE} \end{Bmatrix}$];

B. FUNCTION

The purpose of the FIND NEXT RECORD[S] procedure is to identify the next record(s) that satisfies(y) the given query. The procedure keeps track of the number of records already retrieved using the given query. If a query is being used for the first time, the procedure will automatically start with the first record that satisfies the query.

C. PARAMETERS

1. QUERY ID: Specifies the query that is used for record retrieval.
2. INDEX: Specifies the index number for the query. The default is 1.
3. NUMBER OF RECORDS: Specifies the number of records to be retrieved. All the records retrieved must satisfy the given query. The default for NUMBER OF RECORDS is 1.

4. INTERVAL: Records that satisfy different conjuncts of a query (i.e. search keys connected by '.AND.') are based on the matching of the probabilistically generated record numbers of individual search keys. If the pairwise difference between the record numbers are less than the value given by the INTERVAL parameter, the record numbers arec considered to be matched. The default value for INTERVAL is 1.
5. ADDRESS: This is a user supplied FORTRAN variable or array for storing the next record address(es). If the number of records to be retrieved is one, then a variable name should be specified. Otherwise, an array name should be specified.
6. ERROR EXIT: Specifies the processing to be performed when an error is detected during execution of the FIND NEXT RECORD[S] built-in procedure. The available options are:
    a. <label> states the next statement to be executed.
    b. STOP SIMULATION means that the simulation is aborted when control returns to the nucleus.
    c. CONTINUE results in execution to proceed as though no error had occurred.
    CONTINUE is the default option.
D. IPSS TRANSLATION
1. for FIND NEXT RECORD statement (one record)
    CALL $NREC1(P1, P2, P3, P4, P5, P6 [,P7])
2. for FIND NEXT RECORDS statement (multiple records)

CALL $NREC2(P1, P2, P3, P4, P5, P6 [,P7])

The reason for having two procedures for this statement is because FORTRAN expects argument P5 to be either a variable or an array. Also since P3 may be a variable such that the number of records to be retrieved is not known till model execution time, P3 can not be used to determine which procedure to call.

where

P1 = \<QRY-ref\>

P2 = $\begin{cases} 1 & \text{if INDEX is not specified} \\ \text{<value-1>} & \text{if INDEX is specified} \end{cases}$

P3 = $\begin{cases} 1 & \text{if NUMBER OF RECORDS is not specified} \\ \text{<value-2>} & \text{if NUMBER OF RECORDS is specified} \end{cases}$

P4 = $\begin{cases} 1 & \text{if INTERVAL is not specified} \\ \text{<value-3>} & \text{if INTERVAL is specified} \end{cases}$

P5 = $\begin{cases} \text{<variable>} & \text{when FIND NEXT RECORD is specified} \\ \text{<array name>} & \text{when FIND NEXT RECORDS is specified} \end{cases}$

P6 = $\begin{cases} 1 & \text{if ERROR EXIT is a label} \\ 2 & \text{if ERROR EXIT is STOP SIMULATION} \\ 3 & \text{if ERROR EXIT is CONTINUE or} \\ & \text{ERROR EXIT is not specified} \end{cases}$

P7 = &\<label\>   if \<label\> is specified.

E. EXAMPLES

Example 1:

IPSS Source --

FIND NEXT RECORD : QUERY ID = SRCH4,
                   INDEX = IX,
                   INTERVAL = 2,
                   ADDRESS = LREC,
                   ERROR EXIT = CONTINUE;

Fortran Source -

CALL $NREC1(SRCH4,IX,1,2,LREC,3)

Example 2:

IPSS Source -

FIND NEXT RECORDS: QUERY ID = SRCH2,
                   INDEX = IN,
                   NUMBER OF RECORDS = 20,
                   ADDRESS = LRECS,
                   ERROR EXIT = 2001;

Where LRECS is a Fortran array.

Fortran Source -

CALL $NREC2(SRCH2,IN,20,1,LRECS,1,&2001)

4.7 FIND LIST LENGTH statement

A. SYNTAX

FIND LIST LENGTH: QUERY ID = <QRY-ref>

        [,INDEX = <value>]

        ,LENGTH = <variable>

        [,ERROR EXIT = $\left\{ \begin{array}{l} <label> \\ STOP\ SIMULATION \\ CONTINUE \end{array} \right\}$];

B. FUNCTION

    The purpose of the FIND LIST LENGTH statement is to get the length of the list of records that has been identified by the FIND NEXT RECORD[S] statement.

C. PARAMETERS

1. QUERY ID: Specifies the query facility.
2. INDEX: Specifies the index of the query. The default for INDEX is 1.
3. LENGTH: Specifies a Fortran variable for storing the length of the list of records that has been retrieved by the given query.
4. ERROR EXIT: Specifies the processing to be performed when an error is detected during execution of the FIND LIST LENGTH Built-in procedure. The available options are:
    a. <label> states the next statement to be executed.
    b. STOP SIMULATION means that the simulation is aborted when control returns to the nucleus.
    c. CONTINUE results in execution to proceed as though no error had occurred.

CONTINUE is the default option.

D. IPSS TRANSLATION

CALL $LISTL(P1, P2, P3, P4 [,P5])

where

P1 = <QRY-ref>

P2 = { 1   if INDEX is not specified }
     { <value-1> if INDEX is specified

P3 = <variable>

P4 = { 1   if ERROR EXIT is a label
     { 2   if ERROR EXIT is STOP SIMULATION }
     { 3   if ERROR EXIT is CONTINUE or
             ERROR EXIT is not specified

P5 = &<label>   if <label> is specified.

E. EXAMPLES

Example 1:

IPSS Source --

FIND LIST LENGTH: QUERY ID = SRCH2,

                LENGTH = CURLEN;

Fortran Source --

CALL $LISTL(SRCH1,1,CURLEN,3)

Example 2:

IPSS Source --

FIND LIST LENGTH: QUERY ID = QRYA,
                  INDEX = IA,
                  LENGTH = LEN,
                  ERROR EXIT = 100;

Fortran Source --

CALL $LISTL(QRYA,IA,LEN,1,&100)

5.0 Modeling Facilities

The IPSS/REL execution facilities consists of the following statements.

* Attribute
* Distribution Function
* Search Key
* Query
* Create/Destroy Query
* Find Next Record
* Query List Length
* Define Query Statistics

5.1 The ATTRIBUTE Statement

A. PURPOSE

The ATTRIBUTE statement defines one or more attribute facilities. The distribution of attribute and values within the logical record address space of a file is defined by the attribute facility. These distributions are used in a search procedure during model execution to locate the logical records that contain the given attribute.

3. SYNTAX

ATTRIBUTE:

$$ID = \begin{cases} \text{<identifier>} \\ \text{<identifier>, [NUMBER=] <integer>} \end{cases}$$

[,DISTRIBUTION =

([[FIRST =] $\begin{cases} \text{FIRST} \\ \text{<value-1>} \\ \text{DF(<DF-id-1>)} \\ \text{PROC(<PROC-ref-1>)} \end{cases}$]

,[[NEXT =] $\begin{cases} \text{NEXT} \\ \text{<value-2>} \\ \text{DF(<DF-id-2>)} \\ \text{PROC(<PROC-ref-2>)} \end{cases}$]

,[[LAST =] $\begin{cases} \text{LAST} \\ \text{<value-3>} \\ \text{DF(<DF-id-3>)} \\ \text{PROC(<PROC-ref-3>)} \end{cases}$]

)]

,[[NUMBER=] $\begin{cases} \text{NUMBER} \\ \text{<value-4>} \\ \text{DF(<DF-id-4>)} \\ \text{PROC(<PROC-ref-4>)} \end{cases}$]

[,VALUES= $\begin{cases} \text{<value-5>} \\ \text{PROC(<PROC-ref-5>)} \\ \text{DF(<DF-id-5>)} \\ \text{UNIFORM[} \begin{cases} \text{.DISCRETE} \\ \text{.CONTINUOUS} \end{cases} \text{]} \\ \text{([MIN=] <value-6>,} \\ \text{[MAX=] <value-7>)} \end{cases}$];

C. SEMANTICS

The parameters associated with the ATTRIBUTE statement have the following meanings.

1. ID: Specifies the external identifier(s) of the attribute(s).

2. DISTRIBUTION: Specifies the three distributions associated with an attribute. The subparameters

have the following meanings:

a. FIRST: identifies the first occurrence probability distribution function value, Fx(.), for the attribute. During model execution, this pdf is used to locate the first file record that contains the given attribute. The availabe options are:

    i. FIRST states that the first record in a file always contains the attribute, i.e.,

$$Fx(.) = \begin{cases} 0 & \text{if } x < 1 \\ 1 & \text{if } x >= 1 \end{cases}$$

    ii. <value-1> states that the record number given by <value-1> is the first record that contains the attribute, i.e.,

$$Fx(.) = \begin{cases} 0 & \text{if } x < \text{value}(1) \\ 1 & \text{if } x >= \text{value}(1) \end{cases}$$

    iii. DF(<DF-id-1>) states that the named DF facility is used to define the first occurrence value.

    iv. PROC(<PROC-ref-1>) states that the named Procedure facility is used to define the first occurrence value.

b. NEXT: states by what means the next occurrence pdf values, Rx(.), associated with the attribute are to be generated. During model execution this pdf is used to compute inter-record distances. The available options are:

i. NEXT states the next record that contains the same attribute is always equal to the current record location plus 1, i.e.,

$$Rx(.) = \begin{cases} 0 & \text{if } x < 1 \\ 1 & \text{if } x >= 1 \end{cases}$$

ii. <value-2> states that the next record to contain the same attribute is always equal to the current record location plus the current value found in <value-2>, i.e.,

$$Rx(.) = \begin{cases} 0 & \text{if } x < value(2) \\ 1 & \text{if } x >= value(2) \end{cases}$$

iii. DF(<DF-id-2>) states that a DF facility is used to generate the next occurrence values.

iv. PROC(<PROC-ref-2>) states that an IPSS Procedure facility is used to define the next occurrence values.

C. LAST: identifies the last occurrence pdf, Lx(.), for the attribute. During model execution, the last occurrence pdf is used to locate the last record that contains the given attribute.

i. LAST states that the last record of a FILE or RECORD TYPE always contains the attribute, i.e.,

$$Lx(.) = \begin{cases} 0 \text{ if } x < \text{ last record number} \\ 1 \text{ if } x >= \text{ last record number} \end{cases}$$

ii. <value-3> states that the record number given by <value-3> is the last record that contains the attribute, i.e.,

$$Lx(.) = \begin{cases} 0 \text{ if } x < \text{ value(3)} \\ 1 \text{ if } x >= \text{ value(3)} \end{cases}$$

iii. DF(<DF-id-3>) states that a DF facility is used to define the last occurrence pdf.

iv. PROC(<PROC-ref-3>) states that an IPSS facility is used to define the last occurrence pdf.

D. NUMBER: specifies the number of occurrences pdf, $Nx(.)$, for the attribute. During model execution, the number of occurrences pdf is used to compute the number of records that contain the given attribute The abailable options are:

i. NUMPER states that the number of records that contain the attribute is equal to the size of the related FILE or RECORD TYPE, i.e.,

$$Nx(.) = \begin{cases} 0 \text{ if } x < \text{ file size} \\ 1 \text{ if } x >= \text{ file size} \end{cases}$$

ii. <value-4> specifies that the number of records containing the attribute is equal to <value-4>, i.e.,

0 if x < value(4)

$$N_x(.) = 1 \text{ if } x >= value(4)$$

   iii. DF(<DF-id-4>) states that a DF facility
        is used to define the number of occurrences pdf.
   iv. PROC(<PROC-ref-4>) states that an IPSS procedure
       is used to define the number of occurrences pdf.
3. VALUES: Specifies the distribution of possible values
   for the attribute. During model execution, the value
   pdf, $V_x(.)$, is used to compute values for the given
   attribute. The subparameters have the following meanings
   a. <value-5> states that that the only possible
      value for the attribute is <value-5>, i.e.,

      $$V_x(.) = \begin{cases} 0 \text{ if } x < value(5) \\ 1 \text{ if } x >= value(5) \end{cases}$$

   b. DF(<DF-id-5>) states that a DF facility is used
      to define the value pdf.
   c. PROC(<PROC-ref-5>) states that an IPSS procedure is
      used to define the value pdf.
   d. UNIFORM specifies that the values of the attribute
      are uniformly distributed between the minimum value
      <value-6> and the maximum value <value-7>. The
      available options are:
      i. DISCRETE states that the distribution is
         a discrete uniform distribution, i.e.,

         $$V_x(.) = \begin{array}{l} 0 \quad \text{if } x < value(6) \\ (x-value(6)+1)/(value(7)-value(6)+1) \\ \quad \text{if } value(6) <= x <= value(7) \end{array}$$

$$\qquad\qquad 0 \qquad\qquad \text{if } x > value(7)$$

ii. CONTINUOUS specifies that the distribution is a continuous uniform distribution, i.e.,

$$Vx(.) = \begin{cases} 0 & \text{if } x <= value(6) \\ (x-value(6))/(value(7)-value(6)) & \\ & \text{if } value(6) < x < value(7) \\ 0 & \text{if } x >= value(7) \end{cases}$$

The default is no value pdf. That is the attribute has a null value.

The $COMM conventions to be observed are shown in table A-5.

TableA-5
$COMM conventions for ATTRIBUTE statement

ATTRIBUTE Statement	$COMM Location	Value		when called
		Dimension	Data Type	
FIRST	1	logical records	integer	A
NEXT	1	logical records	integer	B
LAST	1	logical records	integer	A
NUMBER	1	logical records	integer	A
VALUES	1	mode of attr.	integer	B

A - Invoked each time attribute facility is referenced through the CREATE QUERY statement during execution time.

B - Invoked each time attribute facility is referenced through the FIND NEXT RECORD statement during execution time.

5.2 The DISTRIBUTION FUNCTION (DF) Statement

A. PURPOSE

The DF statement is used to define cumulative probability distribution functions. When a DF is referenced during execution time, an occurrence of the associated random variate is generated.

B. SYNTAX

```
DISTRIBUTION FUNCTION  :
DF
```

ID= <identifier>

$$[, \text{MODE} = \begin{Bmatrix} \text{DISCRETE} \\ \text{CONTINUOUS} \end{Bmatrix}]$$

$$[, \text{RV DATA TYPE} = \begin{Bmatrix} \text{INTEGER} \\ \text{REAL} \\ \text{DP} \end{Bmatrix}]$$

$$, \text{RV VALUE} = \begin{Bmatrix} (\text{<value-element>}\ldots) \\ \text{<IPSS-pdf>} \end{Bmatrix}$$

$$[, \text{RNG SEED} = \begin{Bmatrix} \text{<value-1>} \\ \text{IPSS SEED} \end{Bmatrix}];$$

where

$$\text{<value-element>} = \begin{Bmatrix} ([\text{RV ELEMENT=}] \text{<value-2>}, \\ [\text{FN ELEMENT=}] \text{<value-3>}) \end{Bmatrix}$$

<IPSS-pdf> = <IPSS-rng-name>[(<parameter-list>)]

C. SEMANTICS

The parameters associated with the DF statement have the following meanings.

1. ID: Specifies the external identifier of the DF.
2. MODE: Specifies the mode of the DF. The available options are:

a. DISCRETE: Specifies that the DF is a discrete
      distribution.
   b. CONTINUOUS: Specifies that the DF is a continuous
      distribution.
3. RV DATA TYPE: Specifies the data type for the random
   variate associated with the distribution function.
   The available options are:
   a. INTEGER: States that the returned random variates
      will be of integer format.
   b. REAL: States that the returned random variates
      will be of real format.
   c. DP: States that the returned random variate will
      be of double precision format.
   The default for RV DATA TYPE is REAL.
4. RV VALUE: defines the distribution function for the
   DF facility. i.e., the vaules for the random variate
   and the corresponding probabilities of their occurrences. The available options are:
   a. ((<value-element>...): Specifies a list of value
      elements. Each value element is composed of
      a random variate element <value-2> and a function
      element <value-3>. The random variate element
      gives the value of the random variable and the
      function element gives the corresponding cumulative
      probability. The following describes the use
      of these entries. Let x be the random variate,
      Fx(.) be the distribution function and suppose

there are n value elements in the form of
(V(1), P(1), V(2), P(2),...,V(n),P(n)).
If the DF is discrete, then the following formulae
applies:

$$Fx(.) = \begin{cases} P(1) & \text{if } x \le V(1) \\ P(2) & \text{if } V(1) < x \le V(2) \\ \cdot \\ \cdot \\ \cdot \\ P(n) & \text{if } V(n-1) < x \le V(n) \end{cases}$$

This DF is illustrated in figure 27. If the
DF is continuous, then the following formulae
applies:

$$Fx(.) = \begin{cases} 0 & \text{if } x \le V(1) \\ P(k+1) + \dfrac{(x-V(k-1))(P(k)-P(k-1))}{(V(k)-V(k-1))} \\ \quad \text{if } V(k-1) < x \le V(k) \\ \quad \text{for } k=2,3,...,n-1 \\ 1 & \text{if } x > V(n) \end{cases}$$

This DF is illustrated in figure 28.

b. <IPSS-pdf>: Specifies that an IPSS built-in
probability distribution function is used to
define the distribution function. A standard
set of commonly used pdf's such as: binomial,
normal, exponential, geometric, will be implemented as IPSS built-in pdf's.

5. RNG SEED: Specifies a seed to be used by the random

number generator. The available options are:

a. <value-1>: States that <value-1> will be used as seed.

b. IPSS SEED: States that an IPSS defined seed will be used.

The default for RNG SEED is IPSS SEED.

The $COMM conventions to be observed when a JF is referenced is given in Table A-6 .

Table A-6.
$COMM conventions for DF statement

DF Statement	$COMM Location	Value Dimension	Value Data Type
RANDOM VARIATE	1 2**	random variate type	integer*, real or DP

* Data type is dependent on the RV DATA TYPE of the DF definition.

** Location 2 is used when DP is specified as the RV DATA TYPE.

5.3 The SEARCH KEY Statement

A. PURPOSE

The SEARCH KEY statement is used to identify the search requirements relating to an attribute. A search key is defined as an attribute and a set of conditions on the values of the attribute. Search keys are combined to form queries in the QUERY statement.

B. SYNTAX

SEARCH KEY:

ID = <identifier>

,ATTRIBUTE = <ATTR-id>

$$[,VALUES= \left\{ \begin{array}{l} \text{<value-1>} \\ \text{ALL [ATTR VALUES]} \\ \text{(<condition>, <value-2>)} \\ \text{LIST(<value-3> [,<value-4>] ...)} \\ \text{RANGE([MIN=] <value-5>,} \\ \text{\quad [MAX=] <value-6>)} \\ \text{PROC(<PROC-ref>)} \\ \text{GPROC(<GPROC-ref>)} \end{array} \right\} \quad] ;$$

where

$$\text{<condition>} = \left\{ \begin{array}{l} \text{LT} \\ \text{LE} \\ \text{EQ} \\ \text{GE} \\ \text{GT} \\ \text{NE} \end{array} \right\}$$

C. SEMANTICS

The parameters associated with the SEARCH KEY statement have the following meanings.

1. ID: Specifies the external identifier of the search key.

2. ATTRIBUTE: Specifies an attribute name. This name

links the search key with a corresponding attribute
defined using the ATTRIBUTE statement.
3. VALUES: Specifies the conditions on the values of
the attribute. The available options are:
   a. <value-1> states that the attribute must have
      a value equal to <value-1>.
   b. ALL [ATTR VALUES]: states that the attribute can
      take on all possible values.
   c. (<condition>, <value-2>) states a condition
      on the attribute. The options LT, LE, EQ,
      GE, GT and NE specifies that the value
      of the attribute must be "less than", "less than
      or equal", "equal", "greater than or equal",
      "greater than" or "not equal" to the value
      represented by <value-2> or PROC or OF.
   d. LIST(<value-3> [,<value-4>]...) states that the
      attribute can have any of the values given in
      the list.
   e. RANGE(<value-5>,<value-6>) states that the attribute
      can have any value between the minimum <value-5>
      and the maximum value <value-6>.
   f. PROC(<PROC-ref>) identifies that an IPSS procedure
      is used to generate a list of possible values for
      the attribute. The procedure returns in $COMM(1)
      the length of the list and the values in the list
      are stored in $COMM(2) through $COMM(256).
   g. GPROC(<GPROC-ref>) identifies that an IPSS global

procedure is used to generate a list of possible values for the attribute. The procedure returns in $COMM(1) the length of the list and the values of the list are stored in $COMM(2) through $COMM(256).

The default for the VALUES parameter is ALL. That is any attribute value will satisfy the search key.

Table A-7 identifies the $COMM communication conventions to be followed if a Procedure or Global Procedure is used to supply a list of values for the SEARCH KEY.

Table A-7
$COMM conventions for SEARCH KEY statement

SEARCH KEY Statement	$COMM Location	Value		when called
		Dimension	Data Type	
value list	1	size of list	real	*
	2	values of RV type	real	*
	.	.	.	.
	.	.	.	.
	.	.	.	.
	256	values of RV type	real	*

* - Invoked each time search key facility is referenced during execution.

5.4 The QUERY Statement

A. PURPOSE

The QUERY statement is used to identify the search keys and logical operators ('AND', 'OR', 'NOT') used to build a query. This statement can define any query expressable as a boolean expression (propositional calculus expression).

B. SYNTAX

```
QUERY:
ID = <identifier>,
{EXPRESSION} = ( <sub-expr-1>, [ .OR. <sub-expr-2>]...)
{FORM     }

[,STATISTICS =
     NO
    {(YES [,FREQ INTERVALS = <int-value-1>]    } ];
    {     [,DISPLAY = ([TABLE][,HISTOGRAM])])  }
```

where

<sub-expr> = [.not.] <SK-id-1> [..and.[.not.]<SK-id-2>]...

C. SEMANTICS

The parameters associated with the QUERY statement have the following meanings.

1. ID: Specifies the external identifier of the query.
2. EXPRESSION/FORM: Specifies one or more sub-expressions' connected by the logical operator '.OR.'. Each sub-expression consists of one or more search keys, <SK-id>, connected by the logical operator '.AND.'. Each search key can optionally have the logical operator '.NOT.' in front of it.
3. STATISTICS: Specifies whether inter-record distance

statistics for the given query are to be collected.
The sub-parameters have the following meanings:
a. FREQ INTERVALS: States the number of frequency classes for the inter-record distance statistics.
b. DISPLAY: Specifies the display format for the inter-record distance statistics. These statistics can be displayed in the form of a frequency TABLE or a HISTOGRAM.

The default is NO statistics. If YES is specified, the default number of frequency intervals is 10 and the default DISPLAY is to print both the frequency table and histogram.

5.5 CREATE and DESTROY QUERY Statement

A. SYNTAX

CREATE   QUERY:
DESTROY

QUERY ID = <QRY-ref> [,INDEX = <integer>]

$$\left[, \left\{ \begin{array}{ll} \text{DS FILE} & = \left\{ \begin{array}{l} \text{<DS.FILE-ref>} \\ \text{<DS-ref>} \end{array} \right\} \\ \text{SCHEMA REC} & = \left\{ \begin{array}{l} \text{<SCHEMA.REC-ref>} \\ \text{<SCHEMA-ref>} \end{array} \right\} \end{array} \right\} \right]$$

$$\left[, \text{ERROR EXIT} = \left\{ \begin{array}{l} \text{<label>} \\ \text{STOP SIMULATION} \\ \text{CONTINUE} \end{array} \right\} \right];$$

B. FUNCTION

The purpose of the CREATE QUERY procedure is to create for the named QUERY facility a copy of its associated query structure definition. The copy is placed in a pre-defined area of the model's transaction array ($TRANS). Once copied, simulation functions involving the Query facility can occur. The definition remains valid until the issuing of a DESTROY QUERY statement for the same query facility.

C. PARAMETERS

1. QUERY ID: Names the Query facility which is to be created or destroyed. An error condition occurrs if a non-Query facility is referenced.
2. INDEX: Each copy of the query facility is given an index number. This number is specified by the user. The default index is 1. If the index references an already created query, the old copy of the query is destroyed.

3. DS FILE: Specifies the internal identifier of the data-set file which is being accessed. When only <DS-ref> is specified, the data-set's "prime" file subfacility is assumed.

4. SCHEMA REC: Specifies the internal identifier of the schema record-tye which is being accessed. When only <SCHEMA-ref> is specified, the schema's "prime" record-type subfacility is assumed.

5. ERROR EXIT: Specifies the processing to be performed when an error is detected during execution of the CREATE or DESTROY QUERY Built-in procedures. The available options are:

   a. <label> states the next statement to be executed.

   b. STOP SIMULATION means that the simulation is aborted when control returns to the nucleus.

   c. CONTINUE results in execution to proceed as though no error had occurred.

   CONTINUE is the default option.

D. IPSS TRANSLATION

CALL $QRY(P1, P2, P3, P4, P5)

[IF ($COMM(1).NE.0) P6]*

where

$$P1 = \begin{cases} 1 & \text{if CREATE QUERY} \\ 2 & \text{if DESTROY QUERY} \end{cases}$$

P2 = <QRY-ref>

$$P3 = \begin{cases} 1 & \text{if index is not specified} \\ \text{<integer>} & \text{if index is specified} \end{cases}$$

$$P4 = \begin{cases} \text{<DS.FILE-ref>} & \text{if DS FILE is specified} \\ \text{<DS-ref>} & \text{if DS is specified} \\ 0 & \text{if otherwise} \end{cases}$$

$$P5 = \begin{cases} \text{<SCHEMA.REC-ref>} & \text{if DS FILE is specified} \\ \text{<SCHEMA-ref>} & \text{if DS is specified} \\ 0 & \text{if otherwise} \end{cases}$$

$$P6 = \begin{cases} \text{GO TO <label>} & \text{if ERROR EXIT=<label>} \\ \text{CALL \$ABORT} & \text{if ERROR EXIT=STOP SIMULATION} \end{cases}$$

* This statement is omitted when ERROR EXIT=CONTINUE is specified or the parameter is not specified.

E. EXAMPLES

Example 1:

IPSS Source --

CREATE QUERY: QUERY ID = QRYX,

　　　　　　　INDEX = ID,

　　　　　　　DS FILE = D21;

Fortran Source -

CALL $QRY(1,QRYX,ID,D21,0)

Example 2:

IPSS Source -

DESTROY QUERY: QUERY ID = QRYZ,

　　　　　　　 INDEX = IX,

　　　　　　　 DS FILE = DS21,

　　　　　　　 ERROR EXIT = STOP SIMULATION;

Fortran Source -

CALL $QRY(2,QRYZ,IX,DS21,0)

IF ($COMM(1).NE.0) CALL $ABORT

5.6 FIND NEXT RECORD Statement

A. SYNTAX

FIND NEXT RECORD[S]:

QUERY ID = <QRY-ref>

[, INDEX = <int-expr-1>]

[, OPTION = $\left\{ \begin{array}{l} \text{FIRST} \\ \text{NEXT} \\ \text{<int-expr-2>} \end{array} \right\}$]

[, [NUMBER OF] RECORDS = <int-expr-3>]

[, $\left\{ \begin{array}{l} \text{VALUE SPREAD} = \text{<real-expr>}] \\ \text{INTERVAL} \end{array} \right\}$

, $\left\{ \begin{array}{l} \text{RECORD ID} = \text{<int-var>} \\ \text{RECORD IDS} = ([\text{NUMBER}=] \text{<int-expr-4>}, \\ \qquad\qquad [\text{ARRAY}=] \text{<int-array>}) \end{array} \right\}$

[, NO RECORD STATEMENT = $\left\{ \begin{array}{l} \text{NEXT} \\ \text{<label-1>} \end{array} \right\}$]

[, ERROR EXIT = $\left\{ \begin{array}{l} \text{<label>} \\ \text{STOP SIMULATION} \\ \text{CONTINUE} \end{array} \right\}$];

B. FUNCTION

The purpose of the FIND NEXT RECORD[S] procedure is to identify the next record(s) that satisfies(y) the given query. The procedure keeps track of the number of records already retrieved using the given query. If a query is being used for the first time, the procedure will automatically start with the first record that satisfies the query.

C. PARAMETERS

1. QUERY ID: Specifies the query that is used for record retrieval.

2. INDEX: Specifies the index number for the query. The

default is 1.
3. OPTION: Specifies the search strategy. The available options are:
   a. FIRST: Start the search process from the first logical record address.
   b. NEXT: Start the search process from the next sequential logical record address after the previously retrieved record.
   c. <int-expr-1> Start the search process from the logical record address which is given by <int-expr-1>.

   The default for OPTION is NEXT.
4. NUMBER OF RECORDS: Specifies the number of records to be retrieved. All the records retrieved must satisfy the given query. The default for NUMBER OF RECORDS is 1.
5. VALUE SPREAD or INTERVAL: Records that satisfy different conjuncts of a query (i.e. search search keys connected by ' .AND. ') are based on the matching of the probabilistically generated record numbers of individual search keys. If the pairwise difference between the record numbers are less than the value given by the INTERVAL parameter, the record numbers arec considered to be matched. The default value for INTERVAL is 1.
6. RECORD ID: Specifies a user supplied Fortran variable for storing the next logical record address.

7. RECORD IDS: Specifies a user supplied Fortran array for storing the next logical record address. The dimension of the array is equal to <int-expr-3>.
8. NO RECORD STATEMENT: Specifies the processing to be performed when no more record satisfies the given query. The available options are:
   a. NEXT: States that the next IPSS or Fortran statement is to be executed.
   b. <label-1>: Specifies that <label-1> is the next statement to be executed.

   The default for NO RECORD STATEMENT is NEXT.
9. ERROR EXIT: Specifies the processing to be performed when an error is detected during execution of the FIND NEXT RECORD[S] Built-in procedure. The available options are:
   a. <label> states the next statement to be executed.
   b. STOP SIMULATION means that the simulation is aborted when control returns to the nucleus.
   c. CONTINUE results in execution to proceed as though no error had occurred.

   CONTINUE is the default option.

D. IPSS TRANSLATION

CALL $NREC(P1, P2, P3, P4, P5, P6, P7, P8)

[IF ($COMM(2).NE.0) GO TO <label-1>]*

[IF ($COMM(1).NE.0) P9]**

where

P1 = <QRY-ref>

P2 = $\begin{cases} 1 & \text{if INDEX is not specified} \\ \text{<int-expr-1>} & \text{if INDEX is specified} \end{cases}$

P3 = $\begin{cases} 0 & \text{if NEXT is specified} \\ 1 & \text{if FIRST is specified} \\ \text{<int-expr-2>} & \text{if <int-expr-2> is specified} \end{cases}$

P4 = $\begin{cases} 0 & \text{if NUMBER OF RECORDS is not specified} \\ \text{<int-expr-3>} & \text{if NUMBER OF RECORDS is specified} \end{cases}$

P5 = $\begin{cases} 1 & \text{if INTERVAL is not specified} \\ \text{<real-expr>} & \text{if INTERVAL is specified} \end{cases}$

P6 = $\begin{cases} \text{<int-var>} & \text{if RECORD ID is specified} \\ 0 & \text{if RECORD ID is not specified} \end{cases}$

P7 = $\begin{cases} \text{<int-expr-4>} & \text{if NUMBER is specified} \\ 0 & \text{otherwise} \end{cases}$

P8 = $\begin{cases} \text{<int-array>} & \text{if ARRAY is specified} \\ 0 & \text{otherwise} \end{cases}$

P9 = $\begin{cases} \text{GO TO <label>} & \text{if ERROR EXIT=<label-2>} \\ \text{CALL SABORT} & \text{if ERROR EXIT=STOP SIMULATION} \end{cases}$

* This statement is omitted when NO RECORD STATEMENT= NEXT is specified or when the parameter is not present.

** This statement is omitted when ERROR EXIT=CONTINUE is specified or when the parameter is not present.

E. EXAMPLES

Example 1:

IPSS Source --

FIND NEXT RECORD : QUERY ID = SRCH4,

                INDEX = IX,

                OPTION = FIRST,

                INTERVAL = 2,

                RECORD ID = LREC,

                ERROR EXIT = 1401;

Fortran Source -

```
CALL $NREC(SRCH4,IX,1,0,2,LREC,0,0)
IF ($COMM(2).NE.0) GO TO 1401
```

Example 2:

IPSS Source -

FIND NEXT RECORDS: QUERY ID = SRCH2,
                   INDEX = IN,
                   OPTION=NEXT,
                   NUMBER OF RECORDS = 20,
                   RECORD IDS = (NUMBER=5,
                                 ARRAY=LRECS),
                   ERROR EXIT = 2001;

Fortran Source -

```
CALL $NREC(SRCH2,IN,0,20,1,0,5,LRECS)
IF ($COMM(1).NE.0) GO TO 2001
```

5.7 QUERY LIST LENGTH function

A. SYNTAX

&QUERY.LIST.LENGTH(<QRY-ref> [,<QRY-index>])

B. FUNCTION

The purpose of the FIND LIST LENGTH statement is to get the length of the list of records that has been identified by the FIND NEXT RECORD[S] statement.

C. PARAMETERS

1. <QRY-ref>: Specifies the query facility.
2. <QRY-index>: Specifies the index of the query. The default for INDEX is 1.

D. IPSS TRANSLATION

&QLEN(P1, P2)

where

P1 =   <QRY-ref>

P2 = $\begin{cases} 1 & \text{if INDEX is not specified} \\ \text{<QRY-index>} & \text{if INDEX is specified} \end{cases}$

E. EXAMPLES

Example 1:

IPSS Source --

CURLEN = &QUERY.LIST.LENGTH(QRY5,2)

Fortran Source --

CURLEN = &QLEN(QRY5,2)

Example 2:

IPSS Source --

```
NUMREC = &QUERY.LIST.LENGTH(QRY3)
                LENGTH = LEN,
                ERROR EXIT = 100;
```
Fortran Source --
```
NUMREC = &QLEN(QRY3,1)
```

5.8 DEFINE QUERY STATISTICS Statement

A. PURPOSE

The DEFINE QUERY STATISTICS Statement creates IPSS internal tables for the collection of inter-record distance statistics.
Two types of query statistics are printed at the end of a simulation run. The ACTIVE QUERY STATISTICS describe queries that are still in an active state when the simulation model terminates. The CUMULATIVE QUERY STATISTICS describe the cumulative statistics about each querry. Figure $fig3 to Figure $fig6 illustrates display formats for the query statistics.

B. SYNTAX

```
{DEFINE QUERY STATISTICS} :
{DEF     QRY    STAT    }

{FREQUENCY TABLE} = {YES [,{TABLE SIZE=<integer>} ]}
{FREQ T3L       }   {NO    {TBL   SIZE=<integer>}  }

,{HISTOGRAM} = {YES [,{HISTOGRAM SIZE=<integer>} ]};
 {HIST    }   {NO    {HIST      SIZE=<integer>}  }
```

C. SEMANTICS

The parameters associated with the DEFINE QUERY STATISTICS statement have the following meanings.

1. FREQUENCY TABLE: For each query, a frequency table of inter-record distance is printed as part of the query statistics. The table can be omitted by specifying 'NO' for this parameter.

2. TABLE SIZE: The frequency table size or the number of frequency classes is specified by this parameter.

The default table size is 10.

3. HISTOGRAM: For each query, a histogram of inter-record distances is printed as part of the query statistics. The histogram can be omitted by specifying 'NO' for this parameter.

4. HISTOGRAM SIZE: The size of the histogram, i.e., the number of columns, is specified by this parameter. The default size is 10.

APPENDIX B

Sample Run of an IPSS/REL Model

The computer printout of a model used to test the relational extensions is given in this appendix. The computer printout includes the following parts:

1. IPSS Source Code

    This is code for a model that contains all the IPSS/REL statements. Various options of these statements are illustrated. Included in this code is a call to the IPSS library listing facilities. A set of IPSS internal tables used by the configuration component is listed. These tables were used to verify the implementation of the IPSS parsers.

2. FORTRAN Code

    A sample listing of the Fortran code generated by the IPSS parsers is given. The diagnostics given by the Fortran compiler is also included.

3. FORTRAN Directed Printout

    This is a listing of results printed using user defined Fortran statements. For each query, a listing of records required by that query is given. This listing is the data base workload. Also included in the printout are internal tables used by IPSS/REL to keep track of the user query statistics.

4. IPSS/REL Statistics

   A sample of the cumulative workload statistics collected by IPSS/REL. These statistics are automatically collected and printed. Included in these statistics are: active query statistics and cumulative query statistics. The active query statistics describe queries that are still active at the end of the simulation run. The cumulative statistics describe all queries processed during the simulation. Both sets of statistics give the distribution of inter-record distances in frequency table format and histogram format.

INFORMATION PROCESSING SYSTEM SIMULATOR
STANDARD INPUT STREAM LISTING
DATE ... 10/17/79

```
INPUT CARD IMAGE                                                              INPUT    ALT INPUT  MEMBER
........10........20........30........40........50........60........70........80  SEQ-NO   LEV SEQ-NO REF-NO

DEFINE CONFIGURATION:NAME=CF,COMPILE=YES,DISPOSITION=KEEP;            00000010     1
                                                                      00000020     2
DATA SET: ID=CFINDX;                                                  00000030     3                  1
                                                                      00000040     4
ATTRIBUTE: ID=ATTR1, DISTRIBUTION=(FIRST=1,NEXT=1,LAST=40);           00000050     5                  2
                                                                      00000060     6
ATTRIBUTE: ID=ATTR2, DISTRIBUTION=(FIRST=2,NEXT=2,LAST=40);           00000070     7                  3
                                                                      00000080     8
ATTRIBUTE: ID=ATTR3, DISTRIBUTION=(FIRST=1,NEXT=2,LAST=40);           00000090     9                  4
                                                                      00000100    10
                                                                      00000110    11
                                                                      00000120    12
PDF: NAME=DIST1, MODE=DISCRETE,                                       00000130    13                  5
    TABLE=((1, 0.1), (2, 0.5), (3, 1));                               00000140    14                  6
                                                                      00000150    15
PDF: NAME=DIST2, MODE=CONTINUOUS,                                     00000160    16                  7
    TABLE=((4.0, 0.0), (5.0, 0.3), (7.0, 0.8), (9.0, 1.0));           00000170    17                  8
                                                                      00000180    18
PDF: NAME=DIST3, TABLE=((0.5, 0.2), (11.5, 0.6), (12, 1.0));          00000190    19                  9
                                                                      00000200    20
SEARCH KEY: ID=SKEY1,ATTRIBUTE=ATTR1;                                 00000210    21                 10
                                                                      00000220    22
SEARCH KEY: ID=SKEY2,ATTRIBUTE=ATTR2;                                 00000230    23                 11
                                                                      00000240    24
........10........20........30........40........50........60........70........80
```

PAGE 1

INFORMATION PROCESSING SYSTEM SIMULATOR
STANDARD INPUT STREAM LISTING
DATE ... 10/17/78

INPUT CARD IMAGE		INPUT SEQ-NO	ALT INPUT LEV SEQ-NO	MEMBER REF-NO
.....10........20........30........40........50........60........70........80				
SEARCH KEY: ID=SKEY3,ATTRIBUTE=ATR3;	00000250	25		12
	00000260	26		13
QUERY: ID=QRY1, EXPRESSION=SKEY1;	00000270	27		
	00000280	28		14
QUERY: ID=QRY2, EXPRESSION=SKEY2;	00000290	29		
	00000300	30		15
QUERY: ID=QRY3, EXPRESSION=SKEY3;	00000310	31		
	00000320	32		16
QUERY: ID=QRY12, EXPRESSION=SKEY1.AND.SKEY2;	00000330	33		
	0000C340	34		17
QUERY: ID=QRY13, EXPRESSION=SKEY1.AND.SKEY3;	00000350	35		
	00000360	36		18
QUERY: ID=QRY23, EXPRESSION=SKEY2.AND.SKEY3;	00000370	37		
	00000380	38		19
QUERY: ID=QRY2N, EXPRESSION=.NOT.SKEY2;	00000390	39		
	00000400	40		20
QUERY: ID=QRY023, EXPRESSION=SKEY2.OR.SKEY3;	00000410	41		
	00000420	42		21
PROCEDURE: NAME=CYCLE9, TYPE=SUBROUTINE;	00000430	43		
COMMON /RNUM/ RNUM	00000440	44		22
REAL RCOM(256)	00000450	45		23
REAL RNUM	00000460	46		24
EQUIVALENCE (RCOM(1),SYSCOM(1))	00000465	47		25
RCOM(1)=1.0+AMOD(RNUM,10.0)	00000470	48		26
.....10........20........30........40........50........60........70........80				

PAGE 2

INFORMATION PROCESSING SYSTEM SIMULATOR
STANDARD INPUT STREAM LISTING
DATE ... 10/17/78

INPUT CARD IMAGE	INPUT SEQ-NO	ALT INPUT LEV SEQ-NO	MEMBER REF-NO
`........10........20........30........40........50........60........70........80`			
`RNUM=RNUM+1`	00000480	49	27
`RETURN`	00000490	50	28
`END: PROCEDURE;`	00000500	51	29
	00000510	52	
`ATTRIBUTE: ID=ATTR4, DISTRIBUTION=(FIRST=1,NEXT=1,LAST=100,`	00000520	53	30
`               VALUES=PROC(CYCLE9));`	00000530	54	31
	00000540	55	
`SEARCH KEY: ID=SKEY4, ATTRIBUTE=ATTR4, VALUE=1;`	00000550	56	32
	00000560	57	
`SEARCH KEY: ID=SKEY5, ATTRIBUTE=ATTR4, VALUE=LIST(2,4,7);`	00000570	58	33
	00000580	59	
`SEARCH KEY: ID=SKEY6, ATTRIBUTE=ATTR4, VALUE=(GE,5);`	00000590	60	34
	00000600	61	
`SEARCH KEY: ID=SKEY7, ATTRIBUTE=ATTR4, VALUE=(LT,8);`	00000610	62	35
	00000620	63	
`SEARCH KEY: ID=SKEY8, ATTRIBUTE=ATTR4, VALUE=RANGE(2,5);`	00000630	64	36
	00000640	65	
`SEARCH KEY: ID=SKEY9, ATTRIBUTE=ATTR4, VALUE=ALL;`	00000650	66	37
	00000660	67	
`QUERY: ID=QRY4, EXPRESSION=SKEY4;`	00000670	68	38
	00000680	69	
`QUERY: ID=QRY5, EXPRESSION=SKEY5;`	00000690	70	39
	00000700	71	
`QUERY: ID=QRY6, EXPRESSION=SKEY6;`	00000710	72	40
`........10........20........30........40........50........60........70........80`			

INFORMATION PROCESSING SYSTEM SIMULATOR
STANDARD INPUT STREAM LISTING
DATE ... 10/17/78

PAGE   4

```
........10........20........30........40........50........60........70........80      INPUT    ALT INPUT  MEMBER
                    INPUT CARD IMAGE                                                   SEQ-NO    LEV SEQ-NO REF-NO

QUERY: ID=QRY7, EXPRESSION=SKEY7;                                          00000720      73                41
                                                                           00000730      74
                                                                           00000740      75
QUERY: ID=QRY8, EXPRESSION=SKEY8;                                          00000750      76                42
                                                                           00000760      77
                                                                           00000770      78
QUERY: ID=QRY9, EXPRESSION=SKEY9;                                          00000780      79
                                                                           00000790      80                43
                                                                           00000800      81
QUERY: ID=Q456, EXPRESSION=SKEY4 .OR. SKEY5 .OR. SKEY6;                    00000810      82                44
                                                                           00000820      83
QUERY: ID=Q4567,EXPRESSION=.NOT.SKEY4 .AND. .NOT.SKEY5 .OR.                 00000830      84
       SKEY6 .AND. SKEY7;                                                  00000840      85                45
                                                                           00000850      86
QUERY: ID=Q4TO9,EXPRESSION=    SKEY4 .AND. .NOT.SKEY5 .AND. SKEY7           00000860      87                46
       .OR. SKEY9 .AND. .NOT.SKEY7                                         00000865      88
       .OR. SKEY8 .AND. SKEY6                                              00000867      89                47
       .OR. SKEY1 .AND. .NOT.SKEY6 .AND.                                   00000870      90                48
            SKEY8 .AND. .NOT. SKEY5                                        00000880      91
       .OR. SKEY5 .AND. SKEY6;                                             00000890      92                49
                                                                           00000900      93
EXO SERVICE: ID=CFIPL, NAME=CFIPL$;                                        00000910      94                50
END: DECLARATIONS;                                                         00000920      95                51
END: INITIALIZATION;                                                                                       52
INVOKE: SERVICE=ATST$;                                                     00000930      96                53
WAIT RETURN: SERVICE=ATST;                                                                                 54
                                                                                                           55
                                                                                                           56
                                                                                                           57
........10........20........30........40........50........60........70........80
```

INFORMATION PROCESSING SYSTEM SIMULATOR
STANDARD INPUT STREAM LISTING
DATE ... 10/17/78
PAGE 5

```
       INPUT CARD IMAGE
....10........20........30........40........50........60........70........80    INPUT   ALT INPUT  MEMBER
                                                                                 SEQ-NO  LEV SEQ-NO REF-NO

END: EXO SERVICE;                                                      00000940    97                58

ENDO SERVICE: ID = ATST, NAME = ATST$;                                 00000950    98                59
  COMMON /RNUM/ RNUM                                                   00000960    99                60
  REAL RNUM                                                            00000965   100                61
  REAL*8 R8TIME/10.0D+00/                                              00000967   101                62
  INTEGER RECLST(10)                                                   00000970   102                63
END: DECLARATIONS;                                                     00000980   103                64
END: INITIALIZATION;                                                   00000990   104                65
C                                                                      00001000   105                66
  CREATE QUERY: QUERY ID=QRY1, INDEX=1, DATA SET=CFINDX,               00001010   106                67
                FILE=PRIME, ERROR EXIT=CONTINUE;                       00001020   107                68
C                                                                      00001030   108                69
  WRITE(6,130)                                                         00001040   109                70
130 FORMAT('1')                                                        00001050   110                71
C                                                                      00001060   111                72
120 CONTINUE                                                           00001070   112                73
  FIND NEXT RECORD: QUERY ID=QRY1, INDEX=1,                            00001080   113                74
                    NUMBER OF RECORDS=1, INTERVAL=1,                   00001090   114                75
                    ADDRESS=IREC, ERROR EXIT=STOP SIMULATION;          00001100   115                76
  WRITE(6,140) QRY1, IREC                                              00001110   116                77
140 FORMAT(' QUERY DEF=',I4,' REC NUMBER=',I4)                         00001120   117                78
  IF (IREC.NE.-1) GO TO 120                                            00001130   118                79
C                                                                      00001140   119                80
....10........20........30........40........50........60........70........80    00001150   120
```

INFORMATION PROCESSING SYSTEM SIMULATOR
STANDARD INPUT STREAM LISTING
DATE ... 10/17/78

PAGE 6

	INPUT CARD IMAGE		INPUT	ALT INPUT	MEMBER
	.....10........20........30........40........50........60........70........80		SEQ-NO	LEV SEQ-NO	REF-NO
C$	DESTROY QUERY@ QUERY ID=QRY1, INDEX=1;	00001160	121		81
C		00001170	122		82
	CREATE QUERY: QUERY ID=QRY2, INDEX=1;	00001180	123		83
	WRITE(6,130)	00001190	124		84
220	CONTINUE	00001200	125		85
	FIND NEXT RECORD: QUERY ID=QRY2, INDEX=1, ADDRESS=IREC;	00001210	126		86
	WRITE(6,140) QRY2, IREC	00001220	127		87
	IF (IREC.NE.-1) GO TO 220	00001230	128		88
C		00001240	129		89
	CREATE QUERY: QUERY ID=QRY3, INDEX=1;	00001250	130		90
	WRITE(6,130)	00001260	131		91
320	CONTINUE	00001270	132		92
	FIND NEXT RECORD: QUERY ID=QRY3, INDEX=1, ADDRESS=IREC;	00001280	133		93
	WRITE(6,140) QRY3, IREC	00001290	134		94
	IF (IREC.NE.-1) GO TO 320	00001300	135		95
C		00001310	136		96
	CREATE QUERY: QUERY ID=QRY12, INDEX=1;	00001320	137		97
	WRITE(6,130)	00001330	138		98
420	CONTINUE	00001340	139		99
	FIND NEXT RECORD: QUERY ID=QRY12, INDEX=1, ADDRESS=IREC;	00001350	140		100
	WRITE(6,140) QRY12, IREC	00001360	141		101
	IF (IREC.NE.-1) GO TO 420	00001370	142		102
C		00001380	143		103
	CREATE QUERY: QUERY ID=QRY13, INDEX=1;	00001390	144		104

.....10........20........30........40........50........60........70........80

```
         .......10........20........30........40........50........60........70........80       INPUT    ALT INPUT   MEMBER
                              INPUT CARD IMAGE                                                  SEQ-NO   LEV SEQ-NO  REF-NO

             WRITE(6,130)                                                                       00001400             145         105
     520     CONTINUE                                                                           00001410             146         106
             FIND NEXT RECORD: QUERY ID=QRY13, INDEX=1, ADDRESS=IREC;                           00001420             147         107
             WRITE(6,140) QRY13, IREC                                                           00001430             148         108
             IF (IREC.NE.-1) GO TO 520                                                          00001440             149         109
     C                                                                                          00001450             150         110
             CREATE QUERY: QUERY ID=QRY23, INDEX=1;                                             00001460             151         111
             WRITE(6,130)                                                                       00001470             152         112
     620     CONTINUE                                                                           00001480             153         113
             FIND NEXT RECORD: QUERY ID=QRY23, INDEX=1, ADDRESS=IREC;                           00001490             154         114
             WRITE(6,140) QRY23, IREC                                                           00001500             155         115
             IF (IREC.NE.-1) GO TO 620                                                          00001510             156         116
     C$      DESTROY QUERY@ QUERY ID=QRY23; INDEX=1;                                            00001520             157         117
     C                                                                                          00001530             158         118
             CREATE QUERY: QUERY ID=QRY2N, INDEX=1;                                             00001540             159         119
             WRITE(6,130)                                                                       00001550             160         120
     720     CONTINUE                                                                           00001560             161         121
             FIND NEXT RECORD: QUERY ID=QRY2N, INDEX=1, ADDRESS=IREC;                           00001570             162         122
             WRITE(6,140) QRY2N, IREC                                                           00001580             163         123
             IF (IREC.NE.-1) GO TO 720                                                          00001590             164         124
     C                                                                                          00001600             165         125
             CREATE QUERY: QUERY ID=QRY023, INDEX=1;                                            00001610             166         126
             WRITE(6,130)                                                                       00001620             167         127
     820     CONTINUE                                                                           00001630             168         128
         .......10........20........30........40........50........60........70........80
```

INFORMATION PROCESSING SYSTEM SIMULATOR
STANDARD INPUT STREAM LISTING
DATE ... 10/17/78

```
         INPUT CARD IMAGE
.........10........20........30........40........50........60........70........80      INPUT   ALT INPUT   MEMBER
                                                                                        SEQ-NO  LEV SEQ-NO  REF-NO

      FIND NEXT RECORD: QUERY ID=QRY023, INDEX=1, ADDRESS=IREC;              00001640   169                 129
      WRITE(6,140) QRY023, IREC                                              00001650   170                 130
      IF (IREC.NE.-1) GO TO 820                                              00001660   171                 131
C                                                                            00001670   172                 132
      CALL $ATTBL                                                            00001680   173                 133
      RNUM=0.0                                                               00001685   174                 134
      CREATE QUERY: QUERY ID=QRY4, INDEX=1;                                  00001690   175                 135
      CALL $ATTBL                                                            00001700   176                 136
      WRITE(6,1000) QRY4                                                     00001710   177                 137
 1000 FORMAT('1QUERY DEF=',I4,/,'0RECORDS =')                                00001720   178                 138
 1010 FIND NEXT RECORDS: QUERY ID=QRY4, INDEX=1,                             00001730   179                 139
                NUMBER OF RECORDS=10, ADDRESS=RECLST;                        00001740   180                 140
      WRITE(6,1020) (RECLST(IX),IX=1,10)                                     00001750   181                 141
 1020 FORMAT(' ',10(I4,2X))                                                  00001760   182                 142
      IF (RECLST(10).NE.-1) GO TO 1010                                       00001770   183                 143
      CALL $ATTBL                                                            00001780   184                 144
      FIND LIST LENGTH: QUERY ID=QRY4, LENGTH=LEN;                           00001790   185                 145
      WRITE(6,1030) LEN                                                      00001800   186                 146
 1030 FORMAT('0TOTAL # OF RECORDS=',I4)                                      00001810   187                 147
C$    DESTROY QUERY@ QUERY ID=QRY4, INDEX=1;                                 00001820   188                 148
C$    CALL $ATTBL                                                            00001830   189                 149
C                                                                            00001840   190                 150
      WRITE (6,1000) QRY5                                                    00001850   191                 151
      RNUM=0.0                                                               00001855   192                 152
.........10........20........30........40........50........60........70........80
```

PAGE 8

```
                INPUT CARD IMAGE                                    INPUT    ALT INPUT   MEMBER
.....10........20........30........40........50........60........70........80        SEQ-NO   LEV SEQ-NO  REF-NO

     CREATE QUERY: QRY ID=QRY5, IND=1;                              00001860    193              153
1100: FIND NEXT RECORDS: QRY ID=QRY5, IND=1, ADD=RECLST,            00001870    194              154
                        NUMBER OF RECORDS=10;                       00001880    195              155
      WRITE (6,1020) (RECLST(IX), IX=1,10)                          00001890    196              156
      IF (RECLST(10).NE.-1) GO TO 1100                              00001900    197              157
      FIND LIST LENGTH: QUERY ID=QRY5, INDEX=1, LENGTH=LEN;         00001910    198              158
      WRITE(6,1030) LEN                                             00001920    199              159
C                                                                   00001930    200              160
      WRITE (6,1000) QRY6                                           00001940    201              161
      RNUM=0.0                                                      00001945    202              162
      CREATE QUERY: QRY ID=QRY6, IND=1;                             00001950    203              163
1200: FIND NEXT RECORDS: QRY ID=QRY6, IND=1, ADD=RECLST,            00001960    204              164
                        NUMBER OF RECORDS=10;                       00001970    205              165
      WRITE (6,1020) (RECLST(IX), IX=1,10)                          00001980    206              166
      IF (RECLST(10).NE.-1) GO TO 1200                              00001990    207              167
      FIND LIST LENGTH: QUERY ID=QRY6, INDEX=1, LENGTH=LEN;         00002000    208              168
      WRITE(6,1030) LEN                                             00002010    209              169
C                                                                   00002020    210              170
      WRITE (6,1000) QRY7                                           00002030    211              171
      RNUM=0.0                                                      00002035    212              172
      CREATE QUERY: QRY ID=QRY7, IND=1;                             00002040    213              173
1300: FIND NEXT RECORDS: QRY ID=QRY7, IND=1, ADD=RECLST,            00002050    214              174
                        NUMBER OF RECORDS=10;                       00002060    215              175
      WRITE (6,1020) (RECLST(IX), IX=1,10)                          00002070    216              176
.....10........20........30........40........50........60........70........80
```

INFORMATION PROCESSING SYSTEM SIMULATOR
STANDARD INPUT STREAM LISTING
DATE ... 10/17/78

INPUT CARD IMAGE		INPUT SEQ-NO	ALT INPUT LEV SEQ-NO	MEMBER REF-NO
`.....10........20........30........40........50........60........70........80`				
`      IF (RECLST(10).NE.-1) GO TO 1300`	`00002080`	217		177
`      FIND LIST LENGTH: QUERY ID=QRY7, INDEX=1, LENGTH=LEN`	`00002090`	218		178
`      WRITE(6,1030) LEN`	`00002100`	219		179
`C`	`00002110`	220		180
`      WRITE (6,1000) QRY8`	`00002120`	221		181
`      RNUM=0.0`	`00002125`	222		182
`      CREATE QUERY: QRY ID=QRY8, IND=1;`	`00002130`	223		183
`1400: FIND NEXT RECORDS: QRY ID=QRY8, IND=1, ADD=RECLST,`	`00002140`	224		184
`      NUMBER OF RECORDS=10;`	`00002150`	225		185
`      WRITE (6,1020) (RECLST(IX), IX=1,10)`	`00002160`	226		186
`      IF (RECLST(10).NE.-1) GO TO 1400`	`00002170`	227		187
`      FIND LIST LENGTH: QUERY ID=QRY8, INDEX=1, LENGTH=LEN;`	`00002180`	228		188
`      WRITE(6,1030) LEN`	`00002190`	229		189
`C`	`00002200`	230		190
`      WRITE (6,1000) QRY9`	`00002210`	231		191
`      RNUM=0.0`	`00002215`	232		192
`      CREATE QUERY: QRY ID=QRY9, IND=1;`	`00002220`	233		193
`1500: FIND NEXT RECORDS: QRY ID=QRY9, IND=1, ADD=RECLST,`	`00002230`	234		194
`      NUMBER OF RECORDS=10;`	`00002240`	235		195
`      WRITE (6,1020) (RECLST(IX), IX=1,10)`	`00002250`	236		196
`      IF (RECLST(10).NE.-1) GO TO 1500`	`00002260`	237		197
`      FIND LIST LENGTH: QUERY ID=QRY9, INDEX=1, LENGTH=LEN;`	`00002270`	238		198
`      WRITE(6,1030) LEN`	`00002280`	239		199
`C`	`00002290`	240		200
`.....10........20........30........40........50........60........70........80`				

INFORMATION PROCESSING SYSTEM SIMULATOR
STANDARD INPUT STREAM LISTING
DATE ... 10/17/78

PAGE 11

INPUT CARD IMAGE ....10........20........30........40........50........60........70........80	INPUT SEQ-NO	ALT INPUT LEV SEQ-NO	MEMBER REF-NO
WRITE (6,1000) Q456 00002300	241		201
RNUM=0.0 00002305	242		202
CREATE QUERY: QRY ID=Q456, IND=1; 00002310	243		203
1600: FIND NEXT RECORDS: QRY ID=Q456, IND=1, ADD=RECLST, 00002320	244		204
NUMBER OF RECORDS=10; 00002330	245		205
WRITE (6,1020) (RECLST(IX), IX=1,10) 00002340	246		206
IF (RECLST(10).NE.-1) GO TO 1600 00002350	247		207
FIND LIST LENGTH: QUERY ID=Q456, INDEX=1, LENGTH=LEN; 00002360	248		208
WRITE(6,1030) LEN 00002370	249		209
C 00002380	250		210
WRITE (6,1000) Q4567 00002390	251		211
RNUM=0.0 00002395	252		212
CREATE QUERY: QRY ID=Q4567, IND=1; 00002400	253		213
1700: FIND NEXT RECORDS: QRY ID=Q4567, IND=1, ADD=RECLST, 00002410	254		214
NUMBER OF RECORDS=10; 00002420	255		215
WRITE (6,1020) (RECLST(IX), IX=1,10) 00002430	256		216
IF (RECLST(10).NE.-1) GO TO 1700 00002440	257		217
FIND LIST LENGTH: QUERY ID=Q4567, INDEX=1, LENGTH=LEN; 00002450	258		218
WRITE(6,1030) LEN 00002460	259		219
C 00002470	260		220
WRITE (6,1000) Q4T09 00002480	261		221
RNUM=0.0 00002485	262		222
CREATE QUERY: QRY ID=Q4T09, IND=1; 00002490	263		223
1800: FIND NEXT RECORDS: QRY ID=Q4T09, IND=1, ADD=RECLST, 00002500	264		224
........10........20........30........40........50........60........70........80			

INFORMATION PROCESSING SYSTEM SIMULATOR
STANDARD INPUT STREAM LISTING
DATE ... 10/17/78

INPUT CARD IMAGE ....10.........20.........30.........40.........50.........60.........70.........80	INPUT SEQ-NO	ALT INPUT LEV SEQ-NO	MEMBER REF-NO
NUMBER OF RECORDS=10;	00002510	265		225
WRITE (6,1020) (RECLST(IX), IX=1,10)	00002520	266		226
IF (RECLST(10).NE.-1) GO TO 1800	00002530	267		227
FIND LIST LENGTH: QUERY ID=Q4TO9, INDEX=1, LENGTH=LEN;	00002540	268		228
WRITE(6,1030) LEN	00002550	269		229
CALL $ATTBL	00002555	270		230
C CALL $FQSTA	00002557	271		231
C	00002560	272		232
PROCESS: TIME=R8TIME;	00002570	273		233
C	00002580	274		234
END: ENDO SERVICE;	00002590	275		235
END:CONFIGURATION;	00002600	276		236
LIST CONFIGURATION: LIBRARY=SYSTEM, MEMBER=CF,	00002610	277		
OPTIONS=(FAC DIRECTORY, FAC);	00002620	278		

PAGE 12

INFORMATION PROCESSING SYSTEM SIMULATOR
STANDARD INPUT STREAM LISTING
DATE ... 10/17/78

LIBRARY NAME = SYSTEM   LIBRARY LISTING .... (OPTION = CONFIGURATION)
MEMBER NAME = CF

*** FACILITY DIRECTORIES ***
TABLE OF CONTENTS

.. FACILITY NAME ..	MNEMONIC	$NAM-START	NUMBER-ENTRIES
PROCEDURE	PROC	1	4
CONTROL UNIT	CU	0	0
TASK CONTROL POINT	TCP	0	0
IO PROCESSOR	IOP	0	0
DATA CHANNEL	DC	0	0
VOLUME	VOL	0	0
CENTRAL PROCESSOR	CP	0	0
CHAIN	CHN	0	0
BUFFER	BUF	0	0
DATA SET	DS	5	1
ATTRIBUTE	ATR	6	4
ATTRIBUTE LIST	ATL	10	26
ACCESS MECHANISM	AM	0	0
MAIN STORAGE	MS	0	0
EXO SERVICE	EXS	36	1
ENDO SERVICE	ENS	37	1
DEVICE	DV	0	0
EVENT	EV	0	0

INFORMATION PROCESSING SYSTEM SIMULATOR
STANDARD INPUT STREAM LISTING
DATE ... 10/17/78
LIBRARY LISTING ... (OPTION = CONFIGURATION)
MEMBER NAME = CF

*** FACILITY DIRECTORIES ***

LIBRARY NAME = SYSTEM

$NAM DIRECTORY

FACILITY NAME	TYPE	$DIR START	NUM	FACILITY NAME	TYPE	$DIR START	NUM	FACILITY NAME	TYPE	$DIR START	NUM	FACILITY NAME	TYPE	$DIR START	NUM	FACILITY NAME	TYPE	$DIR START	NUM	FACILITY NAME	TYPE	$DIR START	NUM
CYCLE9	1	0	1	DIST1	1	0	1	DIST2	1	0	1	DIST3	1	0	1	CFINDX	10	1	1	ATTR1	11	2	1
ATTR2	11	3	1	ATTR3	11	4	1	ATTR4	11	16	1	QRY023	12	15	1	QRY1	12	8	1	QRY12	12	11	1
QRY13	12	12	1	QRY2	12	9	1	QRY2N	12	14	1	QRY23	12	13	1	QRY3	12	10	1	QRY4	12	23	1
QRY5	12	24	1	QRY6	12	25	1	QRY7	12	26	1	QRY8	12	27	1	QRY9	12	28	1	Q4T09	12	31	1
Q456	12	29	1	Q4567	12	30	1	SKEY1	12	5	1	SKEY2	12	6	1	SKEY3	12	7	1	SKEY4	12	17	1
SKEY5	12	18	1	SKEY6	12	19	1	SKEY7	12	20	1	SKEY8	12	21	1	SKEY9	12	22	1	CFIPL	15	32	1
ATSI	16	33	1																				

INFORMATION PROCESSING SYSTEM SIMULATOR
STANDARD INPUT STREAM LISTING
DATE ... 10/17/78

LIBRARY LISTING ... (OPTION = CONFIGURATION)
MEMBER NAME = CF

PAGE 15

LIBRARY NAME = SYSTEM

*** FACILITY DIRECTORIES ***

$DIR DIRECTORY

FACIL TY ST	$NAME ADDR	IN-DEX	...$DEF... ADDR MADDR	FACIL TY ST	$NAME ADDR	IN-DEX	...$DEF... ADDR MADDR	FACIL TY ST	$NAME ADDR	IN-DEX	...$DEF... ADDR MADDR	FACIL TY ST	$NAME ADDR	IN-DEX	...$DEF... ADDR MADDR
10 0	5	1	7	11 0	6	1	13	11 0	7	1	32	11 0	8	1	51 0
12 1	27	1	70	12 1	28	1	87	12 1	29	1	104	12 2	11	1	121 0
12 2	14	1	131	12 2	17	1	141	12 2	12	1	151	12 2	13	1	164 0
12 2	16	1	177	12 2	15	1	190	12 2	10	1	200	11 0	9	1	213 0
12 1	30	1	232	12 1	31	1	249	12 1	32	1	275	12 1	33	1	292 0
12 1	34	1	309	12 1	35	1	326	12 2	18	1	343	12 2	19	1	353 0
12 2	20	1	363	12 1	21	1	373	12 2	22	1	383	12 2	23	1	393 0
12 2	25	1	403	12 2	26	1	419	12 2	24	1	438	15 0	36	1	484 0
16 0	37	1	492												

INFORMATION PROCESSING SYSTEM SIMULATOR
STANDARD INPUT STREAM LISTING
DATE ... 10/17/78

LIBRARY LISTING ... (OPTION = CONFIGURATION)
MEMBER NAME = CF

PAGE 16

LIBRARY NAME = SYSTEM

*** FACILITY DEFINITIONS ***

TYPE	NAME	IND	$DEF	REL-ADDR		......01......02......03......04......05......06......07......08......09......10
DS	CFINDX	1	7	1 -	10	0A0000000060000 0005001000000000 0000000000000001
ATR	ATTR1	1	13	1 -	10	0B0000000130000 0006000200000000 0000000100000001 0000000000000000 0000000100000000
				11 -	20	00000000100000028 0000000000000000 0000000000000000 00000000
ATR	ATTR2	1	32	1 -	10	0B0000000130000 0007000300000000 0000000100000002 0000000000000000 0000000200000000
				11 -	20	00000000100000028 0000000000000000 0000000000000000 00000000
ATR	ATTR3	1	51	1 -	10	0B0000000130000 0003000400000000 0000000100000001 0000000000000000 0000000200000000
				11 -	20	00000000100000028 0000000000000000 0000000000000000 00000000
ATR	ATTR4	1	213	1 -	10	0B0000000130000 0009001000000000 0000000100000000 0000000000000001 0000000100000000
				11 -	20	00000000100000064 0000000000000000 0000000000000000 00000000
ATL	QRY023	1	200	1 -	10	0C0200000000D000 000A000F00000000 0000000000000000 4040404040400001 00000000
				11 -	20	000000000E2D2C5E8 F3400068
ATL	QRY1	1	121	1 -	10	0C0200000000A000 0008000800000000 4040404040400000 0000000100000000 E2D2C5E8F1400046
ATL	QRY12	1	151	1 -	10	0C0200000000D000 000C000800000000 4040404040400000 0000000200000000 E2D2C5E8F1400046
				11 -	20	00010000E2D2C5E8 F2400057
ATL	QRY13	1	164	1 -	10	0C0200000000D000 000D000C00000000 4040404040400000 0000000200000000 E2D2C5E8F1400046
				11 -	20	00010000E2D2C5E8 F3400068
ATL	QRY2	1	131	1 -	10	0C02000000000A000 000E000900000000 4040404040400000 0000000100000000 E2D2C5E8F2400057
ATL	QRY2N	1	190	1 -	10	0C0200000000A0000 000F000E00000000 4040404040400000 0000000100000001 E2D2C5E8F2400057
ATL	QRY23	1	177	1 -	10	0C0200000000D0000 0010000D00000000 4040404040400000 0000000200000000 E2D2C5E8F2400057
				11 -	20	00010000E2D2C5E8 F3400068
ATL	QRY3	1	141	1 -	10	0C0200000000A000 0011000A00000000 4040404040400000 0000000100000000 E2D2C5E8F3400068
ATL	QRY4	1	343	1 -	10	0C02000000000A000 0012001700000000 4040404040400000 0000000100000000 E2D2C5E8F4400068

......01......02......03......04......05......06......07......08......09......10

INFORMATION PROCESSING SYSTEM SIMULATOR
STANDARD INPUT STREAM LISTING
DATE ... 10/17/78

LIBRARY LISTING ... (OPTION = CONFIGURATION)
MEMBER NAME = CF

LIBRARY NAME = SYSTEM

PAGE 17

*** FACILITY DEFINITIONS ***

TYPE	NAME	IND	$DEF	REL-ADDR	......01......02......03......04......05......06......07......08......09......10
ATL	QRY5	1	353	1 - 10	0C0200000000A0000 0013001800000000 4040404040400000 0000000100000000 E2D2C5E8F54000F9
ATL	QRY6	1	363	1 - 10	0C0200000000A0000 0014001900000000 4040404040400000 0000000100000000 E2D2C5E8F6400113
ATL	QRY7	1	373	1 - 10	0C0200000000A0000 0015001A00000000 4040404040400000 0000000100000000 E2D2C5E8F7400124
ATL	QRY8	1	383	1 - 10	0C0200000000A0000 0016001B00000000 4040404040400000 0000000100000000 E2D2C5E8F8400135
ATL	QRY9	1	393	1 - 10	0C0200000000A0000 0017001C00000000 4040404040400000 0000000100000000 E2D2C5E8F9400146
ATL	Q4T09	1	438	1 - 10	0C0200002E0000 0018001F00000000 4040404040400000 00000000D0000000 E2D2C5E8F44000E8
				11 - 20	00010001E2D2C5E8 F54000F900010000 E2D2C5E8F7400124 00000000E2D2C5E8 F9400146000100001
				21 - 30	E2D2C5E8F7400124 00000000E2D2C5E8 F8400135000100000 0000000E2D2C5E8
				31 - 40	F14000460001000001 E2D2C5E8F6400113 0001000E2D2C5E8 F8400135000100001
				41 - 50	00000000E2D2C5E8 F54000F900010000 E2D2C5E8F6400113
ATL	Q456	1	403	1 - 10	0C02000001000000 0019001D00000000 4040404040400000 0000000300000000 E2D2C5E8F44000E8
				11 - 20	0000000E2D2C5E8 F54000F900000000 E2D2C5E8F6400113
ATL	Q4567	1	419	1 - 10	0C0200000130000 001A001E00000000 4040404040400000 0000000400000001 E2D2C5E8F44000E8
				11 - 20	00010001E2D2C5E8 F54000F900000000 E2D2C5E8F6400113 0010000E2D2C5E8 F7400124
ATL	SKEY1	1	70	1 - 10	0C010000110000 0018000500000000 C1E3E3D9F1400000 0001000000000000 00000000J0000000
				11 - 20	000000000000000000 00000000000000000 000000000000000000 00000000
ATL	SKEY2	1	87	1 - 10	0C010000110000 001C00060000000 C1E3E3D9F24000020 G001000000000000 00000000000000000
				11 - 20	000000000000000000 000000000000000000 00000000000000000 00000000
ATL	SKEY3	1	104	1 - 10	0C010000110000 001D00070000000 C1E3E3D9F3400033 0001000000000000 00000000000000000
				11 - 20	000000000000000000 000000000000000000 00000000000000000 00000000
ATL	SKEY4	1	232	1 - 10	0C010000110000 001E001100000000 C1E3E3D9F4400005 0002000300000001 0000000100000000
				11 - 20	000000000000000000 000000000000000000 00000000000000000 00000000

INFORMATION PROCESSING SYSTEM SIMULATOR
STANDARD INPUT STREAM LISTING
DATE ... 10/17/78

PAGE   18

LIBRARY LISTING ... (OPTION = CONFIGURATION)
MEMBER NAME = CF

LIBRARY NAME = SYSTEM

*** FACILITY DEFINITIONS ***

```
TYPE NAME  IND $DEF REL-ADDR        ......01......02......03......04......05......06......07......08......09......10
ATL  SKEY5  1  249   1 -  10        0C010000001A0000 001F001200000000 C1E3E3D9F4400005 0003000000000000 0000000000000000
                    11 -  20        0000000000000000 0000000000000000 0000000000000000 0000003000000001 0000000200000000
                    21 -  30        0000000100000004 0000000000000001 0000000700000000
ATL  SKEY6  1  275   1 -  10        0C010000000110000 0020001300000000 C1E3E3D9F4400005 0002000400000001 0000000500000000
                    11 -  20        0000000000000000 0000000000000000 0000000000000000 00000000
ATL  SKEY7  1  292   1 -  10        0C010000000110000 0021001400000000 C1E3E3D9F4400005 0002000100000001 0000000800000000
                    11 -  20        0000000000000000 0000000000000000 0000000000000000 00000000
ATL  SKEY8  1  309   1 -  10        0C010000000110000 0022001500000000 C1E3E3D9F4400005 0004000000000000 0000000000000000
                    11 -  20        0000000100000002 0000000000000001 0000000500000000 00000000
ATL  SKEY9  1  326   1 -  10        0C010000000110000 0023001600000000 C1E3E3D9F4400005 0001000000000000 0000000000000000
                    11 -  20        0000000000000000 0000000000000000 0000000000000000 00000000
EXS  CFIPL  1  484   1 -  10        0F0000000030000  0024002000000000 0000000200010002 0000000100000000
ENS  AISI   1  492   1 -  10        1000000000080000 0025002100000000 0000000100000003 0000000100000000

                                    ......01......02......03......04......05......06......07......08......09......10
......10......20......30......40......50......60......70......80
```

INFORMATION PROCESSING SYSTEM SIMULATOR
STANDARD INPUT STREAM LISTING
DATE ... 10/17/78

```
........10........20........30........40........50........60........70........80    INPUT    ALT INPUT   MEMBER
                        INPUT CARD IMAGE                                            SEQ-NO   LEV SEQ-NO  REF-NO

                                                                        00002630     279
DEFINE DATA BASE: NAME=DB,COMPILE=YES,DISPOSITION=KEEP;                 00002640     280
DEVICE: ID=DUMMY;                                                       00002650     281          1
END: DATA BASE;                                                         00002660     282          2

DEFINE EXOGENOUS EVENT STREAM: NAME=EX,COMPILE=YES,                     00002670     283
       DISPOSITION=KEEP;                                                00002680     284
EXOGENOUS EVENT: ID=EXIPL,TIME=PROC(EXIPL$)                             00002690     285
PROCEDURE: NAME=EXIPL$,TYPE=SUBROUTINE;                                 00002700     286          1
C                                                                       00002710     287          2
      REAL*8 ITIME                                                      00002720     288          3
      DATA ITIME /0.0D+00/                                              00002730     289          4
      SYSCOM(1)=0                                                       00002740     290          5
      CALL $SREAL(ITIME,SYSCOM,34)                                      00002750     291          6
      ITIME=ITIME+1.0D+20                                               00002760     292          7
      RETURN                                                            00002770     293          8
END: PROCEDURE;                                                         00002780     294          9
END: EXOGENOUS EVENT STREAM;                                            00002790     295         10
                                                                        00002800     296         11
DEFINE MODEL: ID=OCLC,COMPONENTS=(CF(SYSTEM.CF),DB(SYSTEM.DB),           00002810     297
              EX(SYSTEM.EX));                                           00002820     298
EQUATE: CF=CFIPL,EX=EXIPL;                                              00002830     299
SIMULATE: STREAM=START,TRACE=OFF,STOP=(EVENTS=1),                       00002840     300          1
          ERROR=(TERMINATE=2,STATISTICS=YES);                           00002850     301          2
                                                                        00002860     302          3
........10........20........30........40........50........60........70........80
```

INFORMATION PROCESSING SYSTEM SIMULATOR
STANDARD INPUT STREAM LISTING
DATE ... 10/17/78

PAGE   20

```
........10........20........30........40........50........60........70........80    INPUT    ALT INPUT   MEMBER
INPUT CARD IMAGE                                                                     SEQ-NO   LEV SEQ-NO  REF-NO

END: MODEL;                                                              00002870    303                 4
```

```
FORTRAN IV G1   RELEASE 2.0        DIST3              DATE = 78290         22/50/54          PAGE 0001

0001            SUBROUTINE DIST3
0002            COMMON /SYSCOM/ SYSCOM
0003            REAL SYSCOM(256)
0004            REAL $UNFM, PERCNT
0005            REAL V(003), P(003)
0006            DATA V(001) /0.5/
0007            DATA P(001) /0.2/
0008            DATA V(002) /11.5/
0009            DATA P(002) /0.6/
0010            DATA V(003) /12.0/
0011            DATA P(003) /1.0/
0012            PERCNT = $UNFM(0.0, 1.0, 1)
0013            DO 10 K = 1, 003
0014            IF (PERCNT.LE.P(K)) GO TO 20
0015     10     CONTINUE
0016     20     SYSCOM(1)=V(K)
0017            RETURN
0018            END
```

```
FORTRAN IV G1  RELEASE 2.0          DIST3              DATE = 78290        22/50/54

*OPTIONS IN EFFECT*  NOTERM,NOID,EBCDIC,SOURCE,NOLIST,NODECK,LOAD,NOMAP,NOTEST
*OPTIONS IN EFFECT*  NAME = DIST3  , LINECNT = 60
*STATISTICS*  SOURCE STATEMENTS =   18,PROGRAM SIZE =    418
*STATISTICS*  NO DIAGNOSTICS GENERATED
```

```
FORTRAN IV G1   RELEASE 2.0         CYCLE9          DATE = 78290      22/50/54      PAGE 0001

0001          SUBROUTINE CYCLE9
0002          COMMON /$CFDEF/ $CFDEF
0003          COMMON /$TRANS/ $TRANS
0004          COMMON /$CDS/ $CDS
0005          COMMON /SYSCOM/ SYSCOM
0006          COMMON /SYSVAR/ SYSVAR
0007          COMMON /SYSINF/ SYSINF
0008          COMMON /SYSIM/ $CLOCK,$CLK1,$CLK2
0009          COMMON /$CFFAC/ CFINDX,ATTRI,ATTR2,ATTR3,ATTR4
     @,QRY023,QRY1,QRY5,QRY6,QRY12,QRY13,QRY2,QRY2N,QRY8,QRY23,QRY3
     @,QRY4,QRY5,SKEY1,SKEY2,QRY6,QRY7,QRY8,QRY9,Q4T09,Q456
     @,Q4567,SKEY8,SKEY9,CFIPL,ATST,SKEY3,SKEY4,SKEY5,SKEY6,SKEY7
0010          INTEGER CFINDX,ATTR1,ATTR2,ATTR3,ATTR4,QRY023
     @,QRY1,QRY12,QRY13,QRY2,QRY2N,QRY3,QRY3
     @,QRY4,QRY5,QRY6,QRY7,QRY8,QRY9,Q4T09
     @,Q456,Q4567,SKEY7,SKEY8,SKEY9,CFIPL,ATST,SKEY4,SKEY5
     @                                   ,SKEY6
0011          INTEGER $CFDEF(1),$TRANS(1),$CDS(1),SYSCOM(256)
0012          INTEGER SYSVAR(256),SYSINF(40)
0013          REAL*8 $CLOCK,$CLK1,$CLK2
0014          COMMON /$SYSPAR/ SYSPAR,$SYSPAR
0015          INTEGER SYSPAR(256)
0016          INTEGER SYSID,SYSTRC,SYSPCT,SYSON
0017          EQUIVALENCE (SYSINF(4),SYSPCT),(SYSINF(28),SYSTRC)
0018          DATA SYSON/1/
0019          COMMON /RNUM/ RNUM                                          00000440
0020          REAL RCOM(256)                                              00000450
0021                                                                      00000460
0022          EQUIVALENCE (RCOM(1),SYSCOM(1))                             00000465
0023          RCOM(1)=1.0+AMOD(RNUM,10.0)                                 00000470
0024          RNUM=RNUM+1                                                 00000480
0025          RETURN                                                      00000490
0026          END
```

FORTRAN IV G1 RELEASE 2.0   CYCLE9   DATE = 78290   22/50/54   PAGE 0002

OPTIONS IN EFFECT NOTERM,NOID,EBCDIC,SOURCE,NOLIST,NODECK,LOAD,NOMAP,NOTEST
OPTIONS IN EFFECT NAME = CYCLE9 , LINECNT = 60
STATISTICS SOURCE STATEMENTS =   26,PROGRAM SIZE =   364
STATISTICS NO DIAGNOSTICS GENERATED

```
FORTRAN IV G1  RELEASE 2.0                CFIPL$                  DATE = 78290        22/50/54             PAGE 0001

0001           SUBROUTINE CFIPL$
0002           COMMON /$CFDEF/ $CFDEF
0003           COMMON /$TRANS/ $TRANS
0004           COMMON /$CDS/ $CDS
0005           COMMON /SYSCOM/ SYSCOM
0006           COMMON /SYSVAR/ SYSVAR
0007           COMMON /SYSINF/ SYSINF
0008           COMMON /SYSTIM/ $CLOCK,$CLK1,$CLK2
0009           COMMON /$SAVE/$SAVE
0010           COMMON /$CFAC/ CFINDX,ATTR1  ,ATTR2  ,ATTR3  ,ATTR4
              @,QRY023,QRY1  ,QRY2  ,QRY13 ,QRY2  ,QRY7  ,QRY8  ,QRY2N ,QRY23 ,QRY3
              @,Q4567 ,SKEY1 ,SKEY2 ,ATST  ,SKEY3 ,SKEY4 ,SKEY8 ,SKEY9 ,Q4T09 ,Q456
              @,SKEY8 ,SKEY9 ,CFIPL ,SKEY5 ,SKEY6 ,SKEY7
0011           INTEGER CFINDX,ATTR1  ,ATTR2  ,ATTR3  ,ATTR4  ,QRY023
              @,QRY1  ,QRY12 ,QRY13 ,QRY2  ,QRY2N ,QRY23 ,QRY3
              @,Q4567 ,QRY5  ,QRY6  ,QRY7  ,QRY8  ,QRY9  ,Q4T09
              @,SKEY6 ,SKEY7 ,SKEY8 ,SKEY9 ,CFIPL ,ATST  ,SKEY5
0012           INTEGER $SAVE(128),$ASRIX,$NSA
0013           INTEGER $CFDEF(1),$TRANS(1),$CDS(1),SYSCOM(256)
0014           INTEGER SYSVAR(256),SYSINF(40)
0015           REAL*8 $CLOCK,$CLK1,$CLK2,SYSNAM
0016           COMMON /SYSPAR/ SYSPAR
0017           INTEGER SYSPAR(256)
0018           INTEGER SYSID,SYSTRC,SYSPCT,SYSON
0019           EQUIVALENCE (SYSINF(4),SYSPCT),(SYSINF(28),SYSTRC)
0020           DATA SYSON/1/,SYSNAM/'CFIPL$'/
0021           CALL $CREATI(SYSVAR(1),1),CFIPL )
0022           CALL $SADR(SYSVAR(1),1)
0023           $NSA = SYSINF(5) - 32
0024           IF($NSA.EQ.0) GO TO 30002
0025           DO 30001 $ASRIX = 1,$NSA
0026  30001    $TRANS($SYSVAR(1)+3)+$ASRIX) = $SAVE($ASRIX)
0027  30002    CONTINUE
0028           IF (SYSTRC .EQ. SYSON) CALL $TRACE(2,SYSNAM)
0029           RETURN
0030  30010    IF (SYSTRC .EQ. SYSON) CALL $TRACE(2,SYSNAM)
0031           CALL ATST$
0032           CALL $INVOK(1)
0033           CALL $WAITR(ATST$,1,&30021)
0034  30020    CALL $SADR(SYSPCT,002)
0035           RETURN
0036  30021    CONTINUE
0037           CALL $TERM(SYSPCT)
0038           RETURN
0039           ENTRY SYS001(SYSID,*)
0040           IF (SYSTRC .EQ. SYSON) CALL $TRACE(2,SYSNAM)
0041           GO TO(30010,30020),SYSID
0042           RETURN 1
0043           END
```

FORTRAN IV G1 RELEASE 2.0   CFIPL$ DATE = 78290   22/50/54   PAGE 0002

OPTIONS IN EFFECT NOTERM,NOID,EBCDIC,SOURCE,NOLIST,NODECK,LOAD,NOMAP,NOTEST
OPTIONS IN EFFECT NAME = CFIPL$, LINECNT = 60
STATISTICS SOURCE STATEMENTS =   43,PROGRAM SIZE =   966
STATISTICS NO DIAGNOSTICS GENERATED

FORTRAN IV G1 RELEASE 2.0   ATST$ DATE = 78290   22/50/54   PAGE 0001

```
0001            SUBROUTINE ATST$
0002            COMMON /$CFDEF/ $CFDEF
0003            COMMON /$TRANS/ $TRANS
0004            COMMON /$CDS/$CDS1/ $CDS1 /$CDS2/ $CDS2
0005            COMMON /SYSCOM/ SYSCOM
0006            COMMON /SYSVAR/ SYSVAR
0007            COMMON /SYSINF/ SYSINF
0008            COMMON /SYSIM/ $CLOCK,$CLK1,$CLK2
0009            COMMON /$SAVE/ $SAVE
0010            COMMON /$CFFAC/ CFINDX,ATTR1 ,ATTR2 ,ATTR3 ,ATTR4 ,QRY1
               @,QRY23,QRY1 ,QRY12 ,QRY13 ,QRY2 ,QRY2N ,QRY23 ,QRY3
               @,QRY4 ,QRY5 ,QRY6 ,QRY7 ,QRY8 ,QRY9 ,QRY4T9 ,QRY456
               @,Q4567,SKEY1 ,SKEY2 ,SKEY3 ,SKEY4 ,SKEY5 ,SKEY6 ,SKEY7
               @,SKEY8,SKEY9 ,CFIPL ,ATST
0011            INTEGER CFINDX,ATTR1 ,ATTR2 ,ATTR3 ,ATTR4 ,QRYQ23
               @,QRY1 ,QRY12 ,QRY13 ,QRY2 ,QRY2N ,QRY23 ,QRY3
               @,QRY4 ,QRY5 ,QRY6 ,QRY7 ,QRY8 ,QRY9 ,QRY4T9 ,QRY456
               @,Q4567,SKEY1 ,SKEY2 ,SKEY3 ,SKEY4 ,SKEY5
               @,SKEY6,SKEY7 ,SKEY8 ,SKEY9 ,CFIPL ,ATST
0012            INTEGER $SAVE(128),$NSA,$ASRIX
0013            INTEGER $CFDEF(1),$TRANS(1),$CDS1(1),$CDS1(1),$CDS2(1)      00000965
0014            INTEGER SYSCOM(256),SYSVAR(256),SYSINF(50)                  00000967
0015            REAL*8 $CLOCK,$CLK1,$CLK2,SYSNAM                            00000980
0016            INTEGER SYSPAR(256)
0017            INTEGER SYSID,SYSTRC,SYSPCT,SYSON
0018            EQUIVALENCE (SYSINF(4),SYSPCT),(SYSINF(28),SYSTRC)
0019            DATA SYSON/1/,SYSNAM/'ATST$ '/
0020            COMMON /RNUM/'RNUM
0021            REAL RNUM
0022            DATA R8TIME/10.0D+00/
0023            INTEGER RECLST(10)
0024            CALL $CREAT(SYSVAR(1),1,ATST  )                             00001010
0025            CALL $SADR(SYSVAR(5),1,1)
0026            $NSA = SYSINF(5) - 32
0027            IF($NSA .EQ. 0) GO TO 30002
0028            DO 30001 $ASRIX = 1,$NSA
0029   30001    $TRANS(SYSVAR(1)+3I+$ASRIX) = $SAVE($ASRIX)
0030   30002    CONTINUE
0031            IF (SYSTRC .EQ. SYSON) CALL $TRACE(2,SYSNAM)
0032            RETURN
0033   30010    IF (SYSTRC .EQ. SYSON) CALL $TRACE(2,SYSNAM)
0034   C
0035            CALL $CRQRY(QRY1,1,CFINDX,1,-1,1,3,1)                       00001040
0036   C                                                                    00001050
0037    130     WRITE(6,130)                                                00001060
0038    120     FORMAT('1')                                                 00001070
0039            CONTINUE                                                    00001080
0040    140     CALL $NREC1(QRY1,1,1,1,0,IREC,2)
0041            WRITE(6,140) QRY1,' REC ',IREC                              00001130
0042            FORMAT(6,140) QRY1, DEF=',I4,' REC NUMBER=',I4)             00001140
0043            IF (IREC.NE.-1) GO TO 120                                   00001150
0044   C$       DESTROY QUERY@  QUERY ID=QRY1, INDEX=1;                     00001160
                                                                            00001170
0045            CALL $CRQRY(QRY2,1,-1,-1,1,3,1)                             00001190
0046            WRITE(6,130)
```

FORTRAN IV G1   RELEASE 2.0   ATST$ DATE = 78290   22/50/54   PAGE 0002

```
0045   220  CONTINUE                                          00001200
0046        CALL $NREC1(QRY2,1,1,1,0,IREC,3)                  00001220
0047        WRITE(6,140) QRY2,1,QRY2,IREC                     00001230
0048        IF (IREC.NE.-1) GO TO 220                         00001240
0049   C                                                      00001260
0050        CALL $CRQRY(QRY3,1,-1,1,-1,1,3,1)                 00001270
0051        WRITE(6,130)                                      00001280
0052   320  CONTINUE                                          00001290
0053        CALL $NREC1(QRY3,1,1,1,0,IREC,3)                  00001300
0054        WRITE(6,140) QRY3,1,QRY3,IREC                     00001310
        IF (IREC.NE.-1) GO TO 320                             
0055        WRITE(6,130)                                      00001330
0056        CALL $CRQRY(QRY12,1,-1,1,-1,1,3,1)                00001340
0057   420  CONTINUE                                          00001360
0058        CALL $NREC1(QRY12,1,1,1,0,IREC,3)                 00001370
0059        WRITE(6,140) QRY12,IREC                           00001380
0060        IF (IREC.NE.-1) GO TO 420                         
0061   C    CALL $CRQRY(QRY13,1,-1,1,-1,1,3,1)                00001400
0062        WRITE(6,130)                                      00001410
0063   520  CONTINUE                                          
0064        CALL $NREC1(QRY13,1,1,1,0,IREC,3)                 00001430
0065        WRITE(6,140) QRY13,IREC                           00001440
0066        IF (IREC.NE.-1) GO TO 520                         00001450
0067   C    CALL $CRQRY(QRY23,1,-1,1,-1,1,3,1)                00001470
0068        WRITE(6,130)                                      00001480
0069   620  CONTINUE                                          
0070        CALL $NREC1(QRY23,1,1,1,0,IREC,3)                 00001500
0071        WRITE(6,140) QRY23,IREC                           00001510
        IPLIREC.NE.-1) GO TO 620                              00001520
0072   C$   DESTROY QUERY@ QUERY ID=QRY23, INDEX=1;           00001530
0073        CALL $CRQRY(QRY2N,1,-1,1,-1,1,3,1)                00001550
0074        WRITE(6,130)                                      00001560
0075   720  CONTINUE                                          
0076        CALL $NREC1(QRY2N,1,1,1,0,IREC,3)                 00001580
0077        WRITE(6,140) QRY2N,IREC                           00001590
0078        IF (IREC.NE.-1) GO TO 720                         00001600
0079   C    CALL $CRQRY(QRYO23,1,-1,1,-1,1,3,1)               00001620
0080        WRITE(6,130)                                      00001630
0081   820  CONTINUE                                          
0082        CALL $NREC1(QRYO23,1,1,1,0,IREC,3)                00001650
0083        WRITE(6,140) QRYO2,IREC                           00001660
0084        IF (IREC.NE.-1) GO TO 820                         00001670
0085   C    CALL $ATTBL                                       00001680
0086        RNUM=0.0                                          00001685
0087        CALL $CRQRY(QRY4,1,-1,1,-1,1,3,1)                 
0088        CALL $ATTBL                                       
0089        WRITE(6,1000) QRY4                                00001700
0090   1000 FORMAT(' IQUERY DEF=',I4,/,'0RECORDS =')           00001710
0091   1010 CALL $NREC2(QRY4,1,10,1,0,RECLST,3)               00001720
        WRITE(6,1020) (RECLST(IX),IX=1,10)                    
0092   1020 FORMAT(' ',10(14,2X))                             00001750
0093        IF (RECLST(10).NE.-1) GO TO 1010                  00001760
0094                                                          
```

```
FORTRAN IV G1    RELEASE 2.0           ATS1$              DATE = 78290        22/50/54           PAGE 0003

0095                   CALL $ATTBL                                            00001780
0096                   CALL $LISTL(QRY4,1,LEN,3)                              00001800
0097              1030 WRITE(6,1030) LEN                                      00001810
0098            C$     FORMAT(';TOTAL # OF RECORDS=',I4)                      00001820
                C$     DESTROY QUERY@ QUERY ID=QRY4, INDEX=1;                 00001840
                C      CALL $ATTBL                                            00001850
                                                                              00001855
0099                   WRITE (6,1000) QRY5                                    00001890
0100                   RNUM=0.0                                               00001900
0101                   CALL $CRQRY(QRY5,1,1,-1,1,-1,2,1,3,1)
0102                   CALL $NREC2(QRY5,1,10,1,0,RECLST,3)                    00001920
0103                   WRITE(6,1020) (RECLST(IX),IX=1,10)                     00001930
0104                   IF (RECLST(10).NE.-1) GO TO 1100                       00001940
0105                   CALL $LISTL(QRY5,1,LEN,3)                              00001945
0106              1100 WRITE(6,1030) LEN
0107              C                                                           00001980
0108                   WRITE (6,1000) QRY6                                    00001990
0109                   RNUM=0.0
0110                   CALL $CRQRY(QRY6,1,1,-1,1,-1,2,1,3,1)                  00002010
0111                   CALL $NREC2(QRY6,1,10,1,0,RECLST,3)                    00002020
0112                   WRITE (6,1020) (RECLST(IX),IX=1,10)                    00002035
0113                   IF (RECLST(10).NE.-1) GO TO 1200
0114                   CALL $LISTL(QRY6,1,LEN,3)                              00002070
                  1200 WRITE(6,1030) LEN                                      00002080
0115              C
0116                   WRITE (6,1000) QRY7                                    00002100
0117                   RNUM=0.0                                               00002120
0118                   CALL $CRQRY(QRY7,1,1,-1,1,-1,2,1,3,1)                  00002125
0119                   CALL $NREC2(QRY7,1,10,1,0,RECLST,3)
0120                   WRITE (6,1020) (RECLST(IX),IX=1,10)                    00002160
0121                   IF (RECLST(10).NE.-1) GO TO 1300                       00002170
0122                   CALL $LISTL(QRY7,1,LEN,3)
                  1300 WRITE(6,1030) LEN                                      00002190
0123              C                                                           00002210
0124                   WRITE (6,1000) QRY8                                    00002215
0125                   RNUM=0.0
0126                   CALL $CRQRY(QRY8,1,1,-1,1,-1,2,1,3,1)                  00002250
0127                   CALL $NREC2(QRY8,1,10,1,0,RECLST,3)                    00002260
0128                   WRITE (6,1020) (RECLST(IX),IX=1,10)
0129                   IF (RECLST(10).NE.-1) GO TO 1400                       00002280
0130                   CALL $LISTL(QRY8,1,LEN,3)                              00002290
                  1400 WRITE(6,1030) LEN                                      00002300
0131              C                                                           00002305
0132                   WRITE (6,1000) QRY9
0133                   RNUM=0.0                                               00002340
0134                   CALL $CRQRY(QRY9,1,1,-1,1,-1,2,1,3,1)                  00002350
0135                   CALL $NREC2(QRY9,1,10,1,0,RECLST,3)
0136                   WRITE (6,1020) (RECLST(IX),IX=1,10)
0137                   IF (RECLST(10).NE.-1) GO TO 1500
0138                   CALL $LISTL(QRY9,1,LEN,3)
                  1500 WRITE(6,1030) LEN
0139              C
0140                   WRITE (6,1000) Q456
0141                   RNUM=0.0
0142                   CALL $CRQRY(Q456,1,1,-1,1,-1,2,1,3,1)
0143                   CALL $NREC2(Q456,1,10,1,0,RECLST,3)
0144              1600 IF (RECLST(10).NE.-1) GO TO 1600
```

```
FORTRAN IV G1   RELEASE 2.0          ATST$              DATE = 73290       22/50/54         PAGE 0004

0145              CALL $LIST(Q456,1,LEN,3)                         00002370
0146              WRITE(6,1030) LEN                                00002380
     C                                                             00002390
0147              WRITE (6,1000) Q4567                             00002395
0148        1700  CALL $CRQRY(Q4567,1,-1,-1,1,3,1)
0149              RNUM=0.0
0150              CALL $NREC2(Q4567,1,1,0,RECLST,3)                00002430
0151              WRITE (6,1020) (RECLST(IX),IX=1,3)               00002440
0152              IF(RECLST(10).NE.-1) GO TO 1700
0153              CALL $LIST(Q4567,1,LEN,3)                        00002460
0154              WRITE(6,1030) LEN                                00002470
     C                                                             00002480
0155              WRITE (6,1000) Q4T09                             00002485
0156              RNUM=0.0
0157        1800  CALL $CRQRY(Q4T09,1,-1,-1,-1,1,3,1)
0158              CALL $NREC2(Q4T09,1,1,0,RECLST,3)                00002520
0159              WRITE (6,1020) (RECLST(IX),IX=1,3)               00002530
0160              IF(RECLST(10).NE.-1) GO TO 1800                  00002550
0161              CALL $LIST(Q4T09,1,LEN,3)                        00002555
0162              WRITE(6,1030) LEN                                00002557
0163              CALL $ATTBL                                      00002560
     C            CALL $FQSTA
     C
0164              CALL $SADR(SYSPCT,002)
0165              CALL $PRCSSIRBTIME,0)
0166              RETURN
0167       30020  CONTINUE                                         00002580
     C
0168              CALL $TERM(SYSPCT)
0169              RETURN
0170              ENTRY SYS002(SYSID,*)
0171              IF (SYSTRC.EQ.SYSON) CALL $TRACE(2,SYSNAM)
0172              GO TO(30010,30020),SYSID
0173              RETURN 1
0174              END
```

FORTRAN IV G1 RELEASE 2.0   ATST$ DATE = 78290   22/50/54   PAGE 0005

OPTIONS IN EFFECT NOTERM,NOID,EBCDIC,SOURCE,NOLIST,NODECK,LOAD,NOMAP,NOTEST
OPTIONS IN EFFECT NAME = ATST$, LINECNT = 60
STATISTICS SOURCE STATEMENTS =   174,PROGRAM SIZE =   4878
STATISTICS NO DIAGNOSTICS GENERATED

```
FORTRAN IV G1   RELEASE 2.0          $CFPR1          DATE = 74290        22/50/54        PAGE 0001

0001          SUBROUTINE $CFPR1
0002          COMMON /$CFFAC/ CFINDX,ATTR1 ,ATTR2 ,ATTR3 ,ATTR4
     @ ,QRY23,QRY1  ,QRY12 ,QRY13 ,QRY2N ,QRY9  ,Q4T09 ,QRY3
     @ ,Q4567,SKEY1 ,SKEY12,SKEY3 ,SKEY2 ,SKEY5 ,SKEY6 ,Q456
     @ ,SKEY8,SKEY9 ,CFIPL ,AIST                         ,SKEY7
0003          INTEGER CFINDX,ATTR1 ,ATTR2 ,ATTR3 ,ATTR4 ,QRY023
     @ ,QRY1 ,QRY12 ,QRY13 ,QRY2  ,QRY2N ,QRY23 ,QRY3
     @ ,QRY4 ,QRY5  ,QRY6  ,QRY7  ,QRY8  ,QRY9  ,Q4T09
     @ ,Q456 ,Q4567 ,SKEY1 ,SKEY2 ,SKEY3 ,SKEY4 ,SKEY5
     @ ,SKEY6,SKEY7 ,SKEY8 ,SKEY9 ,CFIPL ,AIST
0004    1     CALL CYCLE9
0005          RETURN
0006          ENTRY $CFPR(SYSIND,*)
0007          INTEGER SYSIND
0008          GO TO (1), SYSIND
0009          RETURN 1
0010          END
```

FORTRAN IV G1 RELEASE 2.0 $CFPR1   DATE = 78290   22/50/54   PAGE 0002

OPTIONS IN EFFECT NOTERM,NOID,EBCDIC,SOURCE,NOLIST,NODECK,LOAD,NOMAP,NOTEST
OPTIONS IN EFFECT NAME = $CFPR1 , LINECNT = 60
STATISTICS SOURCE STATEMENTS = 10,PROGRAM SIZE = 434
STATISTICS NO DIAGNOSTICS GENERATED

QUERY DEF= 190 REC NUMBER= 1
QUERY DEF= 190 REC NUMBER= 3
QUERY DEF= 190 REC NUMBER= 5
QUERY DEF= 190 REC NUMBER= 7
QUERY DEF= 190 REC NUMBER= 9
QUERY DEF= 190 REC NUMBER= 11
QUERY DEF= 190 REC NUMBER= 13
QUERY DEF= 190 REC NUMBER= 15
QUERY DEF= 190 REC NUMBER= 17
QUERY DEF= 190 REC NUMBER= 19
QUERY DEF= 190 REC NUMBER= 21
QUERY DEF= 190 REC NUMBER= 23
QUERY DEF= 190 REC NUMBER= 25
QUERY DEF= 190 REC NUMBER= 27
QUERY DEF= 190 REC NUMBER= 29
QUERY DEF= 190 REC NUMBER= 31
QUERY DEF= 190 REC NUMBER= 33
QUERY DEF= 190 REC NUMBER= 35
QUERY DEF= 190 REC NUMBER= 37
QUERY DEF= 190 REC NUMBER= 39
QUERY DEF= 190 REC NUMBER= -1

QUERY DEF= 200 REC NUMBER= 1
QUERY DEF= 200 REC NUMBER= 2
QUERY DEF= 200 REC NUMBER= 3
QUERY DEF= 200 REC NUMBER= 4
QUERY DEF= 200 REC NUMBER= 5
QUERY DEF= 200 REC NUMBER= 6
QUERY DEF= 200 REC NUMBER= 7
QUERY DEF= 200 REC NUMBER= 8
QUERY DEF= 200 REC NUMBER= 9
QUERY DEF= 200 REC NUMBER= 10
QUERY DEF= 200 REC NUMBER= 11
QUERY DEF= 200 REC NUMBER= 12
QUERY DEF= 200 REC NUMBER= 13
QUERY DEF= 200 REC NUMBER= 14
QUERY DEF= 200 REC NUMBER= 15
QUERY DEF= 200 REC NUMBER= 16
QUERY DEF= 200 REC NUMBER= 17
QUERY DEF= 200 REC NUMBER= 18
QUERY DEF= 200 REC NUMBER= 19
QUERY DEF= 200 REC NUMBER= 20
QUERY DEF= 200 REC NUMBER= 21
QUERY DEF= 200 REC NUMBER= 22
QUERY DEF= 200 REC NUMBER= 23
QUERY DEF= 200 REC NUMBER= 24
QUERY DEF= 200 REC NUMBER= 25
QUERY DEF= 200 REC NUMBER= 26
QUERY DEF= 200 REC NUMBER= 27
QUERY DEF= 200 REC NUMBER= 28
QUERY DEF= 200 REC NUMBER= 29
QUERY DEF= 200 REC NUMBER= 30
QUERY DEF= 200 REC NUMBER= 31
QUERY DEF= 200 REC NUMBER= 32
QUERY DEF= 200 REC NUMBER= 33
QUERY DEF= 200 REC NUMBER= 34
QUERY DEF= 200 REC NUMBER= 35
QUERY DEF= 200 REC NUMBER= 36
QUERY DEF= 200 REC NUMBER= 37
QUERY DEF= 200 REC NUMBER= 38
QUERY DEF= 200 REC NUMBER= 39
QUERY DEF= 200 REC NUMBER= 40
QUERY DEF= 200 REC NUMBER= -1

QUERY DEF= 419

RECORDS =	5	6	7	8	9	10	13	15	16
3	18	19	20	23	25	26	27	28	29
17	33	35	36	37	38	39	40	43	45
30	47	48	49	50	53	55	56	57	58
46	60	63	65	66	67	68	69	70	73
59	76	77	78	79	80	83	85	86	87
75	89	90	93	95	96	97	93	99	100
88	-1	-1	-1	-1	-1	-1	-1	-1	-1
-1									

TOTAL # OF RECORDS= 70

QUERY DEF= 438
RECORDS =

1	3	5	7	8	9	10	11	13	15
17	18	19	20	21	23	25	27	28	29
30	31	33	35	37	38	39	40	41	45
47	48	49	50	51	55	57	58	59	60
61	65	67	68	69	70	71	75	77	78
79	80	81	85	87	88	89	90	91	95
97	98	99	100	-1	-1	-1	-1	-1	-1

TOTAL # OF RECORDS= 64

QUERY TABLE

QUERY ID	QUERY INDEX	DATA SET	FILE	SCHEMA	REC TYPE	QUERY COUNT	DISP. SUM	DISP. SUM SQ
121	1	7	1	1	1	40	39.00	39.00
131	1	-1	1	1	1	20	38.00	76.00
141	1	-1	1	1	1	20	38.00	76.00
151	1	-1	1	1	1	20	38.00	76.00
164	1	-1	1	1	1	20	30.00	70.00
177	1	-1	1	1	1	20	38.00	76.00
190	1	-1	1	1	1	40	39.00	39.00
200	1	-1	1	1	1	100	90.00	900.00
343	1	-1	1	1	1	30	95.00	275.00
353	1	-1	1	1	1	60	93.00	204.00
363	1	-1	1	1	1	70	96.00	47.00
383	1	-1	1	1	1	40	99.00	99.00
393	1	-1	1	1	1	100	99.00	99.00
403	1	-1	1	1	1	90	97.00	117.00
438	1	-1	1	1	1	64	99.00	207.00

QUERY TABLE (FREQUENCIES)

QUERY ID	QUERY INDEX	LOC	MIN DISP	MAX DISP	FREQ 1	FREQ 2	FREQ 3	FREQ 4	FREQ 5	FREQ 6	FREQ 7	FREQ 8	FREQ 9	FREQ 10
121	1	40	1.00	1.00	39	0	0	0	0	0	0	0	0	0
131	1	40	2.00	1.00	19	0	0	0	0	0	0	0	0	0
141	1	39	2.00	1.00	19	0	0	0	0	0	0	0	0	0
151	1	40	2.00	1.00	19	0	0	0	0	0	0	0	0	0
164	1	39	1.00	1.00	19	0	0	0	0	0	0	0	0	0
177	1		1.00	1.00	19	0	0	0	0	0	0	0	0	0
190	1	39	2.00	1.00	19	0	0	0	0	0	0	0	0	0
200	1	40	10.00	1.00	39	0	0	0	0	0	0	0	0	0
343	1	97	1.00	1.00	9	0	0	0	0	0	0	0	0	0
353	1	100	2.00	5.00	100	0	0	1	0	0	0	0	0	0
363	1	97	1.00	4.00	50	0	0	0	0	0	0	0	0	0
383	1	95	1.00	7.00	60	0	0	0	0	0	0	0	9	9
393	1	100	-1.00	-1.00	30	0	0	0	0	0	0	0	0	0
403	1	100	1.00	2.00	99	0	0	0	0	0	0	0	0	9
419	1	100	1.00	3.00	50	0	0	0	0	0	0	0	0	0
438	1	100	1.00	4.00	39	0	0	18	1	0	0	0	0	6

SEARCH KEY TABLE

QUERY ID	QUERY INDEX	CUR. REC	N/L SWITCH	N/L REC	COUNT	.NOT.	POS REC	ATTR DEF	VALUE
121	1	-9	F	40	41	0	-1	13	-.00000E+71
131	1	-9	F	40	21	0	-1	32	-.00000E+71
141	1	-9	F	40	41	0	-1	51	-.00000E+71
151	1	-9	F	40	41	0	-1	13	-.00000E+71
164	1	-9	F	40	41	0	-1	32	-.00000E+71
177	1	-9	F	40	21	0	-1	51	-.00000E+71
190	1	-9	F	40	21	0	-1	32	-.00000E+71
200	1	-9	F	40	22	1	-1	32	-.00000E+71
343	1	-9	F	40	21	0	-1	51	-.00000E+71
353	1	-9	F	100	101	0	-1	2213	-.00000E+71
363	1	-9	F	100	101	0	-1	2213	-.00000E+71
373	1	-9	F	100	101	0	-1	2213	-.00000E+71
383	1	-9	F	100	101	3	-1	2213	-.00000E+71
393	1	-9	F	100	102	0	-1	2213	-.00000E+71
403	1	-9	F	100	101	1	101	2213	-.00000E+71
419	1	-9	F	100	101	0	-1	2213	-.00000E+71
438	1	-9	F	100	102	1	101	2213	-.00000E+71
438	1	-9	F	40	41	0	-1	213	-.00000E+71

PAGE 1

INFORMATION PROCESSING SYSTEM SIMULATOR
MODEL SIMULATION PHASE
POST SIMULATION STATISTICS

PART A — GENERAL STATISTICS

CURRENT CLOCK TIME   10.00
TIME OF LAST RESET   0.0   TIME SINCE LAST RESET   10.00
TIME OF LAST SIMULATE   0.0   TIME SINCE LAST SIMULATE 10.00

NUMBER OF EVENT OCCURRENCES PROCESSED
   EXIPL   1

NUMBER OF I/O CALLS
SEEK   0   SEARCH   0   SET SECTOR   0   BACKSPACE   0   ERASE   0
REWIND   0   DTRAN-DASD 0   DTRAN-TAPE   0   DTRAN-UR   0   DTRAN-UNSP   0

NUMBER OF SIMULATION-TIME ERRORS   0

INFORMATION PROCESSING SYSTEM SIMULATOR

MODEL SIMULATION PHASE

POST SIMULATION STATISTICS

PART G1 - ACTIVE QUERY STATISTICS

QUERY NAME   QRY1   QUERY INDEX   1

DATA SET (FILE NUMBER)   = CFINDX (FILE 1)
CURRENT RECORD NUMBER   = 40
TOTAL NUMBER OF RECORDS   = 40
MIN. INTER-RECORD DISTANCE = 1.000
MEAN INTER-RECORD DISTANCE = 1.000
STD. INTER-RECORD DISTANCE = 0.0

INTER-RECORD DISTANCE FREQUENCY TABLE

FREQ. CLASS	INTERVAL START	INTERVAL MEAN	INTERVAL END	FREQ.
1	0.50	1.00	1.50	39
2	1.50	2.00	2.50	0
3	2.50	3.00	3.50	0
4	3.50	4.00	4.50	0
5	4.50	5.00	5.50	0
6	5.50	6.00	6.50	0
7	6.50	7.00	7.50	0
8	7.50	8.00	8.50	0
9	8.50	9.00	9.50	0
10	9.50	10.00	10.50	0

INFORMATION PROCESSING SYSTEM SIMULATOR
MODEL SIMULATION PHASE
POST SIMULATION STATISTICS
PART G1 - ACTIVE QUERY STATISTICS
INTER-RECORD DISTANCE HISTOGRAM

```
FREQUENCY  39    0    0    0    0    0    0    0    0    0    0
           39    *
           38    *
           37    *
           36    *
           35    *
           34    *
           33    *
           32    *
           31    *
           30    *
           29    *
           28    *
           27    *
           26    *
           25    *
           24    *
           23    *
           22    *
           21    *
           20    *
           19    *
           18    *
           17    *
           16    *
           15    *
           14    *
           13    *
           12    *
           11    *
           10    *
            9    *
            8    *
            7    *
            6    *
            5    *
            4    *
            3    *
            2    *
            1    *
INTERVAL    1    2    3    4    5    6    7    8    9   10
CLASS
```

PAGE 3

INFORMATION PROCESSING SYSTEM SIMULATOR
MODEL SIMULATION PHASE
POST SIMULATION STATISTICS
PART G1 - ACTIVE QUERY STATISTICS

QUERY NAME   QRY5   QUERY INDEX   1

CURRENT RECORD NUMBER   =   97
TOTAL NUMBER OF RECORDS   =   30
MIN. INTER-RECORD DISTANCE =   2.000
MAX. INTER-RECORD DISTANCE =   5.000
MEAN INTER-RECORD DISTANCE =   3.276
STD. INTER-RECORD DISTANCE =   1.229

INTER-RECORD DISTANCE FREQUENCY TABLE

FREQ. CLASS	INTERVAL START	INTERVAL MEAN	INTERVAL END	FREQ.
1	1.50	2.00	2.50	10
2	2.50	3.00	3.50	10
3	3.50	4.00	4.50	1
4	4.50	5.00	5.50	9
5	5.50	6.00	6.50	0
6	6.50	7.00	7.50	0
7	7.50	8.00	8.50	0
8	8.50	9.00	9.50	0
9	9.50	10.00	10.50	0
10	10.50	11.00	11.50	0

INFORMATION PROCESSING SYSTEM SIMULATOR
MODEL SIMULATION PHASE
POST SIMULATION STATISTICS
PART G1 - ACTIVE QUERY STATISTICS
INTER-RECORD DISTANCE HISTOGRAM

```
FREQUENCY  10    10    10     0     0     0     0     0     0     0
       10   |*****|*****|     |     |     |     |     |     |     |
        9   |*****|*****|*****|     |     |     |     |     |     |
        8   |*****|*****|*****|     |     |     |     |     |     |
        7   |*****|*****|*****|     |     |     |     |     |     |
        6   |*****|*****|*****|     |     |     |     |     |     |
        5   |*****|*****|*****|     |     |     |     |     |     |
        4   |*****|*****|*****|     |     |     |     |     |     |
        3   |*****|*****|*****|     |     |     |     |     |     |
        2   |*****|*****|*****|     |     |     |     |     |     |
        1   |*****|*****|*****|     |     |     |     |     |     |
            -------------------------------------------------------
INTERVAL      1     2     3     4     5     6     7     8     9    10
CLASS
```

INFORMATION PROCESSING SYSTEM SIMULATOR
MODEL SIMULATION PHASE
POST SIMULATION STATISTICS
PART G1 - ACTIVE QUERY STATISTICS

QUERY NAME   QRY6   QUERY INDEX   1

CURRENT RECORD NUMBER   =   100
TOTAL NUMBER OF RECORDS   =   60
MIN. INTER-RECORD DISTANCE =   1.000
MAX. INTER-RECORD DISTANCE =   5.000
MEAN INTER-RECORD DISTANCE =   1.610
STD. INTER-RECORD DISTANCE =   1.433

INTER-RECORD DISTANCE FREQUENCY TABLE

FREQ. CLASS	INTERVAL START	INTERVAL MEAN	INTERVAL END	FREQ.
1	0.50	1.00	1.50	50
2	1.50	2.00	2.50	0
3	2.50	3.00	3.50	0
4	3.50	4.00	4.50	0
5	4.50	5.00	5.50	0
6	5.50	6.00	6.50	9
7	6.50	7.00	7.50	0
8	7.50	8.00	8.50	0
9	8.50	9.00	9.50	0
10	9.50	10.00	10.50	0

PAGE 20

INFORMATION PROCESSING SYSTEM SIMULATOR
MODEL SIMULATION PHASE
POST SIMULATION STATISTICS
PART G1 - ACTIVE QUERY STATISTICS
INTER-RECORD DISTANCE HISTOGRAM

```
FREQUENCY    50    0    0    0    0    0    0    0    0    0    0
EACH * EQUALS 2 POINTS
         50  *
         48  *
         46  *
         44  *
         42  *
         40  *
         38  *
         36  *
         34  *
         32  *
         30  *
         28  *
         26  *
         24  *
         22  *
         20  *
         18  *
         16  *
         14  *
         12  *
         10  *
          8  *
          6  *                                ****
          4  *
          2  *
             ------------------------------------------------------
INTERVAL      1    2    3    4    5    6    7    8    9    10
CLASS
```

INFORMATION PROCESSING SYSTEM SIMULATOR
MODEL SIMULATION PHASE
POST SIMULATION STATISTICS
PART G1 - ACTIVE QUERY STATISTICS

QUERY NAME   Q4567   QUERY INDEX   1

CURRENT RECORD NUMBER   =   100
TOTAL NUMBER OF RECORDS   =   70
MIN. INTER-RECORD DISTANCE =   1.000
MAX. INTER-RECORD DISTANCE =   3.000
MEAN INTER-RECORD DISTANCE =   1.406
STD. INTER-RECORD DISTANCE =   0.709

INTER-RECORD DISTANCE FREQUENCY TABLE

FREQ. CLASS	INTERVAL START	INTERVAL MEAN	INTERVAL END	FREQ.
1	0.50	1.00	1.50	50
2	1.50	2.00	2.50	10
3	2.50	3.00	3.50	9
4	3.50	4.00	4.50	0
5	4.50	5.00	5.50	0
6	5.50	6.00	6.50	0
7	6.50	7.00	7.50	0
8	7.50	8.00	8.50	0
9	8.50	9.00	9.50	0
10	9.50	10.00	10.50	0

PAGE 30

INFORMATION PROCESSING SYSTEM SIMULATOR

MODEL SIMULATION PHASE

POST SIMULATION STATISTICS

PART G1 - ACTIVE QUERY STATISTICS

INTER-RECORD DISTANCE HISTOGRAM

```
FREQUENCY  50      10      9       0       0       0       0       0       0       0
EACH * EQUALS 2 POINTS
         50 *
         48 *
         46 *
         44 *
         42 *
         40 *
         38 *
         36 *
         34 *
         32 *
         30 *
         28 *
         26 *
         24 *
         22 *
         20 *
         18 *
         16 *
         14 *
         12 *
         10 *     *
          8 *     *    *
          6 *     *    *
          4 *     *    *
          2 *     *    *
            -----------------------------------------------------------------
INTERVAL    1     2     3     4     5     6     7     8     9     10
CLASS
```

INFORMATION PROCESSING SYSTEM SIMULATOR
MODEL SIMULATION PHASE
POST SIMULATION STATISTICS
PART G1 - ACTIVE QUERY STATISTICS

QUERY NAME   Q4T09   QUERY INDEX   1

CURRENT RECORD NUMBER   = 100
TOTAL NUMBER OF RECORDS   =   64
MIN. INTER-RECORD DISTANCE =   1.000
MAX. INTER-RECORD DISTANCE =   4.000
MEAN INTER-RECORD DISTANCE =   1.571
STD. INTER-RECORD DISTANCE =   0.904

INTER-RECORD DISTANCE FREQUENCY TABLE

FREQ. CLASS	INTERVAL START	INTERVAL MEAN	INTERVAL END	FREQ.
1	0.50	1.00	1.50	39
2	1.50	2.00	2.50	18
3	2.50	3.00	3.50	0
4	3.50	4.00	4.50	6
5	4.50	5.00	5.50	0
6	5.50	6.00	6.50	0
7	6.50	7.00	7.50	0
8	7.50	8.00	8.50	0
9	8.50	9.00	9.50	0
10	9.50	10.00	10.50	0

INFORMATION PROCESSING SYSTEM SIMULATOR

MODEL SIMULATION PHASE

POST SIMULATION STATISTICS

PART G1 - ACTIVE QUERY STATISTICS

INTER-RECORD DISTANCE HISTOGRAM

```
FREQUENCY  39    18     0     6     0     0     0     0     0     0
       39 |*
       38 |*
       37 |*
       36 |*
       35 |*
       34 |*
       33 |*
       32 |*
       31 |*
       30 |*
       29 |*
       28 |*
       27 |*
       26 |*
       25 |*
       24 |*
       23 |*
       22 |*
       21 |*
       20 |*
       19 |*
       18 |*   *
       17 |*   *
       16 |*   *
       15 |*   *
       14 |*   *
       13 |*   *
       12 |*   *
       11 |*   *
       10 |*   *
        9 |*   *
        8 |*   *
        7 |*   *
        6 |*   *     *
        5 |*   *     *
        4 |*   *     *
        3 |*   *     *
        2 |*   *     *
        1 |*   *     *
          ----------------------------------------------------------
INTERVAL   1    2     3     4     5     6     7     8     9    10
CLASS
```

INFORMATION PROCESSING SYSTEM SIMULATOR

MODEL SIMULATION PHASE

POST SIMULATION STATISTICS

PART G2 - CUMULATIVE QUERY STATISTICS

QUERY NAME   QRY5

TOTAL NUMBER OF QUERIES   =   1.000
MEAN NO. OF REC. PER QUERY =   30.000
STD. NO. OF REC. PER QUERY =   0.0
MIN. INTER-RECORD DISTANCE =   2.000
MAX. INTER-RECORD DISTANCE =   5.000
MEAN INTER-RECORD DISTANCE =   3.276
STD. INTER-RECORD DISTANCE =   1.229

INTER-RECORD DISTANCE FREQUENCY TABLE

FREQ. CLASS	INTERVAL START	INTERVAL MEAN	INTERVAL END	FREQ.
1	1.50	2.00	2.50	10
2	2.50	3.00	3.50	10
3	3.50	4.00	4.50	0
4	4.50	5.00	5.50	0
5	5.50	6.00	6.50	9
6	6.50	7.00	7.50	0
7	7.50	8.00	8.50	0
8	8.50	9.00	9.50	0
9	9.50	10.00	10.50	0
10	10.50	11.00	11.50	0

PAGE 50

INFORMATION PROCESSING SYSTEM SIMULATOR

MODEL SIMULATION PHASE

POST SIMULATION STATISTICS

PART G2 - CUMULATIVE QUERY STATISTICS

INTER-RECORD DISTANCE HISTOGRAM

```
FREQUENCY  10    10    10     0     0     0     0     0     0     0
       10   *
        9   *     *
        8   *     *
        7   *     *     *
        6   *     *     *
        5   *     *     *
        4   *     *     *
        3   *     *     *
        2   *     *     *
        1   *     *     *
           ------------------------------------------------------------
INTERVAL    1     2     3     4     5     6     7     8     9     10
CLASS
```

PAGE 51

References

ABRA77 Abrams, M.D., And Tren, S., "A Methodology for Interactive Computer Service Measurement," *Communications of the ACM,* Vol. 20, No. 12. December 1977, pp. 936-99.

ARON69 Aron, J.D., "Information Systems in Perspective," *ACM Computing Surveys,* Vol. 1, No. 4. December 1969, pp. 214-23.

BERZ71 Berztiss, A.T., *Data Structures: Theory and Practice,* Academic Press, 1971.

BORO77 Borovits, I., and Ein-Dor, P., "Cost/Utilization: A Measure of System Performance," *Communications of the ACM,* Vol. 20, No. 3. March 1977, pp. 185-91.

BOYS75 Boyse, J.W., and Wern, D.R., "A Straightforward Model for Computer Performance Prediction," *ACM Computing Surveys,* Vol. 7, No. 2. June 1975, pp. 73-93.

BROW79 Brownsmith, J.D., "A Methodology for the Performance Evaluation of Data Base Systems: An Extension of the IPSS Methodology," Ph.D. Dissertation, The Ohio State University, 1979.

BUCC79 Bucci, G., and Streeter, D., "A Methodology for the Design of Distributed Information Systems," *Communications of the ACM,* Vol. 22, No. 4. April 1979.

CARD75 Cardenas, A.F., "Analysis and Performance of Inverted Data Base Structures," *Communications of ACM,* Vol. 18, No. 5. May 1975, pp. 253-63.

CARD73 Cardenas, A.F., "Evaluation and Selection of File Organization—A Model and System," *Communications of the ACM,* Vol. 16, No. 9. September 1973, pp. 540-48.

CHOW75 Chow, J.V., "What You Need to Know About DBMS," *Journal of System Management,* Part I: Vol. 25, No. 5. May 1975, pp. 22-27; Part II: Vol. 25, No. 6. June 1975, pp. 28-35.

CHAN69 Chandor, A., Graham, J., and Williamson, R., *Practical System Analysis,* New York: G.P. Putnams' Sons Publishing Co., 1969.

CHAN76 Chandy, K.M. and Hewes, J.E., "File Allocation in Distributed Systems," *Proceedings of the International Symposium on Computer Performance, Modeling, Measurement, and Evaluation,* ACM Publishing Department, March 1976, pp. 10-13.

References

CODA73   CODASYL Data Description Language Committee, *CODASYL Data Description Language Journal of Development.* NBS Handbook 113, 1973.

CODD70   Codd, E.F., "A Relational Model of Data for Large Shared Data Banks," *Communications of the ACM,* Vol. 13, No. 6. June 1970.

COUG73   Couger, J.P., "Evaluation of Business System Analysis Techniques," *ACM Computing Surveys,* Vol. 5, No. 3. September 1973, pp. 167-98.

DATE75   Date, C.J., *An Introduction to Data Base Systems,* Addison-Wesley, 1975.

DBTG71   *Data Base Task Group of CODASYL Programming Language Committee Report,* April 1971.

DELU68   DeLutis, T.G., and Braker, W.E., "Information Structure Characterization by Attribute Analysis," West Lafayette, Indiana: Purdue University, 1968.

DELU76   Delutis, T.G., "The Information Processing System Simulator," *Proceedings of the 9th Annual Simulation Symposium,* Tampa, Florida, March 1976.

DELU77a   Delutis, T.G., "A Methodology for the Performance Evaluation of Information Processing Systems," Final Report, National Science Foundation Grant Number GN36622, March 1977, also published as OSU-CISRC-TR-77-2, March 1977, Columbus, Ohio: Department of Computer and Information Science, The Ohio State University.

DELU77b   Delutis, T.G., Rush, J.E., and Wong, P.M., "The Modeling of a Large, On-Line, Real-time Information System," *Proceedings of the 10th Annual Simulation Symposium,* Tampa, Florida, March 1977.

DELU78   DeLutis, T.G., *The Information Processing System Simulator (IPSS): Language Syntax and Semantics, I and II,* Columbus, Ohio: The Ohio State University, 1978.

DELU79   Delutis, T.G., Johnston, K.B., Rush, J.E., and Wong, P.M., "A Simulation Model for Information System Design, Evaluation and Planning," *Proceedings of the 12th Annual Simulation Symposium,* Tampa, Florida, March 1979.

DENN72   Denning, P.J., and Graham, G.S., "Protection: Principles and Practice," *AFIPS Comt.,* SJCC 72, Vol. 42, pp. 417-29.

DONO72   Donovan, J.J., *Systems Programming,* McGraw-Hill Book Co., 1972.

EMER72   Emery, J.C. "Where Do We Stand in Implementing Information Systems?" *AFIPS Proceedings,* Vol. 40, SJCC 1972, pp. 1167-70.

ESTR72   Estrin, G., Muntz, R.R., and Uzgolis, R.C., "Modeling, Measurement and Computer Power," *AFIPS Proceedings,* Vol. 40, SJCC 1972, pp. 725-38.

FRAN74   Frank, R.L., and Yamaguchi, K., "A Model for a Generalized Data Access Method," *AFIPS Conference,* Vol. 43. NCC 1974, 45-57.

FRY76   Fry, J.P., and Sibley, E.H., "Evaluation of Data Base Management Systems," *ACM Computing Surveys,* Vol. 8, No. 1. March 1976, pp. 7-42.

GHOS69   Ghosh, S.P., and Senko, M.L., "File Organization: On the Selection of Random Access Index Points for Sequential Files," *Journal ACM,* Vol. 16, No. 4. 1969, pp. 569-79.

References   233

GHOS72 Ghosh, S.P., "File Organization: The Consecutive Retrieval Property," *Communications of the ACM,* U 15, No. 9. September 1972, pp. 802-8.

GHOS75 Ghosh, S.P., "Consecutive Storage of Relevant Recs with Redundancy," *Communications of the ACM,* Vol. 8. August 1975, pp. 464-71.

GRAH73 Graham, R.M., "A Software Design and Evaluation System," *Communications of the ACM,* Vol. 16. February 1973, pp. 110-16.

GREE74 Greenfeld, N.R., "Quantification in a Relational System," *AFIPS Proceedings,* Vol. 43. NCC 1974, pp. 71-76.

KARL61 Karlin, S., *A First Course in Stochastic Processes,* New York: Academic Press, 1961.

KIMB72 Kimbleton, S.R., "Performance Evaluation—A Structured Approach," *AFIPS Proceedings,* Vol. 40, SJCC 1972, pp. 411-15.

KNUT73 Knuth, D.E., *The Art of Computer Programming,* Vol. 1 and Vol. 3, Addison-Wesley Publishing Company, 1973.

KORF66 Korfhage, R.R., *Logic and Algorithms,* John Wiley and Sons, 1966.

KRIE72 Kriebel, C.H., "MIS Technology—A View of the Future." *AFIPS Proceedings,* Vol. 42, SJCC 1972, pp. 1173-85.

KUMA78 Kumar, B., and Davidson, E.S., "Performance Evaluation of Highly Concurrent Computers by Deterministic Simulation," *Communications of the ACM,* Vol. 21, No. 11. November 1978, pp. 904-13.

LEFK69 Lefkovitz, D., *File Structures for On-Line Systems,* New York: Sporten Press, 1969.

LIAS74 Lias, E.J., "On-Line vs. Batch Costs," *Datamation,* Vol. 20, No. 12. December 1974, pp. 69-70.

LOCK74 Lockett, J.A., "Computer Performance Analysis in Mixed On-Line Batch Workloads," *AFIPS Proceedings,* Vol. 43, NCC 1974, pp. 671-676.

LOWE68 Lowe, T.C., "The Influence of Data Characteristics and Usage on Direct Access File Organization," *Journal, ACM,* Vol, 15, No. 4. October 1968, pp. 535-48.

LUM75 Lum, V.Y., Senko, M.E., Wong, C.P., and Ling, H., "A Cost Oriented Algorithm for Data Set Allocation in Storage Hierarchies," *Communications of the ACM,* Vol. 18, No. 6. June 1975, pp. 318-22.

LYON71 Lyon, J.K., *An Introduction to Data Base Design,* John Wiley and Sons, 1971, pp. 1-80.

MADN74 Madnick, S.E., and Donovan, J.J., *Operating Systems,* McGraw-Hill Book Company, 1974.

MART77 Martin, J., *Computer Data Base Organization,* Prentice-Hall Inc., 2nd ed., 1977.

MART75 Martin, M.P., "The Instant Analyst," *Journal of System Management,* Vol. 26, No. 2. February 1975, pp. 13-19.

References

MARU76   Maruyama, K. and Smith, S.E., "Optimal Reorganization of Distributed Space Disk Files," *Communications of the ACM,* Vol. 19, No. 11. November 1976, pp. 634-42.

MEAD67   Meadow, C., *The Analysis of Information Systems,* John Wiley and Sons Publishing Company, 1967.

MOLI74   Molick, P., "Systems Performance Measurements—A Qualitative Base for Management of Computer Systems," *AFIPS Proceedings,* Vol. 43. NCC 974, pp. 677-82.

MORG74   Morgan, H.E., "Optimal Space Allocation on Disk Devices," *Communications of the ACM,* Vol. 17, No. 3. March 1974, pp. 1329-42.

NUNA76   Nunansker, J.F., Konsynski, B.R., Ho. J. and Singer, C., "Computer-Aided Analysis and Design of Information Systems," *Communications of the ACM,* Vol. 19, No. 12. December 1976, pp. 674-85.

OCLC79   OCLC Monographic Reports, *Subject Heading Patterns, Report No. OCLC/RDD/RR-79/1,* Columbus, Ohio: OCLC Inc., 1979.

PARZ62   Parzen, E., *Stochastic Processes,* California: Holden-Dey Press, 1962.

PIEP75   Piepmeier, W.F., "Optimal Balancing of I/O Request to Disks," *Communications of the ACM,* Vol. 18, No. 9. September 1975, pp. 524-27.

ROSE73   Rodriguez-Rosell, J., and Duprey, J.P., "The Design, Implementation, and Evaluation of a Working Set Dispatcher," *Communications of the ACM,* Vol. 16, No. 4. April 1973, pp. 247-53.

ROTH74   Rothnie, J.B., and Lozano, T., "Attribute Base File Organization in a Paged Memory Environment," *Communications of the ACM,* Vol. 17, No. 2. February 1974, pp. 63-69.

SALE73   Salesin, J., "Hierarchical Storage in Information Retrieval," *Communications of the ACM,* Vol. 16, No. 5. May 1973, pp. 291-95.

SALT71   Salton, G., *The Smart Retrieval System—Experiment in Automatic Document Processing,* Prentice-Hall Inc., 1971.

SALT74   Saltzer, J.M., "A Simple Linear Model of Demand Paging Performance," *Communications of the ACM,* Vol. 17, No. 4. April 1974, pp. 181-89.

SCAM75   Scamell, R.W., and Baugh, E.W., "Team Approach to Systems Analysis," *Journal of System Management,* Vol. 26, No. 4. April 1975, pp. 32-35.

SENK71   Senko, M.E., "Details of a Scientific Approach to Information Systems," *Data Base Systems,* Courant Computer Science Symposium, 1971, pp. 143-74.

SEVE74   Severence, P.G., "Identifier Search Mechanisms: A Survey and Generalized Model," *ACM Computing Surveys,* Vol. 6, No. 3. September 1974, pp. 173-75.

SHAW74   Shaw, A.C., *The Logical Design of Operating Systems,* Prentice-Hall Inc., 1974.

SHET74   Shetler, S.C., "Controlled Testing for Computer Performance Evaluation," *AFIPs Proceedings,* Vol. 43. NCC 1974, pp. 693-99.

SHNE73   Shneiderman, B., "Optimal Data Base Reorganization Points," *Communications of the ACM,* Vol. 11, No. 6. June 1973, pp. 362-65.

SIBL73	Sibley, E.H. and Taylor, R.W., "A Data Definition and Mapping Language," *Communications of the ACM,* Vol. 16, No. 12. December 1973, pp. 750-59.
SILE76	Siler, K.F., "A Stochastic Evaluation Model for Data Base Organizations in Data Retrieval Systems," *Communications of the ACM,* Vol. 19, No. 2. February 1976.
SYSR79	The System R Group, "System R: A Relational Data Base Management System," *Computer,* IEEE Computing Society Publication, Vol. 12, No. 5. May 1979, pp. 42-48.
TAGG77	Taggert, W.M., and Tharp, M.O., "A Survey of Information Requirements Analysis Techniques," *ACM Computing Surveys,* Vol. 9, No. 4. December 1977, pp. 273-90.
TIMM73	Timmreck, W.M., *ACM Computing Surveys,* Vol. 5, No. 4. December 1973, pp. 199-222.
TSIC77	Tsichritzis, D.C. and Lochovsky, F.H., *Data Base Management Systems,* Academic Press, 1977.
WEBS62	*Webster's New World Dictionary of American Language,* college Ed., Cleveland and New York: World Publishing Co., 1962.
WHIT69	Whittenbury, J.A., and Schumacher, A.W., *Information System Program Planning,* Alexandria, Virginia: Whittenbury Vaughen Associates, 1969.
ZLOO77	Zloof, M.M., "Query-by-Example: A Data Base Language," *IBM Systems Journal,* Vol. 16, No. 4, 1977, pp. 324-43.

Index

Access time, 24
Accession number, 52
Antisymmetric property, 64
Attribute analysis, 49, 104
Attribute statement, 86
Attribute transformation, 61, 72, 92, 104
Attribute-value pairs, 65; characterization. *See also* Attribute analysis; examples, 6, 8, 31

Benchmarks, 23
Boolean expression, 9, 14, 37, 71, 72. *See also* Propositional calculus

Clustering, 25, 31; efficiency, 94
CODASYL, 40
Comparable property, 64
Conceptual model, 31
Concurrent processing, 24
Content analysis, 6, 9
Counting process, 51
Create query facility, 90

Data Acquisition. *See* Document acquisition
Data Base, 64
    administrator, 37
    Management System. *See* DBMS
    mapping, 33, 37
    organization, 11, 26
    performance. *See* System performance
    reorganization, 12
    response pattern, 61
    traversal, 62
    workload measures. *See* Workload measures
    workload transformation. *See* Attribute Transformation
Data Definition Language. *See* DDL
Data Manipulation Language. *See* DML
Data model, 36. *See also* Relational data model
Data processing system. *See* Information system

Data retrieval efficiency, 103
Data storage, 8
Data sublanguage. *See* DML
Data submodel, 33
DBMS, 20, 26, 33
DBMS approaches, 36, 37, 46
DDL, 33
Descriptor data base, 8
Destroy query facility, 91
Device allocation, 23
Device utilization, 23
Distributed processing, 24
DML, 24, 33, 38
Document acquisition, 6
Document data base, 8

Entity, 31, 62

File, 64
File traversal work function, 75
Find list length facility, 92
Find next record facility, 91, 100
First occurrence PDF, 52, 66, 86, 92
First order predicate calculus, 38
First query occurrence PDF, 73
Frequency table, 83
Future extensions, 16, 101, 102, 103

Get record address statement, 100

Hardware selection, 23
Hierarchical approach, 40

Indexing breadth, 11
Indexing depth, 11
Information Processing System Simulator Relational Extensions. *See* IPSS: REL
Information Processing System Simulator. *See* IPSS
Information structure, 8, 62, 100
Information system, 1
    attributes, 62

238 Index

evolution, 4, 19
examples, 20
functions, 1, 5
general model, 6, 8
modern, 4
on-line, 5, 6, 20
problems, 1, 2
reasons for, 20, 22
traditional, 4, 5, 19
See also DBMS
Information unit, 31
Inter-arrival time, 51, 70
IPSS, 54, 55, 56, 57, 58, 59
    data base access component, 58
    data base structure component, 58
    execution facilities, 56, 58
    model director component, 58, 80
    modeling facilities, 56
    REL, 79
    request stream component, 58, 80
    storage structure component, 58, 80
    system resource component, 58, 80

Last occurrence PDF, 68, 86, 94
Last query occurrence PDF, 73
Logical data base, 33
Logical retrieval efficiency, 102

Methodological algorithms, 14
Methodological components, 14, 63
Multi-attribute, 4, 5

Network approach, 40
Next occurrence PDF, 67, 86, 94. *See also* Renewal process PDF
Next query occurrence PDF, 73
Non-procedural language, 38
Number of occurrences PDF, 52, 68, 86, 94
Number of query occurrences PDF, 73

Object, 14
    examples, 2, 6
    formal definition, 65
    See also Entity; Information unit
Object retrieval work function, 75
On-line system. *See* Information system; on-line
Operation system, 25

Parsers, 80
PDF, 51
PDF statement, 83
Physical data base, 36
Physical retrieval efficiency, 102, 103
Precision ratio, 102
Predicate calculus, 101

Probability distribution function. *See* PDF
Probability function, 51
Probability theory, 49
Procedural language, 38
Propositional calculus, 9, 38, 101

Query, 69
    Analysis, 8
    complexity measure, 25
    content, 62
    language, 6
Query language
    complexity, 9
    selection, 24, 25
    syntax rules, 9
    vocabulary, 9
    See also DML
Query response set, 9
Query statement, 90
Query stream. *See* Workload
Query structure, 62
Query transformation, 61, 70, 71, 104

Random variable, 49
Recall ratio, 101
Reflexive property, 64
Relation, 37
Relational algebra, 38
Relational approach, 37, 101
Relational calculus, 38, 71
Relational data model, 29, 33
Renewal process, 49, 51
Renewal process PDF, 52. *See also* Next occurrence PDF
Research objectives, 2, 12, 14, 17, 99
Retrieval efficiency, 94, 102

Sample space, 49
Search key, 69
Search key statement, 87, 89
Simulation statistics, 94, 95, 105
Software selection, 24
Stochastic process, 49, 51. *See also* Renewal process
Subschema, 46
System analysis, 19, 20
    constraints, 22
    objectives, 22
    tools, 2, 19
System analyst, 19
System development phases, 20
System loading: formal definition, 70
System performance, 11, 19, 26
    parameters, 77
    See also Access time; clustering efficiency; retrieval efficiency

Index

Testing and verification, 80, 105   55
Total ordering, 64
Transformations, 12, 55, 79, 92
   application level, 59
   data base management level, 59
   file management level, 59
   information system level, 58
   secondary storage management level, 59
Transitive property, 64

Uni-attribute, 4
User request pattern, 77

Value PDF, 69, 86

Workload, 2, 10, 12, 14, 26, 62, 100. *See also* System loading
   measures, 75, 76
   transformation. *See* Attribute transformation

Zipf's law, 52